English Discovery of America to 1585

English Discovery of America to 1585

By FRANKLIN T. McCANN

1969
OCTAGON BOOKS
New York

Reprinted 1969
by special arrangement with Franklin T. McCann

OCTAGON BOOKS
A Division of Farrar, Straus & Giroux, Inc.
19 Union Square West
New York, N. Y. 10003

AM

Library of Congress Catalog Card Number: 73-86280

Printed in U.S.A. by
TAYLOR PUBLISHING COMPANY
DALLAS, TEXAS

To ESTHER N. McCANN

Acknowledgments

FOR ACTIVE HELP in the pursuit of a difficult task I am particularly grateful to Professors Oscar J. Campbell and Garrett Mattingly of Columbia University and Dr. John Kirtland Wright of the American Geographical Society. Three fields of knowledge overlap at the point where one must dig for information about *The English Discovery of America to 1585,* and the searcher would be rash indeed who did not ask for special guidance in each. Professor Campbell has given that kind of help in the field of literature, Professor Mattingly in history, and Dr. Wright in geography. My indebtedness to Professor Elliott V. K. Dobbie of Columbia, the late Professor Kirk Bryan of Harvard, and Professors W. R. Patrick and Paul Haines, colleagues at the Alabama Polytechnic Institute, though of a lesser magnitude, is still considerable. Any mistakes of omission or commission are of course my own.

For permission to quote from copyrighted material I am indebted to the kindness of the following publishers and authors: Estate of E. A. N. Arber, for passages from *The First Three English Books on America,* 1885; Cambridge University Press, for Gascoigne's sonnet to Humphrey Gilbert, *Complete Works,* 1907; Clarendon Press, for passages from the Tucker Brooke edition of *The Works of Christopher Marlowe,* 1910, and from the Lupton edition of More's *Utopia,* 1895, and for a passage from the Grierson edition of *The Poems of John Donne,* 1912; Columbia University Press, for the satire from Brant's *The Ship of Fools,* 1944; Hakluyt Society, for passages from Roger Barlow's *A brief summe of Geographie,* 1932, from David Beers Quinn's *The Voyages and Colonizing Enterprises of Sir Humphrey Gilbert,* 1940, and from

Hakluyt's *Divers Voyages*, 1850; Jackson, Son & Co. (Booksellers), Ltd., for passages from Hakluyt's *The Principal Navigations Voyages Traffiques and Discoveries of the English Nation*, 1903–5; the Executor of the late Francis A. Macnutt for passages from Macnutt's translation of Peter Martyr's *De orbe novo*, 1912; Charles J. Sawyer, Ltd., booksellers, representing the Argonaut Press, for passages from Rastell's *Interlude of the Four Elements* as printed in James A. Williamson's *The Voyages of the Cabots and the English Discovery of North America under Henry VII and Henry VIII*, 1929, and for passages from Vilhjalmur Stefansson's *The Three Voyages of Martin Frobisher*, 1938.

For permission to reproduce illustrative material I am indebted to the kindness of the following organizations: American Geographical Society, for the diagram of the Greek universe from Peter Apian's *Cosmographicus*, 1524; Columbia University Press, for Brant's representation of the geographical fool from Brant, *The Ship of Fools*, 1944.

A generous grant from the Alabama Polytechnic Institute has aided materially in the final preparation of the manuscript.

FRANKLIN T. MC CANN

Auburn, Alabama
October 19, 1951

Contents

Illustrations

The Author to the Reader

THIS BOOK is about the English discovery of America up to the time of the planting of the Roanoke colony, the first bona fide English colony in America and consequently a fitting place to stop the pursuit of discovery. Since the word "discovery" as applied to this period is sometimes limited to the voyages, the Reader, to avoid disappointment, should be warned to expect something else here. The voyages are considered, to be sure, yet there is little of salt flavor, no sense of adventuring across a great ocean in a tiny ship toward a chimerical dream-world beyond. "Discovery" is treated objectively, sometimes coldly, as a state of mind in which certain Englishmen progressed from the unknown or the unrecognized (a distinction which Mr. Noah Webster was careful to point out long before my day) to the known. The material objects found along the way are discussed incidentally, with particular emphasis on gold, which Englishmen desired above all other things and never found, within the limits of our period, except in Spanish hands.

The first two chapters are concerned with what Englishmen knew of the earth before Columbus first returned from western shores. Two chapters are required instead of one because of the sharp cleavage between the Greco-Roman fossil earth (and universe), in late medieval time still treated in some books as vigorously alive even though not only dead but also crusted over with a hard growth of legend and mistaken theory, and the changing, generally expanding, earth of trader, lay traveler, and itinerant churchman, which also occasionally found its way into books.

Chapters III, IV, VI, and VIII trace English interest in America from the first rush of enthusiasm which greeted the return of John Cabot in 1497 through the ebb period of the next fifty years and the gradually mounting flood tide of the thirty-eight following to the year 1585. In their pages the voyages do put in an appearance. Chapter III is, however, concerned with voyaging only to a minor degree. Major emphasis is placed upon examining a change in attitude toward America: the realization, first, that America was neither one of the Western Islands nor a part of Asia and, second, that it was something brand new and big, indeed a fourth part of the earth.

Chapter IV, which contains accounts of English voyages to America in the reign of Henry VIII, is shorter than might be expected because the voyages were few and the description scant. The Reader might perhaps find himself interested in such small matters as the stir created in the Spanish harbor of Santo Domingo in 1527 by the sudden appearance of an English ship there and the Sunday-School-picnic aspects of Master Hore's voyage to "Newfoundland" in 1536.

Chapter VI is devoted to English voyages between the reign of Henry VIII and that of Elizabeth, his younger daughter. In these pages, Gentle Reader, you will sail to Russia by way of the frigid and treacherous North Cape and to torrid Africa, but not to America. This digression is that of the Englishmen, not of the Author. Increasing numbers were becoming actively interested in voyaging for gain, and they thought to find that commodity more easily in Russia and Africa than in America.

Chapter VIII deals with the Golden Age of English voyaging to America, an age made possible by the hard experience gained through voyages to the White Sea and the Gold Coast in the years 1552–1558 and by information about America supplied by such a work as Eden's *Decades* (1555). These pages are concerned with the illegal, often piratical, voyages of Hawkins, Drake, and Oxenham to Central and South America and to Mexico, with the lesser known and more informative legal activities of men like

Tomson, Chilton, and Hawks who lived in Mexico and Central America for extended periods, with Ribault's trip to Florida and Georgia, and with the voyages of Frobisher, Gilbert, and Barlowe to points north. Probably the best portions of this chapter, and certainly the freshest, are two wildly enthusiastic descriptive passages: Georgia as seen though the eyes of Ribault, and Roanoke Island as seen by Barlowe.

Chapter VII, "Eden's America," is in a class by itself. It analyzes Eden's *Decades* in order to demonstrate what a wealth of geographical information about America was available in English as early as the year 1555. This travel book describes parts of the east coast of America from the Strait of Magellan to Hudson Bay, enough to convey an unmistakable sense of the vastness, diversity, and wealth of the new continent. Treatment of Perú and Panamá City on the west coast further stresses wealth, especially gold. Eden's long-neglected book, known today only to a few specialists, this Author considers the most important early work relating to the English discovery of America because of the kind and abundance of information made available to the average interested Englishman who could not read Latin. It surely did more to encourage voyaging to America than the better-known work of Hakluyt, which appeared after the impetus toward discovery had already swelled to major proportions.

Chapter IX, "Medieval Concepts of the Earth in a Renaissance World," is closely related to Chapter I. It shows how certain misconceptions associated with or related to the Greco-Roman earth and universe continued to be given credence in sixteenth-century England. Foremost among them was the belief that gold, its growth controlled by the rays of the sun, was restricted to the torrid zone. Evidence of its rooting in English thought is produced. The Author is firmly convinced that this belief is a principal explanation for English failure to explore extensively or settle North America before 1585. The antiquarian-minded Reader will find other matters in these pages, too, to interest him.

Chapters V and X are concerned with the effects of discovery on the English creative imagination. Few works of imaginative literature were stimulated in whole or in part by the English discovery of America within the period named. Two important ones, More's *Utopia* (1516/17) and Rastell's *Interlude of the Four Elements* (c. 1519), appeared abnormally early because of the special qualifications and interests of the authors. Marlowe's *Tamburlaine* (1587–1588), the most important of all, appeared shortly after 1585, its composition retarded by the expectable lag between discovery and the ferment of the creative imagination. The first two, while not void of interest, are strictly black and white productions and meant for meditation, not entertainment. *Tamburlaine's* color, on the other hand, was meant to catch the eye and stir the pulse, and it is just possible that the Author may be able to convey to the Reader his own sense of excitement about it.

CHAPTER I

The Static Three-Part Earth in England
Before the Discovery of America

MAN HAS of necessity taken a special interest in the earth, his natural habitat, from the beginning of his existence. In very early prehistoric time he must have seen it primarily in terms of his own local region, a dry cave in which to live, a spring of clear, cold water to quench his thirst, a hillside where edible fruit grew, a secluded valley where he could find game. At the dawn of his existence man must also have been aware of the universe in a very limited sense, of the heavenly bodies above him, the sun, the moon, and the stars. In the beginning earth and universe may not have been separate entities for him in any sense, constituting rather a single, whole background for living. At a very early date man must have noted the regularity with which day and night replaced each other, and as early as the Neolithic Age he was aware of the summer solstice,[1] after which the days grow shorter instead of longer. Early in historic time he was visualizing a "system" of which the earth was an essential part, though men differed in their concepts of that system. Universe and earth were still closely associated in spite of being thus differentiated, and they remained closely associated down through the ages.

We can hardly understand the English discovery of America before 1585 unless we first consider English knowledge of the earth about the year 1493, when Columbus returned from his first voyage to the "Indies," and somewhat earlier. We can hardly

understand the medieval earth in England unless we also consider
the medieval universe of which it was a part, for they were mu-
tually dependent. Vives, the brilliant Spanish humanist long resident in England, outlined the proper approach in 1531 when he
wrote:

There should be, in the first place, a general explanation, an exposition
or, as it were, a picture of the whole of nature, of the heavens, the
elements, and those things that are in the heavens, and in the elements,
in fire, air, water and earth; so that a full representation and description of the whole earth is included as in a picture.[2]

This Greek universe and its included static, three-part earth,
which were current in medieval England, were primarily, though
not exclusively, the property of the scholar, who was usually also
a churchman. Whether a man could read and write Latin was the
one supreme test of a medieval scholar. Latin works concerned
with universe and earth which were written in England or circulated in England, including some written by Englishmen in France,
may be regarded as revealing to us the knowledge possessed by the
English scholar. Comparable works written in English or translated into English, and known to circulate in England, may by
that token be considered to represent the knowledge available to
the English layman. These two classes of works are our present
source of information. The test by which they are classified is
rough at best, since it does not sufficiently clarify the terms
"scholar" and "layman," but it should still serve here where the
principal intent is to show the kind of knowledge available rather
than to weigh the relative amounts possessed by different types
of readers. The classification should at least serve to emphasize
that some knowledge of universe and earth was finding its way
beyond the scholar in even the loosest sense of the term. Only
the more important works involved need be considered.

Bede's two best known temporal works, De natura rerum (c.
703 A.D.) and De temporum ratione (725 A.D.), far more important
in their day than his ecclesiastical writings, are the earliest to in-

dicate the knowledge of the English scholar. They were written in England and used as texts there and on the continent for centuries. The Greek universe is clearly, though briefly, described in *De natura rerum* [3] and the major regions of the earth are referred to in both works [4] much as they are in Pliny's *Historia naturalis* despite the five centuries intervening. Nothing comparable appeared until the thirteenth century when three works were written within a few years of each other, their composition made possible by the arrival of new knowledge from Greek and Moslem sources during the preceding century. Two of them, the *De sphaera* of Grosseteste and the *Opus majus* of Roger Bacon, were written by Franciscans connected with Oxford University. They had a limited circulation. The third, the *Sphaera mundi* of Sacrobosco, written by an Englishman teaching at the University of Paris, reached a much larger audience. Like the works of Bede, it was used as a text for centuries, both on the continent and in England. It was, in fact, required for the A.B. degree at Oxford in 1409 [5] and probably earlier. The *De sphaera* and the *Sphaera mundi* treated the universe more comprehensively than the works of Bede but were little concerned with the regions of the earth; the *Opus majus* added a good deal to both subjects.

No work on universe and earth was written in English during the Middle Ages with the partial exception of Alfred's Orosius, his ninth century version of Orosius' *apologia* for Christianity called *Historiae adversum paganos* (c. 417 A.D.). Orosius, for the better understanding of his historical examples, devoted a part of Book I to the provinces of the earth, the usual Roman "orbis terrae." Alfred or his scholars, in translating this part into Old English, added some new material about France and much about Germany. Derived from sources other than classical or Moslem texts, it belongs to the changing earth and will be considered in the next chapter.

Four important late medieval works concerned in some measure with universe and earth were translated into English and circulated in England before the beginning of the sixteenth century.

They were the *De proprietatibus rerum* of Bartholomeus Anglicus, Higden's *Polychronicon*, Gossouin's *Image du monde*, and
The Travels of Sir John Mandeville by Jean d'Outremeuse, the
first two written in Latin, the last two in French. Only Higden's
work appeared first in England in the original, the others in France.
Gossouin's *Image du monde* was equally concerned with the Greek
universe and the regions of the earth; the others were concerned
with the universe only incidentally or not at all.

De *proprietatibus rerum*, a very elaborate encyclopedia, was
translated into English by John de Trevisa in 1398. His translation
was printed in England by Wynkyn de Worde in 1495. The work
had a special slant, which was also a limitation. Bartholomew intended it to be a summary of knowledge sufficient only to explain
Scripture and Gloss, and it may have been aimed principally at
students and parish priests. If the translation was so used in England, the knowledge it contained must have had a considerable
circulation, for the parish priests would have passed some of it on
to their flocks. The Greek universe appears, though the discussion
is incidental to theological matters. The early printing of the translation indicates a real and probably continuing need and demand
for it.

Higden's *Polychronicon* or universal history was also translated into English by John de Trevisa in the fourteenth century.
An unnamed translator made another English translation in the
fifteenth century. Caxton printed an edition of the earlier translation, with some revisions, in 1482, and Wynkyn de Worde also
printed it in 1495(?).

Gossouin's *Image du monde*, which contained an unusually good
description of the Greek universe, was translated into English
by Caxton, who published it in England in 1480 or 1481 as *The
Mirrour of the World*. It was so well received that he printed another edition about 1490.

The *Travels of Sir John Mandeville* was twice translated into
English before the end of the fifteenth century. The great popu-
larity of the translation in England during the fifteenth century,

before as well as after the advent of printing, is suggested by the appearance of four English printings at the turn of the century, in 1496, 1499, 1501, and 1503. Sir John Mandeville was of course an imaginary traveler. From time immemorial men have been particularly interested in the exploits of their own countrymen, and it is just possible that the entertainment provided by this work was enhanced for Englishmen because Sir John, the alleged author as well as traveler, was represented as being real and one of them. How Jean d'Outremeuse would have relished the irony of this if he could have lived long enough to note the size of his English audience! Though the emphasis is almost wholly on the regions of the earth, since this is a travel book, there is mention of the round earth of the Greek universe, "for our Lorde made the earth all rounde in the middest of ye fyrmament." [6]

Several of the works mentioned, in addition to Alfred's *Orosius*, drew on sources outside the old texts for information about various regions of the earth, thus exhibiting some awareness of a changing earth. Discussion of this "new" information will in most instances be reserved for the next chapter.

Universe and Earth

The universe described by Sacrobosco [7] was standard for England during the Middle Ages from the time of Bede, though some of the details may have been obscure or entirely lacking that early. It was a great sphere, constructed, like an onion, of a number of shells or hollow spheres having a common center, a round and motionless earth, but unlike an onion it had two principal parts, an inner or "elementary" part which was subject to change and decay and an outer or "ethereal" part which was changeless, eternal, and incorruptible. The inner part extended outward to the orbit of the moon and contained three elements, water, air, and fire, which surrounded the fourth element, earth, as hollow spheres in the order named. The sphere of water was the only incomplete one, being pierced in places by the dry land of the earth. The outer part consisted of nine spheres, the orbits of the seven "planets," of the

moon, Mercury, Venus, the sun, Mars, Jupiter, and Saturn, beginning with the lowest, and the spheres of the fixed stars and the
primum mobile or last heaven. The entire great sphere, with the
notable exception of the earth, had two movements. The *primum
mobile* rotated on its axis from east through west every twenty-
four hours. This was the principal movement. The other spheres
moved in the opposite direction and obliquely, the angle of varia-
tion being 23 degrees. The rate of movement differed for each
"planet." The ninth sphere carried all the others with it in its daily
rotation in spite of their contrary struggle.

Though this universe was in essence Greek, one change had been
made in the region beyond the sphere of Saturn since the days of
Aristotle. For Aristotle the sphere of fixed stars, the eighth sphere,
was the *primum mobile* and rotated daily. Ptolemy changed this.[8]
In order to account for the precession of the equinoxes, he visualized a ninth sphere beyond the sphere of fixed stars. It became the
primum mobile and took over the burden of daily rotation. The
sphere of fixed stars was carried along, but like the "planets" took
on a movement of its own, a very small one, in the opposite direction. There was a thirteenth-century theory of a ninth sphere
without contrary movement between the sphere of fixed stars and
the *primum mobile,* but Sacrobosco shows no awareness of
it.[9]

Medieval Christian theologians, faced with the problem of fitting heaven into this universe, evolved several heavens peopled
with angels of varying degrees; but they were not in agreement
as to the number of heavens, which ranged as high as eleven, nor
where to put them. Peter Apian's sixteenth-century diagram of the
medieval universe presents it in full panoply, complete with ninth
sphere and eleven heavens. This arrangement follows the Greek
practice of having a heaven for each ethereal sphere, starting with
the sphere of the moon, but adds an outer, empyreal heaven, "the
abode of God and all the Elect," and two others for the added ninth
and tenth spheres. Bartholomew followed a different scheme. He
lists [10] seven heavens, *Aereum, Olympium, Igneum, Firmamentu,*

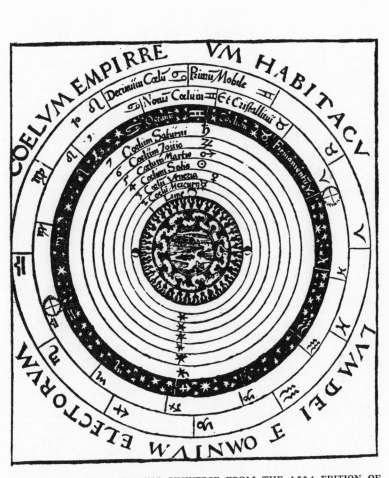

DIAGRAM OF THE MEDIEVAL UNIVERSE FROM THE 1524 EDITION OF
PETER APIAN'S *Cosmographicus*

Aqueum (*Cristallineum*), *Imperium,* and *Celum,* and places *Aereum,* the lowest, in the middle of the element air. During the Middle Ages there was almost as much interest in and difference of opinion about the location of Paradise, and that problem more nearly concerns us because Paradise was commonly supposed to be on earth. But before we turn to this and other regions of the earth, we ought to consider the shape of the earth and other matters relating to the whole.

The motionless earth at the center of the medieval (Greek) universe was round; unmistakably and unequivocally round. Belief in a flat earth was current among the Jews and some Moslems and early Christians. In eastern Europe there were men who believed in the earth of Cosmos, oblong in shape, with a great mountain in the north. Lactantius (fl. 290–300), one of the early Church fathers, argued, perhaps with tongue in cheek, that the earth might be shaped like an egg or might even be oblong and hollow like a boat. There is, however, little reason to think that the medieval Englishman believed that the shape of the earth was anything but round. Bartholomew and Gossouin speak of the earth as being round. Grosseteste, Sacrobosco, and Roger Bacon are at some pains to prove its roundness. The proof they advanced was not original with them but was derived from Greek, Roman, and Moslem sources; it demonstrated that the earth is round in two directions, north-south and east-west, and presumably must then be round in every direction.

Grosseteste argues [11] that if the earth were a plane, all men everywhere would always see the same portion of the sky. In order to show that the earth is round in a north-south direction, he calls attention to the fact that Polaris rises as a man travels north from the equator. That this proof was derived from Moslem scientists is indicated by his use of the city of Arim as a point of departure. Arim was a legendary city which the Moslems believed to be located at the point where the equator is cut by the meridian which passes 10 degrees east of the city of Baghdad. Since day and night appear first to persons in the east and lunar eclipses to those in the west, says Grosseteste, then the earth must also be round in an east-west direction.

Sacrobosco uses the same arguments as Grosseteste and adds others.[12] Thinking more particularly in terms of the four elements than Grosseteste, he presents two arguments to prove that the sphere of water is round as well as the sphere of earth. If this sphere were not round, argues Sacrobosco, the man at the top of the mast and the man on the deck of a ship would both see the shore at the same time whereas, in fact, the man at the top of the mast sees it first. Furthermore, he adds, water is an homogeneous body. Water in very small amounts, as a drop of dew, tends to assume a globular form. Since water is homogeneous, the whole must be similar to its parts. Therefore the element water has assumed the form of a sphere.

The arguments of Roger Bacon are similar to those of Sacrobosco except that they tend to be even more systematic, to fall even more into the pattern of the four elements.[13] Bacon defends the thesis that the principal mass of each of the four elements, earth, water, air, and fire, is convexly spherical on the outside. He too explains how the swelling of the sphere of water enables the sailor on the ship's mast to see land before the sailor on deck, and he, like Sacrobosco, makes it plain that he is referring to the element water in its entirety. Then he goes beyond Sacrobosco. From this he deduces that the surface of the earth under the water must also be spherical. Otherwise there would be a vacuum between the two, and nature abhors a vacuum. His arguments for the sphericity of air and fire follow this line.

That choice bit of Christian doctrine which held that Jerusalem is the middle point of the earth found its way early into medieval England. Adamnan, abbot of Iona, reports [14] Arculf's belief in it, Arculf's authority being that 12th verse of the 74th Psalm which says, "But God, our King, before the ages had wrought salvation in the midst of the earth." When Arculf visited Jerusalem as a pilgrim, he was shown a column said to mark the spot. The position of the spot seems to have moved around through the ages, but be-

lief in the doctrine was quite persistent. Saewulf, an English pilgrim to the Holy Land in 1102 and 1103, reiterates it, reporting
however that the spot is located in the wall outside the head of
the Church of the Holy Sepulchre in Jerusalem. In support of the
doctrine he quotes the same verse from the Psalmist as Arculf, in
slightly different form, "For God is my king of old, working
salvation in the midst of the earth." [15] In the archives of Hereford
Cathedral is a vellum map of the earth, drawn in the latter part of
the thirteenth century (1275–1300), which represents Jerusalem as
the middle of the earth, indicating continuing belief in this doctrine
in England that late. The phrase "midst of the earth" may have
been considered to refer either to the highest point on a motionless, round earth or to the center of the inhabited quarter of the
globe or even to the center of the *known* earth, the "orbis terrae,"
that broad area in southern Europe, northern Africa, and southern
Asia known to the Romans, without regard for curvature.

How much of this round earth is inhabited was a matter of considerable concern in the Middle Ages. The problem was raised by
two Greek concepts, that of four inhabited land masses separated
by impassable oceans and that of a "zoned" earth. The latter was
an essential part of the Greek universe already described; the
former was a separate theory which attached itself to the motionless, round earth before the birth of Christ. Both concepts reached
England before Columbus first sailed for the "Indies."

The concept of four inhabited land masses separated by impassable oceans was propounded by Crates of Mallos in the second
century before Christ and reached western Europe through the
writings of Macrobius and Capella. Crates suggested [16] that the
known earth is one of four, similar, inhabited land masses, separated from each other by two oceans, one encircling the globe
from east to west, the other encircling it from north to south.
The two oceans were regarded as impassable, and they, together
with a fiery, equatorial zone, were thought to seal off each land
mass from the other three. The people supposed to live on three
of these land masses were given special names to distinguish them

from the inhabitants of the known earth. The people living on that land mass lying in the north temperate zone opposite to the known earth were called *antipodes*. Those living on that land mass which lies in the south temperate zone immediately south of the known earth were called *antoikoi*. Those living on the land mass in the south temperate zone which lies opposite to that inhabited by the *antoikoi* were called *antichthones*.

Some of the early Church fathers, like Augustine and Lactantius, argued that if the earth were round and human beings lived on such opposite land masses, these persons would hang by their feet instead of walking on them, trees would send their branches downward, and rain would fall up, patently ridiculous ideas and sufficient ground for rejecting the concept of antipodean beings and perhaps of a round earth too, though Augustine was not quite willing to go that far. More disturbing to the Church was the postulated existence of human beings separated from the known portion of the earth by an impassable ocean. Christ had instructed his disciples to "make disciples of all the nations" (Matthew 28:19). If some nations lived on the opposite side of an impassable ocean they, contrary to the dictates of Scripture, could never hear the message of salvation. Such a situation was, to the Church fathers, intolerable. They could have taken the positive view that the ocean is passable. Instead, they leaned toward the negative one that the other quarters of the globe are not inhabited. Gossouin reflected this attitude in *The Mirrour of the World* when he stated:

Syth we haue vnderstande how the erthe is rounde on all partes as an apple, neuertheles it is not enhabited in alle partyes, whiche is wel knowen, of no peple of the world. And it is not enhabited but in one quarter only, lyke as the philosophres haue enserched, whiche put for to knowe it grete trauayll and estudye.[17]

The Greek universe was marked by five zones, separated by the Tropics of Cancer and Capricorn and the Arctic and Antarctic Circles, extending upward to the sphere of the sun. The traces of these zones on the earth were also called zones. The Greek earth, then, was marked by five zones, two frigid, two temperate, and one central and torrid, all circling the earth as bands about the poles, just as they do today. Today all five are regarded as habitable, although there is no permanent settlement south of the Arctic Circle. In the Middle Ages the two frigid zones were generally considered too cold for living, the torrid zone too hot. These beliefs were taught by such writers on universe and earth as Bede [18] and Sacrobosco [19] and also perpetuated by the poets Virgil [20] and Ovid.[21] Nevertheless they did not go entirely unchallenged, and a man might hold one without the other.

Several English scholars had argued that the torrid zone is habitable before Portuguese mariners braved its heat in the early fifteenth century. Grosseteste, Roger Bacon, and Robertus Anglicus, who lectured in France on Sacrobosco's *Sphaera mundi*, seem to have been persuaded to this view largely by the writings of Avicenna, the great Moslem physician and philosopher who lived two centuries before them. Their arguments were theoretical and logical and not based on experience. Robertus Anglicus treated the subject very elaborately, presenting seven reasons in support of his contention.[22] The equatorial region is not only habitable but good to live in, he says, because, being equidistant from the poles, its heat is tempered by their frigidity; equal day and night temper each other; winter and summer are both short; the sun does not delay long in its zenith at the equator; vapors from the seas and rivers there tend to temper the natural heat, a purely accidental cause; since the rays of the sun and the other planets cause generation, the place where they are the most abundant should be best suited to living; since the more remote lands are from the equator the more uninhabitable they are, the converse must be true. This is a good example of reaching the right conclusion by arguments which are more often wrong than right.

Since the weight of scholastic argument was against the comparable view that the frigid zones are habitable, few scholars dared maintain it. Bacon, like Robertus Anglicus, believed that they are not habitable, arguing that the cold must be very intense because the rays of the sun are longest and weakest there.[23] It is nonsense to believe, as some do, that the shining of the sun there for half a year produces unbearable heat, he says—actually the valid explanation, in extreme form, for the true state of affairs. The only concession he makes is the admission that the intense cold could be modified, as in Italy, by the presence of high mountains.

Evidence that the north frigid zone is habitable was not entirely lacking. Dicuil, the imperturbable and refreshingly impudent Irish scholar of the Carolingian renaissance, knew monks who had spent six months in Iceland [24]—Thule to him—just under the Arctic Circle. Iceland was settled soon after by the Norse who, in the tenth century, also settled Greenland, where they found traces of prior occupation by natives, further evidence of habitableness. In the ninth century Ohthere, the Norwegian, had sailed north of the Arctic Circle into the White Sea, on whose shores he found men living, and told King Alfred of Wessex about it. But this evidence was lost or buried or disregarded or simply not generally available.

Bartholomew, Higden, and Gossouin do not discuss the five zones, and there is only indirect evidence to suggest the attitude toward them of the Englishman who was not a scholar. The chances are that before the fifteenth century he knew little about them and cared less. Belief in the intolerable heat of the torrid zone should not long have survived news of Portuguese discoveries in that zone in Africa during the fifteenth century, but it does seem to have lingered on into the sixteenth. Belief in the intolerable cold of the frigid zones had an even longer life despite numerous English contacts with Iceland in the fifteenth century and English voyages to the White Sea in the century following.

The belief that gold occurs in quantity only near the equator, prevalent in England during the sixteenth century, was much more important in turning Englishmen away from the temperate zone of North America (Canada, the United States, and northern Mexico) than is generally supposed. It stems from the early Greek theory of the origin of metals. According to this theory, as presented by Aristotle in the third book of his *Meteorologica*,[25] metals are formed by the imprisonment within the earth of a somewhat mysterious, vaporous exhalation which is congealed by the "dryness" of earth. This exhalation is one of two produced within the earth by the rays of the sun, the other being a dry exhalation which gives rise to stones that cannot be melted. By the thirteenth century, when Albertus Magnus wrote his *De mineralibus*, all of the "planets" were regarded as having a share in the creation of metals, each body being responsible for one particular metal.[26] The moon was considered to be responsible for the "generation" of silver, Mercury for quicksilver, Venus for copper, the sun for gold, Mars for iron, Jupiter for tin, and Saturn for lead. This concept was a part of the scholarly learning of the late Middle Ages and as such was current in England as well as on the continent. It was only a short step from the belief that the sun is responsible for the generation of gold to the correlative belief that gold occurs in purest form and greatest quantity where the sun's rays are hottest and most direct, along the equator, and another short step to the belief that the Tropics of Cancer and Capricorn are the limits of gold in sufficient quantity to warrant the search for it. The concept in this form was current in England at a time when gold was the principal attraction offered by America.

Regions of the Earth

That portion of the earth's surface known to the Greeks and Romans through actual experience was a narrow belt, called "orbis terrae" or "orbis terrarum" by the Romans, which stretched from Gibraltar on the west to the mouth of the river Ganges on the east. Southward by sea the limits of knowledge were the slight bulge in the African coast just south of the Strait of Gibraltar on the west and, on the east, the mouth of the Red Sea and the island of Taprobane (Ceylon), though an occasional bold trader may have sailed south along the east coast of Africa below Cape Guardfui for a short distance. The great deserts which stretch across northern Africa restricted knowledge of the interior of that continent to the coastal regions immediately south of the Mediterranean. Northward, knowledge began to be vague with Germany, which was considered to extend eastward to the Black Sea. Eastward it blurred and grew dim with Asia Minor and the Holy Land.

This narrow, east-west belt was divided into three parts: Europe, Asia, and a third which the Greeks called Libya and the Romans Africa the Great. We shall call it Africa, the medieval as well as the modern name. The Mediterranean Sea was considered the boundary between Europe and Africa. The river Tanais (Don-Volga) was usually said to separate Europe from Asia. The Nile was looked upon as the boundary between Asia and Africa. Attaching a large slice of eastern Africa to Asia in this manner was markedly different from modern practice but justified by the knowledge available at the time.

By the beginning of the Christian era the Mediterranean Sea was a Roman lake ringed by Roman provinces, which were named and described by such Roman writers as Mela and Pliny with reasonable accuracy. Long after it had in fact disintegrated, this fossil regional earth was presented as if still alive by medieval writers whose chief source of knowledge was Roman works. If they had other sources of knowledge they might show an awareness of such changes as those wrought in Europe by the Goths, the Huns, and the Franks, in Africa by the Moslems. They might also show an awareness that the limits of the known earth were expanding, particularly to the north and east. But this changing and expanding earth, if present, usually appeared as supplementary to rather than in place of the static Roman earth.

The regional earth described to medieval Englishmen by Bede at the beginning of the eighth century was almost exclusively a Roman earth. So was the earth contained in Alfred's *Orosius* except for the addition of valuable new information about France and Germany. This was the earth Bartholomew presented to his readers in the thirteenth century, an earth straight out of Pliny and Isidore of Seville, as nearly up-to-date as Bartholomew could make it by the addition of later information concerning western and northwestern Europe, yet basically the old Roman earth. This, with similar exceptions, was the earth presented by Gossouin and Higden.

Information about the margins of this earth was apt to be more out-of-date in the Middle Ages than that about more accessible regions, vague and garbled, and it might even be crusted over with a layer of the fabulous. This was particularly true with respect to Africa, Asia, and the Western Islands.

The Africa presented by Bartholomew and Higden—and their treatment of it is fairly typical—was Roman or earlier. It included only that portion of northern Africa which extends from the western borders of Egypt west along the Mediterranean to the Atlantic Ocean. Egypt was generally considered a part of Asia during the Middle Ages. The Africa of Bartholomew and Higden included the Roman provinces of Libya, with emphasis on Cyrenaican Libya, and Mauretania. For the Roman province of Africa the Less, lying between Libya and Mauretania, were substituted the older provinces, largely Phoenician in origin, of which it had been made: Tripolitania, Carthage and vicinity, and Numidia. South of these provinces were western Ethiopia and the lands of the Getulians and Garamantes, which had been partly conquered by the Romans. Eastern Ethiopia lay east of the Nile, and its position with respect to the continents of Africa and Asia was poorly defined.

The information given about Africa is a curious mixture of fact and fancy, including some fabulous material about the lesser known parts. Gold and precious stones were actually to be found there, and fruit, corn, and olives, as Bartholomew indicates. There were also lions and camels, and the Troglodytes or Cave-Dwellers did and do live there. But certainly the satyrs and mad "woses" he refers to [27] did not exist nor that strange race described by Higden from Ethiopia, said to be without heads but with eyes and mouths in their breasts.[28] This race probably stems from Pliny's mention [29] of people without necks but having eyes in their shoulders, who live near the Troglodytes, but Higden's reference need not have come directly from this source. Indeed, the difference in phrasing indicates an intermediate source. Bartholomew might conceivably be excused for including fabulous matter on the ground that he was simply explaining terms used in Scripture and Gloss, themselves old, as any encyclopedia does today, but hardly Higden, and actually both writers phrase and arrange such matter as if it were presently true. Higden's picture of Africa is particularly depressing.[30] Africa, he says, is meant to be a wailing place and has the most desert under heaven, more ground rendered unfit for habitation by the heat of the sun than there is in Europe through the blight of cold. The sun is so hot, he continues, that it makes men who live there short of body, black of skin, crisp of hair, and faint of heart through the evaporation of spirits, whereas, in northern parts, the cold encloses the humours in the body where they grow fat and make men tall, light of skin, and courageous. This weird species of physical anthropology was an inevitable corollary of the belief in the Greek universe, to the parts of which the humours were closely related. Gossouin does not discuss Africa as a whole but does say [31] that Libya is rich and well peopled, that Ethiopians are black from the heat of the sun, and that beyond Ethiopia there is nothing but a desert inhabited by serpents and wild beasts, information available in standard Roman works.

Asia was so large and diverse in character that general description was rarely attempted. Instead, the usual procedure was to describe its provinces. These varied in number from work to work, but a reasonably full list might include Arabia, Assyria, Babylonia, Chaldea, Egypt, India, the Earthly Paradise, and Persia. Mandeville also described Mancy and Cathay, the medieval China, but since he drew on a nearly contemporary travel account for that material, discussion will be reserved for the next chapter. Bacon's reference to Cathay will be reserved until later for the same reason. Higden and Gossouin do not refer to China. Bartholomew does speak of a province in the east called Seres where wool is gathered from trees and silk separated from the wool, but that much information about China appeared in classical works. This medieval Asia was not entirely Roman. To the Roman Asia had been added the Earthly Paradise, an imaginary province derived from the Old Testament. Two others were usually included as parts of India. One of them, Ophir, was also derived from the Old Testament; the other, the land of Prester John, grew out of medieval Christian legend. India and the Earthly Paradise aroused more interest than the rest in western Europe during the late Middle Ages and the sixteenth century.

Considerable information about India, much of it stemming from the conquests of Alexander the Great, found its way into classical and medieval works, but the real knowledge was almost buried under a mass of fable. Bartholomew's India [32] is a land of spices, precious stones, and elephants, where live seven-foot giants who never have headache or toothache, men with the heads of hounds, men with eight-toed feet which point backward instead of forward, and, at the head of the Ganges, men without mouths who live on the smell of flowers and wood-apples. The India of Higden [33] is even more fabulous than that of Bartholomew, though they have enough in common to suggest a common source. India, he says, is a land of nightingales, elephants, pepper, precious stones, and hills of gold guarded by dragons, griffins, and wondrous men. There may be found men seven feet tall who neither die nor wail. In that land are pygmies less than two feet tall who fight with cranes, men with heads like dogs, men who live by smell, and men with hollow fingers. Some men in India have many wives, and when such a man dies, his favorite wife is buried with him. All this is set down as fact, with equal emphasis. *The Mirrour of the World* displays the same indiscriminate mixture of fact and fancy with respect to animals, and part of their description reads like a medieval bestiary, emphasizing the heavy reliance on old texts rather than contemporary travel accounts. Ranging side by side through Gossouin's India [34] are the real elephant, sacred white bull, lion, tiger, panther, and rhinoceros and the fabulous centycore and manticore. The centycore is said to be a beast with the breast and thighs of a lion, the ears and feet of a horse, the muzzle of a bear, the voice of a man, and a single horn in the middle of his face. The manticore is described as having the body of a lion, the tail of a scorpion, the face of a man, and a sweet voice by means of which he lures men to their death. Even the real beasts often have some fabulous attributes. The panther is said to have a sweet breath which attracts other beasts to him, presumably to their death. It is said that a rhinoceros can be captured only by a virgin, attractively dressed, at sight of whom he will approach and drop down, falling asleep with his head in her lap.

The legendary land of Prester John is described in some detail in *The Travels of Sir John Mandeville*.[35] Prester John is said to be a Christian, though lacking some of the articles of faith, and "a great Emperour of Inde," whose dynasty is linked to that of the ruler of Cathay. His land is rich and extensive, including many of the islands caused by the "great flods that come out of Paradise." [36] In this fashion Jean d'Outremeuse tied this legendary land to three different regions of the earth, to India, Cathay, and the Earthly Paradise. Despite this substantial mooring, it is in large measure fabulous. It is the land possessed of precious stones so big that plates and cups are made of them. In it is a sea composed solely of moving sand and gravel, which contains edible fish, and into it flows a great flood out of Paradise, without water but full of precious stones, which rushes swiftly three days a week and is quiet the rest of the time. Beyond the flood is a sandy plain where trees appear at sunrise and grow to maturity by noon, at which time they disappear. In the land is a race of wild men with horns on their heads who root like hogs, and popinjays who talk like men.

The elusive land of Ophir takes substantial form on the pages of Bartholomew.[37] It was more attractive to Englishmen of the fifteenth and sixteenth centuries than the land of Prester John because it was reputed to be the land of gold, for which they longed above all other things. Bartholomew places Ophir in India, and though he offers no explanation for the location, it is in-

herent in his statement that the province was named after the
grandson of Heber.

All the accounts of Ophir are based on the short one found in
the Old Testament, in the first book of Kings 9:26–28, 10:11 and
the second book of Chronicles 8:18, 9:10. It relates that some of
Solomon's men, accompanied by sailors furnished by Hiram, king
of Tyre, set sail for Ophir from Eziongeber, in the land of Edom
on the shores of the Red Sea, and brought back 420 or 450 talents of
gold. The accounts differ slightly as to the amount. Mention is also
made of the almug (sandalwood) trees and precious stones of
Ophir.

By the time this tale reached Bartholomew it had picked up a
number of adornments. He describes it as the golden land with the
golden mountains, and says it possesses such precious stones as
crysopas and adamant (diamond), such valuable woods as thuna(?)
and ebony. Sweet spices may also be found there. It is inhabited
by peacocks, apes, and other wondrous beasts. Lions are so numerous and dangerous that visitors who land there stay within
hailing distance of their ship, which stands by prepared to pick
them up in case the lions appear.

The reasons for some of these additions are readily apparent.
The names of precious stones were probably included because of a
natural desire to be specific. In the first book of Kings 10:22 there
is a passage saying that once every three years Solomon's navy
of Tarshish returned, bringing gold, silver, ivory, apes, and peacocks. Some authorities have thought that Tarshish and Ophir
were located near each other, or perhaps were even the same,
hence the products of one might also be the products of the other.
Thus Ophir, in the old accounts, attracted some of the products
of Tarshish.

The linking of the name of Ophir with that of a grandson of
Heber was almost inevitable. In the Middle Ages there was general
Christian belief in the doctrine that after the Great Flood the
three sons of Noah divided the earth among them, that Japheth

took Europe, Shem Asia, and Ham Africa, their descendants holding these vast areas after them. Among the descendants of Shem the book of Genesis 10:29 lists Ophir, the grandson of Heber. Ophir the man, reasoned the medieval Christian, must have ruled Ophir the region, and since he ruled in Asia, by virtue of descent from Shem, the land bearing his name must be in Asia. Where else in that continent should it be but in India, the place from which some of the named precious objects were known to come? Ophir's place in India was, however, an uneasy one, and some voyagers of the fifteenth and sixteenth centuries, including Englishmen, sought it elsewhere.

The Old Testament was also the principal source of information about the character and location of Eden or Paradise. Genesis 2:8 said it was "a garden eastward," and for the medieval inhabitants of western Europe "eastward" meant Asia. Furthermore, the verses immediately following declared that the garden, in which grew every good and fruitful tree, was watered by a river which divided into four streams when it left Eden: the Phison, "which compasseth the whole land of Havilah, where there is gold"; the Gyhon; the Hiddekel or Diglath, "which goeth in front of Assyria"; and the Euphrates. The natural inclination of the reader was to identify the three unfamiliar names with those of other well-known rivers. The Diglath had to be the Tigris to go with the Euphrates. Havilah must be India, because of the gold, and the Phison therefore the Ganges. The Gyhon must be the Nile, so important that it had to be represented among the four. There was some difference of opinion as to how far east in Asia Eden was. Some, like Jean d'Outremeuse, thought it was the farthest point east, "at the beginning of the earth." [38] Others were less definite.

Because Adam and Eve needed no clothes and Eden was a garden the year around, men considered that the climate was temperate. Those who believed in the extreme heat of the torrid zone presumably placed Eden to the north. Roger Bacon reports that some theologians took a different view. Hearing that the Earthly Paradise required an absolutely even temperature, they located it at the equator, where they considered that the heat of day and the coolness of night neutralized each other.[39]

Men were also concerned with the vertical location of Eden, whether it was above and apart from the earth, above but connected to the earth, or simply on earth and no very great distance above it. Jean d'Outremeuse seems to have taken the intermediate view, saying that the Earthly Paradise is the highest point on earth, approaching the sphere of the moon, for Noah's flood did not reach it.[40] A high mountain indeed, yet many writers, both classical and medieval, believed in very high mountains. Higden argues forcibly and convincingly that Paradise must be on earth and not very far above it.[41] Paradise has to be in the elementary part of the universe, he says, because it contains fruit, flowers, and trees similar to those on earth. It cannot exist in the elements fire, air, or water because neither water nor air is capable of sustaining such a burden, and nothing vegetable could possibly survive in the element fire. If Paradise were situated above and apart from the earth, it would not be possible for the four rivers flowing out of Paradise to reach the earth. If Paradise were above the earth yet connected with it, then the earth would be elongate instead of round. Men know that the earth is round, affirms Higden, because in every eclipse of the moon it makes a round shadow. The only place Paradise could be, then, is on the earth, and the only question remaining is where on the surface of the earth it is to be found. There must be space in the eastern portion, he concludes, at least as large as India or Egypt, and there lies Paradise. More than one voyager of the fifteenth and sixteenth centuries looked for it as his eye swept over a new land.

Islands had a special appeal for classical and medieval writers about the earth, some of whom devoted a separate section to them. Being relatively small and entirely surrounded by water, each island or group of islands had an individuality that a political province on land could never possess. Natural features were often striking, repelling or attracting the mariner as the case might be, and fabulous inhabitants or attributes sometimes attached themselves there. The islands of the Mediterranean received most of the attention, but the islands lying on the western edge of the known earth were given a good share, partly because of their remote situation.

For the Romans there were six important Western Islands, which might be single or a group, and no one writer necessarily treated all of them. They were the Fortunate Isles, Britain, Ireland, the Orcades, Thule, and Atlantis. Bartholomew and Higden included all except Atlantis. Gossouin, whose geographical knowledge was quite inferior to theirs, considered only Ireland and Atlantis. These writers added little to what they found in classical accounts. Atlantis is still the great island which, in the time of Plato, sank into the depths of the ocean because of the sins of its inhabitants. The Fortunate Isles are nothing more than those western islands so temperate of climate and fertile of soil that some men believe them to be the seat of the Earthly Paradise. Something has been added to the descriptions of Britain and Ireland but much less than might be expected, and there are fabulous overtones to both. Ireland, in particular, continues to be simply a green place with a mild climate where no snakes can live. The Orcades (Orkneys, Shetlands, and perhaps Faroes) are only islands north of Britain. Thule or Thile, whose identity is in doubt to this day, is the last island of the Western Ocean, six days' sail from Britain, where there is day half the year and night the other half, a description which differs little from that written by Pytheas of Massilia in the fourth century before Christ.

The Changing Three-Part Earth Brought to England Before the Discovery of America

THERE EXISTED in medieval England another regional earth, a changing, growing one, largely the possession of trader and traveler but available to anyone, including the scholar, who traveled or listened to travelers or read accounts of trade and travel later than Roman works. The scope of that earth in the second quarter of the fifteenth century is indicated by a poem,[1] written by an unnamed person about 1437, exhorting Englishmen to control the "narrowe sea" (Strait of Dover and adjacent portions of the English Channel and the North Sea). This "libel" lumbers clumsily along in heroic couplets which are a far cry from the smoothly tripping ones of the master Pope, yet it has strength and manages a graphic picture of the traffic passing that way.

Tall ships from Spain pass through the strait on their way to Flanders, laden with figs, dates, raisins, grain, wine, olive oil, saffron, iron, and mercury. These return to Spain with cotton, woolen, and linen goods, much of the wool from sheep raised in England. Ships from the Baltic sail to Flanders with beer and bacon; copper, silver, and steel; lumber, pitch, flax, and canvas.

Into English ports sail ships from Portugal with products similar to those of Spain, which are traded for English wool and tin, great carracks from Genoa with such luxuries as cloth of gold, silk, and black pepper, and galleons from Venice and Florence with all sorts of spices, sweet wines, and with apes and marmosets for pets. Bristol men return from Iceland, their bottoms loaded with stockfish. Englishmen pass back and forth between England and Brabant, a great market for English wool, where they buy dyes, garlic, onions, and saltfish and rub shoulders in the markets with Frenchmen, Lombards, Genoese, Catalonians, Scots, Spaniards, and Irishmen as well as Flemings, Dutchmen, and traders from the north.

This changing earth was principally western Europe and adjacent islands. It had very little to do with Africa and was only indirectly concerned with Asia. It had been so since prehistoric time.

The island of Britain might conceivably be looked upon as off the beaten path in prehistoric and early historic time because of its position on the western edge of the known earth, remote from the Mediterranean centers of culture. The contrary seems to have been true. The beaten path was the sea, and evidence dug up by the archeologists [2] indicates that Britain was very much on the beaten path as early as the Neolithic Age, when seamen from western France and the Iberian peninsula began to explore the Atlantic coast to the north of them. Many followed the sea route between Ireland and Britain, probably easier to navigate than that between Britain and the continent, which at that time was shallower and narrower than it is now.

Colonists came early from the continent. About 2400 B.C. some moved from northern France across the English Channel into southern Britain. About 2300 B.C. others came from Iberia to form scattered settlements in Ireland and along the entire length of western Britain. At the dawn of the Early Bronze Age colonists came from still another part of the continent to another part of Britain. Between 1900 and 1800 B.C. men possessed of metal beakers moved from the middle and lower Rhinelands across the North Sea to eastern Britain.

Trade between Britain and Ireland became important in the Early Bronze Age (c. 1900–1600 B.C.). Ornaments were fashioned from Wicklow gold. Tools and weapons of copper or bronze were made in Ireland from Irish copper and Cornish tin. These found their way eastward across Britain to adjacent portions of the continent, providing a temporary reversal of the normal direction of movement of products and culture into the island. In the Middle Bronze Age (c. 1600–1000 B.C.) bronze tools and weapons superior to those of Ireland were made in southern Britain, copied after continental models. The presence of Irish gold, amber from Jutland, trinkets and amulets from central Europe, and beads from Egypt in the graves of those Britons who manufactured or traded in these bronze objects indicates the scope of the trade.

In the Late Bronze Age (c. 1000–500 B.C.) and the Early Iron Age (c. 500 B.C. to 50 A.D.) various groups of men, including the iron-using Celts, moved into Britain from the middle Rhinelands, the Alpine fringe, northern France, and Belgium. Though sea-trade with the Iberian peninsula continued, land routes across the continent became increasingly important. Greek traders, especially interested in Cornish tin, developed two routes across France from the Mediterranean to the Bay of Biscay: from Narbo to the head of the Garonne River and down the Garonne to the sea; from Massilia (Marseilles) up the Rhone Valley to the head of the Loire River and down the Loire to the sea. During the Roman occupation of Britain (43 A.D. to c. 450 A.D.) other land routes were added to the north, making it easier to send goods across to London and neighboring harbors in Kent and Essex than to ports in southern Britain.

Soon after the Romans left Britain, the Jutes, the Angles, and the Saxons established themselves there. They dominated most of eastern and southern Britain until the Norman Conquest, though parts of the island were held by Norsemen after the middle of the ninth century. Beginning with the year 787 when, according to the Anglo-Saxon *Chronicle*,[3] three of their ships touched at a port in Dorset, Norse raiders, traders, and settlers often visited Britain. At various times Norsemen actually ruled large portions of Britain and Ireland.

These visitors to the shores of Britain brought with them information about the regions from which they came. The trader left some behind him, if only in the form of foreign products, and he probably left more. The invader or colonist no doubt made a much greater contribution. Even the casual raider left an awareness of strange ships, arms, dress, and physiognomy. To this list must be added the churchman, who brought much of value, even in the early Middle Ages.

Churchmen were particularly active in Britain in the seventh and eighth centuries, in touch with Ireland on the one hand and with Rome on the other. Visitors also came from other parts of the Christian world. Archbishop Theodore, who was ordained in 668, and his friend, Abbot Hadrian, typify the progressive, traveled churchman of the period.[4] They gathered together in Britain a company of scholars interested in metrics, astronomy, and ecclesiastical arithmetic, subjects which ordinarily included some cosmography, in addition to the normal ecclesiastical curriculum. No doubt they studied a Greek universe and a regional earth that was basically Roman. But Theodore had grown up in Asia Minor and Hadrian in Africa. They had left Rome for Britain together, traveling by ship to Marseilles and overland to Arles. There they had parted company temporarily to visit churchmen in the kingdom of the Franks, joining forces again in Britain. Thus their combined experience of contemporary regions of the earth was considerable and should have leavened their study of the static Roman earth.

New Lands

The first English book to show an awareness of the changing face of Europe was Alfred's *Orosius*.[5] The earth revealed there is the Roman earth of Orosius changed only with respect to Europe. Orosius had visualized Europe as divided into two parts, northern and southern, separated from each other by an imaginary and mainly east-west line which followed the courses of the Rhine and the Danube. Alfred added a little to the description of southern Europe and much to that of northern Europe, doing it so un-

obtrusively that, except for the accounts of the voyages of Ohthere and Wulfstan, it is almost impossible to detect the additions
without comparing the two texts page by page.

The only region in southern Europe about which Alfred had
new information was that which is now France, Belgium, and
southern Holland. For Orosius this area was Gallia, and he had
carefully described its four Roman provinces, Gallia Belgica,
Gallia Lugdunensis, Narbonensis, and Aquitania. Many changes
had taken place there in the more than 400 years since Orosius had
written. The Vascones, a Spanish tribe of Basque antecedents, had
moved down from the Pyrenees into southern Aquitania (south-
western France) as far as the Garonne and had there established
Gascony. The Franks had conquered most of central Europe, sup-
planting the names of the Roman provinces in the west with names
of their own until only Aquitania, modified as Aquitaine, remained.
In the southeast this process had reversed itself. There the very
early Roman term "Our Province," applied to the small area
bounded by the Alps, the Mediterranean, and the river Rhone, had
been revived as "Provence." Alfred's information was not exact
or abundant enough to enable him to make accurate, detailed cor-
rections. Indeed, his additions were not entirely consistent and produced a confused mixture of the old and the new. He dropped the
old term "Gallia Lugdunensis," retained "Gallia Belgica," picked
up the new "Aquitaine," changed "Narbonensis" to "Narbonese
country," and added the entirely new terms "Gascons" and "Bur-
gundi." He made his bow to "Provence" by referring to that part
of the Wendel (Mediterranean) Sea bordering the area east of the
Rhone as the "Provence" Sea.

To Orosius' description of northern Europe, however, Alfred
was able to add new information about the Teutonic tribes, particularly with respect to their number and location, that was exact,
detailed, and constructive. Orosius had described northern Europe
in brief and summary fashion. First he gave its boundaries, then he
divided it into three parts, Alania on the east, Dacia and Gothia in

the middle, and Germany on the west. All he could say about Germany was that it contained fifty-four peoples, the most powerful of whom were the Suevi on the west. Alfred added so much new material that, with the accounts of the voyages of Ohthere and Wulfstan included, he increased the length of Orosius' text by about a third. His boundaries for northern Europe are much the same as those of Orosius, but instead of dividing northern Europe into three separate parts, he followed the more general Roman practice and called the whole Germania. For the bare mention of the existence there of fifty-four peoples, he substituted specific treatment of twenty-eight Teutonic tribes, which he located systematically with respect to each other and to certain named natural features, particularly rivers.

The voyages of Ohthere and Wulfstan are remarkable for the distance traveled and the remoteness of the regions visited. Their own accounts of these voyages, which Alfred acknowledges as contemporary, are equally remarkable for clarity and for the almost complete absence of fabulous material. Ohthere, a Norwegian, described two voyages to Alfred, one around the North Cape into the White Sea, the other south to Denmark and the approaches of the Baltic. Wulfstan, an Anglo-Saxon, described a single voyage which took him into the Baltic Sea and along its south coast as far as the mouth of the Vistula River.

Ohthere told Alfred that he was a Northman and said that his curiosity once drove him to make a voyage northward from his home in order to determine three things: the northward extent of the wasteland to the north of his country, where the Fins came for hunting in the winter and sea fishing in the summer; the range of the walrus, whose hide was used for ship ropes; and whether anyone lived north of the wasteland. He sailed north for three days, when he was as far north as the whale hunters (Ohthere considered the walrus a kind of whale) ever went. Then he sailed north another three days to a place where the land inclined due east. There he waited for a west wind which carried him eastward for four days to a place where the land inclined south. There he waited for a north wind which drove him south for five days to the mouth of a great river, beyond which he dared not sail because of the hostile Beormas who lived there. This was the first inhabited land he had encountered since leaving home.

Ohthere regarded himself as a man of some wealth. He owned 600 reindeer and had a few cattle, sheep, swine, and horses besides. Tribute paid by the Fins, he said, formed a large part of the wealth of the Northmen. This tribute was paid in whalebone, ship ropes of seal hide and whale hide, bird feathers, and the skins of wild animals, and each Fin paid according to his birth, the best-born paying the most.

The land of the Northmen, Ohthere said, is long and narrow, the cultivated land being broadest on the south and narrowing northward to three miles. To the east of the cultivated land and parallel to it is a belt of mountains inhabited by the Fins. Beyond the mountains is Sweden and north of Sweden is Cwenland. The Cwenas raid the Northmen with the help of light boats, which enable them to traverse the narrow mountain lakes which lie between.

Ohthere also told Alfred of a voyage he had made south from his shire of Halgoland (in northern Norway) to Sciringesheal (on the Oslo Firth) and Haethum in Denmark. On the way south he had Norway to port and on the starboard first Iraland and then the islands between Iraland and Britain until he came to Sciringesheal. If the word "Iraland" refers to Ireland, then Ohthere had a poorer conception of the relationship of Britain, Ireland, and the neighboring islands than we should expect from so experienced a mariner. If it should be read as "Iceland," a name already in use among Norsemen for the island which now bears it, then Ohthere's geography is correct. South of Sciringesheal he found a great sea (East Sea) running into the land, too broad to see over, and on the opposite side first Jutland, then Seeland. From Sciringesheal he sailed south in five days to the harbor called Haethum, which stands between the Winedas and the Saxons and Angles. For three days Denmark was on his left and a wide sea on his right; two days before he came to Haethum he had on his right Jutland, Seeland, and many islands.

Wulfstan told Alfred that he went from Haethum to Truso in seven days and nights, full sail all the way. On his left were the islands of Langeland, Laaland, Falster, Skaane, Burgendaland (Bjornholm), Biekinge, Meore, Oland, and Gotland. On his right was Weonodland (Winedasland) as far as the mouth of the river Wisle (Vistula) and beyond the Wisle was Witland, which belongs to the Ests. The Wisle flows into the Estmere (Frisches Haff), which is about 15 miles wide. The Ilfing (Elbing River), a tributary of the Wisle, enters it near its mouth, issuing from a lake on the shores of which Truso stands. The Estmere breaks northwest into the sea. Today most of the water of the Vistula pours directly north across its delta into the Baltic, not northeast through the Nogat channel into the Frisches Haff, as Wulfstan said it did. Furthermore, the barrier beach which closes in the Frisches Haff on the north is today breached by a channel on the northeast instead of the northwest where Wulfstan located it. Despite these apparent discrepancies it seems likely that the observations of Wulfstan were accurate. A great river often shifts channels on its delta, and a barrier beach normally fills in one place and breaches another in time of severe storm.

Estland, says Wulfstan, is very large with many towns, and in every town a king. There is a great quantity of honey so that the poor and the slaves drink mead while the king and the richest men drink mares' milk.

Disposition of the dead among the Ests, as described by Wulfstan, was a protracted and hilarious affair, a long and improved Irish wake. The dead man, he says, lies unburned among his friends and relations for a period of one to six months; the greater his wealth the longer the period. This is possible because of the ability of one of the Est tribes to produce cold in the body so that the flesh does not putrefy. During this period there are drinking and sports at the expense of the dead man's estate. On the day of the burning, the property which remains is divided into five or six heaps of unequal size. The largest is placed about a mile from the dead man's house. The others, in ever diminishing size, are laid in between this one and the house. Then the men of the neighborhood assemble at a distance with fast horses and race toward these heaps of chattels, the rider of the swiftest horse taking the first and largest, the second rider taking the next largest, and so on until each heap has been taken. What a man takes he may keep, and on this account fast horses command an outrageous price. After this event the dead man is carried out and burned, along with his weapons and clothes.

This account of a changing and expanding western Europe was lost to medieval Englishmen after the Norman Conquest when the Anglo-Saxon language, in which Alfred's *Orosius* was written, fell into disfavor. It was not made generally available again until the modern era. However, relatively up-to-date descriptions of that part of the continent immediately adjacent to the island of Britain, the area that is now France, Germany, Belgium, and Holland, were available to the English layman in *De proprietatibus rerum* and the *Polychronicon*. Furthermore, trade, military activities in France, and pilgrimages to shrines in Germany, France, Spain, Italy, and the Holy Land made available considerable first-hand information.

Bartholomew [6] and Higden [7] both knew that France was not divided into Gallia Belgica, Gallia Lugdunensis, Narbonensis, and Aquitania but included such provinces as Picardy, Normandy, Brittany, Burgundy, and Gascony. Indeed, they not only mention these and other provinces by name but refer to their principal rivers, chief towns, and important products, and even enumerate the dominant characteristics, physical and emotional, of their inhabitants. They were well aware of the woolen industry in Flanders and Brabant and its importance as a market for English wool. They knew a little about Holland. Bartholomew was even aware of the already vigorous mining industry in Saxony, where so much was eventually learned about minerals, for he speaks of the mountains there "in the whyche stones ben dygged and ben strongly blowen with fyre: and torne to brasse and metall." [8]

Norse regions and Germanic regions bordering the Baltic are described in cursory fashion only in De proprietatibus rerum and the Polychronicon. Intimate details like those which make the accounts of Ohthere and Wulfstan so entertaining are entirely absent. Some of the regions are aptly, though roughly, characterized; others are distorted almost beyond recognition. Higden thought that the Scandinavian peninsula (Norway to him) was an island; [9] Bartholomew knew better than this, for he says that Norway is almost surrounded by water.[10] Higden also looked upon Denmark as an island,[11] and the several islands which are associated with the peninsula do give color to that mistake. He confused the names Denmark and Dacia,[12] which stood for a country north of the Danube and close to the Black Sea. Bartholomew did not consider Denmark an island, but he also mistakenly thought that the names Denmark and Dacia were synonymous.[13]

Iceland, a Norse region and a post-Roman Western Island (unless Pytheas of Massilia had heard of it) is mentioned by both Bartholomew [14] and Higden.[15] By the fourteenth century it had become an important source of fish for the continent, and Higden rightly says that the inhabitants live by fishing. Both speak of the great white bears who fish through the ice, and Higden refers to the huge falcons and gentle goshawks, all of whom could then be found on the island. Neither writer identifies Iceland with the old Thule or Thile but lists the two separately, perhaps because Thule is said to be six days' sail from Britain and Iceland only three. This identification had been made long before in fact, though not in name, by Dicuil in De mensura orbis terrae (825 A.D.).[16] It could not be made by name at that time because Iceland had not yet been so designated. Dicuil related the two unwittingly in correcting two statements he had read about Thule: that the island has six months of day and six months of night, and that the sea around the island is frozen. Certain monks, who had been on Thule from February to August, had told him thirty years before that while it was light enough at night about the time of the summer solstice for a man to work or pick lice from his shirt, there certainly was not continuous day for six months of the year nor night for the other six. They also reported to him that the sea was frozen a day's sail north of the island but not around the island itself. A statement in the *Islendingabok*,[17] one of two early Norse accounts of the settling of Iceland, leaves little doubt that Dicuil's Thule was Iceland: it records that the colonists who first landed on the island found Irish monks already there, who soon left because they did not wish to associate with heathen men.

Greenland and Vinland, a region in America, were both Norse regions in the Middle Ages. Greenland was settled from Iceland and Vinland was visited from Greenland. Greenland is mentioned by neither Bartholomew nor Higden, but Vinland, curiously enough, is mentioned by both. Bartholomew refers to it as "Wynlandia," and Higden calls it "Wyntlandia."

The Norse visits to America are of particular interest to those of us who live here. Two principal accounts of them are to be found in the early Icelandic sagas and histories, one in the *Hauk's Book*[18] and the *Saga of Eric the Red*,[19] the other in the *Flatey Bok*[20] and the *Heimskringla*.[21] Though they differ in some important respects, they possess enough in common to indicate that about 1000 A.D. members of the family of Eric the Red led at least two expeditions to the eastern coast of North America from Greenland, the sojourn of one of the expeditions covering a period of three winters. It is not altogether clear that the visitors planned to settle, but the length of the stay and the presence of women and cattle seem to indicate that they did. They named the regions of the new land Helluland, Markland, Keelness, and Vinland. In Vinland they found wild grapes and volunteer wheat in abundance. M. L. Fernald has suggested[22] that these were not grapes but whortleberries, wineberries ripe in spring instead of summer or fall, not wheat but a grass with edible seeds ("Strand Wheat"). Even so, the name Vinland was an apt one. The Vinland camp of the Greenlanders, so runs the thread of the narrative, could be reached only at high tide. They traded for furs with certain natives whom they called Skraelings, who were frightened at the time of the trading by the bellowing bull of the foreigners. The Skraelings sought unsuccessfully to obtain Norse weapons, first by trade, then by theft, and eventually proved hostile. Thorvald, a son of Eric the Red, was killed in the new land by a Skraeling arrow, and Snorri, son of Karlsefni, who had married into the family of Eric the Red, was born in Vinland. The leaders made large profits through the sale of furs and timber brought back to a cold and almost treeless Greenland. No permanent settlement was established in Vinland or any other part of the new land. Two entries in the Icelandic annals indicate a continuing interest in the new land on the part of the Greenlanders. They relate that in 1121 Bishop Eric of Greenland went in search of Vinland, and that in 1347 a small trading vessel, with seventeen or eighteen men on board, had sailed from Greenland to Markland, then been blown to Iceland as it sought to return from Markland to Greenland.[23]

Near the end of the twelfth century the climate of Greenland, which had been appreciably milder than it is at present, took a turn for the worse.[24] The summer thaw grew progressively shorter, and about the beginning of the fifteenth century the ground became frozen. This condition gradually destroyed the Greenland colonies and with them the one link between western Europe and America. During the late Middle Ages, Iceland had numerous contacts with other Western Islands and with the continent of Europe as far south as Spain and Portugal. This made possible some dissemination of the news of the discovery of Vinland, to Greenlanders the most important region of the new land. But the snapping of the connecting link between America and the "known" earth made for distortion of fact, and the accounts available to the English layman at the end of the fifteenth century were a far cry from the truth. Higden told him that Wyntlandia was a barren island, west of Denmark, inhabited by a barbarous, idol-worshiping people who sold wind to the persons visiting their ports.[25] Bartholomew, too, related the story about selling wind and said that Wynlandia was a land on the continent of Europe, "a countree besydes the mountayns of Norway towarde the east." [26] A more accurate, though still scanty, account was available to the English scholar from the latter part of the eleventh century in the *Descriptio insularum aquilonis* of Adam of Bremen.[27]

New information about Africa was slow to reach any part of western Europe during the Middle Ages with the exception of Saracen Spain. The Mohammedan sweep across northern Africa to the Atlantic coast in the seventh century served for a time to discourage Christian contacts there. The Moslems themselves traveled widely in Africa. They had probably penetrated southward to the Sudan (central Africa just south of the Sahara Desert) and sailed to the island of Madagascar by the eleventh century. In the thirteenth century there was sufficient trade between African ports and those in Italy and Catalonian Spain to provide an avenue for the transmission of such knowledge to England, but there is little evidence that any came. Though some mathematical geography had reached England from Saracen Spain as early as the twelfth century, as we shall see later, new descriptive geography did not follow in its train, either from Spain or any other Moslem source. Nor were later Christian sources more productive. It seems likely that by the latter half of the fourteenth century Genoese mariners had sailed down the west coast of Africa as far as Cape Bojador (just south of the Canaries). In 1434 Gil Eannes, a Portuguese mariner, braved the supposedly impassable heat of the torrid zone and the strong currents and dangerous shoals which guarded Cape Bojador to sail beyond that point. Soon other Portuguese mariners had reached Cape Blanc and Cape Verde (Dakar). The information these men gathered could have been common talk in English ports, to which ships sailed from Italian, Spanish, and Portuguese ports. But if a man wanted it he had to seek it there. It was not to be found in the books available in England in the fifteenth century.

Fresh information concerning Cathay or northern China came to western Europe about the middle of the thirteenth century as an indirect result of the Tartar invasion, which by that time had extended itself as far west as Hungary and the shores of the Adriatic. Louis IX of France sent William of Rubruque, a Franciscan, to gain firsthand knowledge of these frightening newcomers, who threatened to overrun the whole of Europe. Rubruque traveled among them for two years, 1253–1255, apparently penetrating to the interior of Asia. Though he was chiefly concerned with the Tartars, he also picked up some information about the people of Cathay, perhaps in Tangut, which he visited.[28]

Roger Bacon had access to Rubruque's journal, perhaps because both men were Franciscans, and included most of its information about Cathay in his *Opus majus*.[29] East of the land of the Tartars, says Bacon, lies Tangut, then Thebèt (Thibet), then the people called Solangi, and finally Great Cathay, whose inhabitants were formerly called Seres. Its people, he declares, make excellent garments in great quantity, which they export to other lands. They are competent workmen, good physicians, and write with a brush, forming in one character a group of letters which may represent a sentence. Their common money is a card of mulberry bark bearing stamped lines. In the cliffs of Great Cathay live hairy creatures (monkeys) resembling human beings, who walk by leaping and do not speak, whose blood is used for purple dye. Bacon's work was not generally available since he was under suspicion of heresy because of his advanced ideas; consequently the *Opus majus* had a limited circulation in the Middle Ages, even among scholars. But by the second half of the fourteenth century all literate Englishmen, layman and scholar, had a much better source of information about Cathay—and Mancy (southern China) and certain islands (East Indies) as well—in *The Travels of Sir John Mandeville*.

The Travels of Sir John Mandeville, though patently fictitious in such a part as the description of the land of Prester John, was based in large measure on fact, on the journal [30] of Odoric, a Franciscan missionary, who, in the early part of the fourteenth century, had made a journey to China comparable in extent to that of Marco

Polo. Reversing the order of Polo's travels, he went by land from Constantinople through Trebizond, Tabriz, and Baghdad to the Persian Gulf port of Ormuz, thence by boat to the city of Canton in Mancy. On the way he touched at southern India, Ceylon, Sumatra, Java, perhaps Borneo, and Indo-China. From Canton he went by land and canal to Peking in Cathay, going by way of Hang-chow and Nanking.

Mandeville—and it can do no harm to fall in with the little joke of Jean d'Outremeuse and pretend that he was a real person who actually made this journey—was interested in both people and natural products. His Indians are, on the whole, credible. Some of the fabulous races described by Bartholomew, Higden, and Gossouin from India are present, but most of them are said by Mandeville to inhabit neighboring islands, a natural progression as knowledge of India increased. The only one of the East Indies to be given a modern name is Java, and the reader cannot be sure whether it was attached to the present Java or some other island. The names of places have a way of moving around. Anyone who has watched the name "Taprobane" move from Ceylon to Sumatra and "Labrador" from Greenland to the continent of North America must hesitate to make positive identification on the basis of name alone. Mandeville stresses the riches of two of the islands. On Java, he says, grow ginger, cloves, nutmeg, and cinnamon, and the king's palace is lavishly trimmed with gold and silver.[31] Gold and silver are also said to be abundant on Lamory, sometimes identified with Sumatra.[32] Mandeville's description[33] of Mancy and Cathay is almost as wide in scope as that of Marco Polo and has the same magic touch. The reader gets the impression of a vast land not just wealthy but truly civilized, a land of great cities, numerous towns, and broad stretches of cultivated countryside, where people live well and in harmony with one another. The detailed description of the palace of the "great Caane" creates a picture that dazzles the eye. A similarly detailed relation of the laws, practices, and customs of the country gives an impression of great wealth and immense power wisely used.

Thus a new world was made available to the literate Englishman. No wonder the book was popular. It seems likely, however, that *The Travels of Sir John Mandeville* was more often a source of entertainment than of inspiration. Though a copy was carried by Martin Frobisher on his voyage of 1576 in search of a northwest passage to Tartary and Cathay, that voyage was chiefly inspired by later information stemming from Portuguese and Spanish discoveries of the fifteenth and sixteenth centuries.

There is little evidence that *The Book of Ser Marco Polo*,[34] a sounder and more comprehensive work, was widely read in medieval England. The matter-of-fact presentation, so attractive to the serious student, the inclusion of a large number of unfamiliar place names, and the scarcity of fabulous material must have tended to repel those Englishmen who read for pleasure and relaxation. No edition was printed in England in any language until Frampton's English translation from the Spanish of Santaella appeared in London in 1579.

Several additions were made to the Western Islands, some real and others imaginary, in the late Middle Ages. The real islands were the Madeira and Azores. The most important of the imaginary ones [35] were Antilia or Island of the Seven Cities, St. Brandan's Island, and Brazil. They appeared occasionally on the maps of the fourteenth century and often on those of the century following, instruments of knowledge available principally to the specialist, the mariner and the scholar, in England and elsewhere in western Europe.

The Madeira, which were rediscovered by the Portuguese in 1420, were known to Italian sailors before the middle of the fourteenth century. The Azores, scattered over 400 miles of ocean, were discovered by the Portuguese, island by island, between 1432 and 1444. The most easterly island of this archipelago is 800 miles west of Portugal, the nearest continental land. Both the Madeira and Azores may have been visited by the Phoenicians.

Antilia appeared on the maps of the fifteenth century with considerable regularity. It was usually represented as a very large island a long way west of Africa. It was often, but not necessarily, associated with the legendary Island of the Seven Cities, which was said to have been colonized in the eighth century by seven bishops and their followers, who had fled from Spain and Portugal because of the Moslem invasion, each bishop founding a separate and Utopian city.

St. Brandan, abbot of a Benedictine monastery in Ireland, was reputed to have made an extended voyage out over the Atlantic Ocean in 565–573 in search of an ideal island, revealed to him in a dream, where the trees were heavy with fruit and the climate was always mild. The legend of St. Brandan's Island was soon a widespread one. Although the name was sometimes attached to the Canaries or Madeira, the island was long supposed to exist as a separate entity. Gossouin listed it among the "yles of the see" in his *Image du monde*,[36] and it appeared on more than one late medieval map.

The island of Brazil, whose name means red dyewood, was supposed to lie in the Atlantic Ocean a short distance off the coast of Ireland. At least one Bristol mariner set out to find it in the late fifteenth century, and there may have been others. The *Itinerarium* of William of Worcester relates that Thomas Lloyd sailed from Bristol on July 15, 1480, in search of the island of Brazil "beyond the western part of Ireland." [37]

New Techniques

As the three-part earth expanded in the Middle Ages, so skill in navigation grew and developed. Their mutual relationship is obscure, and we can be sure of little else but that each stimulated the other. New techniques were invented and old ones improved. The mariner's compass came into general use. The concepts of latitude and longitude gained some currency. Maps were greatly improved. These matters did not assume importance in England, however, until after the tenth century.

How or when knowledge of the mariner's compass came to western Europe is not known. The earliest notice of it there is to be found in a work by a distinguished English churchman and scholar, the *De naturis rerum*[38] of Alexander Neckham (1157–1217). A foster brother of Richard the Lionhearted, he was first a scholar in England and France, then professor at the University of Paris at the tender age of twenty-three. Later he returned to England and became a monk, afterward abbot, at the Augustinian monastery at Cirencester. How extensively the compass was used by the English mariner in the twelfth century, and even later, is a matter of conjecture.

It was necessary for man to grasp three concepts in order to determine his position on earth in mathematically precise terms, whether on land or sea. He had to understand that the earth is round; that distance on it can be measured in degrees; and that two celestial measurements made from an undetermined point, one of angular distance north or south of the equator (latitude), the other of distance on the equator east or west of a known point (longitude), will fix its position. At least two Greeks, Hipparchus and Ptolemy, had grasped all three. The first concept, belief in a round earth, was in England at least as early as the eighth century, as we have already seen. The other two did not necessarily accompany it. Dicuil, for example, gives numerous distances in his *De mensura orbis terrae*, including the dimensions of the inhabited earth, but he gives them in miles, not degrees. For him latitude meant the "breadth" and longitude the "length" of a given island or province. We cannot be sure that the third concept was in England until the end of the eleventh century, when the spread of Moslem learning made possible its appearance. With it came the astrolabe, an instrument by means of which latitude could be determined on land, and knowledge of the means of determining longitude.

Walcher, prior of Malvern, exhibited a rough knowledge of relative longitude in the last decade of the eleventh century.[39] In 1091, while in Italy, he noted the hour of an eclipse of the moon and, when he returned to England, checked his time against that recorded there, commenting on the difference. If such observations are exact, east-west distance or relative longitude can be accurately determined. He shot one eclipse of the moon with his astrolabe and might conceivably have used the instrument for the determination of the latitude of Malvern.

Additional knowledge was brought to England in the twelfth century by such scholars as Adelard of Bath and Robert of Chester. Robert Grosseteste compiled a treatise on the astrolabe in the thirteenth century. The appearance of Hereford and London on tables of longitude compiled in the twelfth and thirteenth centuries,[40] in which longitude is given with relation to the city of Toledo, indicates that more accurate observations had been made in England at a comparatively early date.

Chaucer's unfinished *Treatise on the Astrolabe*,[41] prepared for "Lyte Lowys my sone," was probably compiled in 1391. Only two of the five parts projected were written. The third part was to have contained, among other things, tables for the latitude and longitude of the stars, the declination of the sun, and the longitude of certain towns and cities. Part I describes the parts of the astrolabe. Part II contains directions for its use. These include instructions for finding the latitude of a locality after the necessary celestial observations have been made, using the observations for the town of Oxford as an illustration. Since Chaucer compiled the treatise only for the instruction of his son, the existence of such a work in English at this time signifies little more than that the knowledge represented was then easily available to an English man of letters. There is no reason to believe that the work circulated widely.

How soon longitude and latitude were used by English mariners for determination of position at sea is another matter. Prior to the discovery of determination of longitude by lunar conjunction, which Pohl credits [42] to Amerigo Vespucci in 1499, lunar eclipses were used for this purpose, events too infrequent to be of real use to the mariner. How often he determined longitude by lunar conjunction, which occurs when the moon passes a planet, we cannot know, though it was probably infrequently. Easy and accurate determination of longitude at sea was not possible without an accurate chronometer, which first became available to the mariner in 1735 through the efforts of John Harrison. Before that time longitude could be approximated by knowing direction of travel and estimating distance traveled. Exact latitude, on the other hand, could be determined by shooting Polaris with astrolabe or quadrant. Accurate observations were hard to make with crude instruments, however, even on a smooth sea, and it seems likely that English pilots made little use of celestial navigation, as the term is understood today, until well into the sixteenth century.

Three types of maps were made in Europe in the late Middle Ages: the uncontrolled sketch map; the portolano or sailing chart, controlled by compass and log; and the map controlled by degrees of latitude and longitude, as suggested by Ptolemy. All of them were drawn more or less to scale.

The sketch map was a highly individual one and subject to the greatest error of the three because lacking in mathematical control. Mathew Paris' map (c. 1250) of Britain is reasonably accurate and represents the best of this type. The Hereford map (c. 1280) of the inhabited earth is very poor, more suitable for mural decoration than a guide to the regions of the earth. The one covers a small area, many parts of which the maker had probably visited. The other covers a very much larger area, and for his information the maker had to rely on legend, Biblical tale, and his own active imagination to supplement his meager geographical knowledge.

The portolano or sailing chart is, in a sense, a sketch map but one probably based on log and compass readings—on measured or estimated distance and known direction. The oldest known copy dates from the beginning of the fourteenth century. The portolano is covered with a net of intersecting straight lines which issue from a number of systematically arranged points. The lines issuing from any given point probably represent compass rather than wind directions. This net apparently had nothing to do with the construction of the map but was devised as an aid in using it. Originally designed for coastwise sailing, particularly in the Mediterranean, the portolano was sometimes expanded into a world-map. How extensively it was used in England before the beginning of the sixteenth century is not known.

The modern, large-scale map is based on the principle of location of position by latitude and longitude astronomically determined and is generally covered with a grid of lines, laid out in terms of degrees, which intersect at right angles except for allowances made for the curvature of the earth. This grid is useful both in constructing the map and in locating points on it after it has been drawn. This principle of construction was laid down in Book I of Ptolemy's *Geography*, which did not reach western Europe until 1409. It seems likely that maps were being drawn on this principle by 1475.[43] Whether any were drawn or used in England in the fifteenth century is not known, but the presence of Ptolemy's work among the books presented to Oxford University on February 25, 1443, by the Duke of Gloucester [44] raises such a possibility.

Two of the new aids to navigation, the mariner's compass and the portolano, played an important part in expanding the three parts of the earth to four. Columbus depended largely on both.[45] Neither would have been necessary if he had followed the old Norse route from Iceland to Greenland to Vinland. Norsemen first found their way to Iceland, Greenland, and probably to America without benefit of compass or sailing chart, simply by being blown there, blown off another, intended course. They probably sailed all the northern waters before the compass reached them, using such a device as the flight of birds to guide them, orienting themselves by the heavenly bodies and prevailing winds when out of sight of land. Dicuil's monkish friends and the Irish monks found in Iceland by the Norse when they first settled there had probably reached their destination by the same means. These devices, common to all mariners from earliest times, were good enough for island-hopping, but for bridging the broad ocean to "Asia" something more reliable, the mariner's compass, was required. The portolano was needed for plotting a course. English mariners certainly were familiar with the one, and probably with the other, before the beginning of the sixteenth century.

CHAPTER III

America, the Fourth Part of the Earth

THE DISCOVERY of America had some effect on most of the medieval concepts of the earth, particularly those associated with the Greek universe and the Roman earth.[1] What that effect was to be in the sixteenth century depended on such factors as the essential validity of the concept, rates of discovery and communication, and the character of the individual receiving the new information.[2] The concept of a three-part earth was one of the first to undergo change, and that change, in this case an addition, took place slowly and by degrees.

Today the earth is considered to be divided into seven parts: Europe, Asia, Africa, North America, South America, Australia, and Antarctica. This classification in its entirety was not possible until after the sixteenth century. Australia did not become a reality until the seventeenth century nor Antarctica until the nineteenth. America emerged as a named continent, the fourth part of the earth, as early as 1507. Name and phrase were first applied to South America, or perhaps the southern part of it, and later were sometimes used to indicate both continents. The terms North America and South America did not come into common use until after the sixteenth century.

It was only natural that America should be regarded as the fourth part of the earth if one had previously believed in a three-part earth. If one started with a different premise, however, he might reach a different result. Enciso and Barlow, for example, the one a Spaniard and the other an Englishman, conceived of the usual three parts as four, Europe, Asia, Africa, and an India which they called "the indie orientale." [3] To these four they added two new ones, "the indies occidentales," [4] the western counterpart of the eastern India, and "the new founde lande," [5] for a final total of six. Such a view was the exception, though the term "new found land" was widely used for that part of North America which fans out from the island of Newfoundland. The usual division was the three-part one, and America was commonly looked upon as an added fourth. Yet this natural expansion of the old concept could not take place immediately. Grasp of the size of America and the fact that it was "new" land had to precede it.

Any informed medieval mariner finding land almost due west of the Canaries and a long way from them, as Columbus had, must believe that he had reached some part of Asia or one of the Western Islands. On his first voyage (1492–1493) Columbus thought he had reached that part of Asia called the Indies or the islands of India, being persuaded to that view by the character of the people and products he found. [6] The Portuguese and the French, however, refused to believe that he had sailed far enough west to reach them. They thought he had found some of the Western Islands and dubbed them Antilles. [7]

Identification of Columbus' islands with any of the recognized Western Islands was not easy. The only one shown on the medieval portolani a long way to the west of Europe was Antilia, and it was shown as a single, large island. The result was a compromise in name, the pluralizing of Antilia, which suggests a belief that the Antilles were derived from the breaking up of the island Antilia, though that explanation is not specifically given. To this day the terms Antilles and West Indies are looked upon as synonymous and are used interchangeably.

At any rate, Columbus took the first step toward establishing America as the fourth part of the earth when he discovered the West Indies, whatever the islands may have been called. By reaching the mainland to the west on his third (1498) and fourth (1502–1503) voyages he also took the second step. The third step was an act of mind rather than a physical discovery, a realization that the mainland was not Asia but new land, and that step Columbus never did take. Other early mariners to America also failed in this, at least for a time. Hojeda, John Cabot, Pinzón, and even Amerigo Vespucci, who was to be the first man on record to take the third step, regarded the mainland as Asia. Vespucci changed his mind in 1501–1502 in the course of a voyage along the east coast of South America which took him almost as far south as the Strait of Magellan. The character of the country and perhaps its southern latitude (all of the mainland of Asia lies north of the equator) moved him to write in a letter to his Florentine friend, Lorenzo di Pier Francesco de' Medici, "we arrived at a new land which, for many reasons that are enumerated in what follows, we observed to be a continent." [8]

Although Vespucci concluded that South America was new land and a continent, he did not actually call it the fourth part of the earth. It remained for Martin Waldseemüller, a German geographer living in Lorraine, to do that.

News of Vespucci's opinion was spread through western Europe by two documents which purported to be his letters but are now generally regarded as forgeries,[9] the *Mundus novus* and the Soderini letter. Both, though forgeries, contained the statement that the land described was new and a continent. It was the Soderini letter that reached Waldseemüller. He was so impressed with what he read that in his *Cosmographiae introductio* (1507) he referred to the new land as the fourth part of the earth and named it America after Vespucci.[10]

The plan of Waldseemüller's *Cosmographiae introductio* is indicative of the difficulties facing one who would write of the regions of the earth at a time when important new discoveries were being made. Waldseemüller had before him at least one of the ancient texts, Priscian's *Periegesis* (sixth century), which described the Roman three-part earth. In addition, he had Ptolemy's *Geography* and the Soderini letter. Ptolemy's *Geography* was indispensable to him in drafting his own world-map, which accompanied the cosmography, because it gave the relative positions of the regions of the earth in degrees of latitude and longitude, but it added little in the way of new regions to those given by Priscian. The Soderini letter, on the other hand, described parts of South America, an entirely new region. Waldseemüller's problem was to combine the information from these sources so that it all made sense. He solved his problem in a way which was simple and at the same time bold. He faithfully described the Roman three-part earth, then referred to the region purportedly described by Vespucci as a fourth part, one unknown to the ancients, and appended the Soderini letter in Latin for the benefit of anyone who wanted detailed information.

Waldseemüller's world-map shows the West Indies, Central America, and part of North America as well as South America, indicating additional sources of information. The map is an item of considerable interest, in part for a major mistake. It shows a middle western passage south of Paria (northeastern Venezuela). Belief in such a passage was not uncommon in the early sixteenth century, but it was usually considered to be west of the Gulf of México and north of Paria. Location of Paria on this map north of the supposed strait seems to restrict the name America to that part of South America south of Paria. It was commonly applied by others to all of South America and sometimes to the whole of the two continents.

The year when Englishmen first began to think of America as the fourth part of the earth cannot be determined with certainty, but it may have been not many years after 1507. There is a known, rather late, outside limit for both South America and North America. Eden called America the fourth part of the earth in 1553, and the evidence indicates that he was referring to both continents. But Alexander Barclay may have been thinking of one or both as new land as early as 1509. If Sebastian Cabot sailed under the English flag in 1509 in search of a northwest passage to Asia, as seems likely, then he and the Englishmen who sponsored him must have been aware at that time that North America was not

Asia but new land. Thomas More almost certainly regarded South America as new land in 1516, and he probably also considered it a continent. John Rastell, More's brother-in-law, probably thought of the two continents together as America and the fourth part of the earth about 1519.

Richard Eden was the first Englishman to write unequivocally of America as the fourth part of the earth. This he did in the epistle to the reader which precedes his translation (1553) of part of the fifth chapter of Münster's cosmography, referring to "*America* with the hole fyrme lande adherent thereunto, which is nowe found to be the fourth parte of the earth." [11] He probably meant to include North America as well as South America. This is not apparent from his quoted statement by itself, but it is clear when that is taken in conjunction with his suggestion that "Regio Baccalearum" and "Terra Florida," names by which parts of North America were then known, might be joined to the "sayde fyrme land" (South America). Though Münster's chapter, which included treatment of America, was entitled "De terris Asiae Maioris," Eden's introductory remarks would surely be understood to correct that. In referring to Regio Baccalearum, Terra Florida, and México in the preface to the reader which introduces his *Decades* (1555), Eden says, "Summe wryters connecte this lande to the firme lande of Asia: But the truth hereof is not yet knowen." [12] This statement could indicate that Eden was wavering from his stand of 1553. It seems likely, however, that this scholarly Englishman was thus simply making a polite bow to the opinion of his fellow scholars and that his intended reader, the English layman, would so interpret the remark.

The early and wide distribution of the *Mundus novus* and the Soderini letter suggests, on a priori grounds, that other scholarly Englishmen must have begun to think of America—certainly South America and probably North America, too—as the fourth part of the earth long before this, and there is some positive evidence in support of such a postulate.

This concept may have been in the mind of Alexander Barclay

when, in *The Ship of Fools* (1509), he wrote in unmistakable terms of the new land, saying:

> For nowe of late hath large londe and grounde
> Ben founde by maryners and crafty gouvernours
> The whiche londes were neuer knowen nor founde
> Byfore our tyme by our predecessours
> And here after shall by our successours
> Parchaunce mo be founde, wherin men dwell
> Of whome we neuer before this same harde tell.[13]

This land is certainly not Asia, sometimes referred to in this period of transition as "new" land, for Asia had been known and found long before Barclay's day, and it seems too large to be one of the Western Islands. This same concept was almost certainly in the mind of John Rastell when he wrote the *Interlude of the Four Elements* (c. 1519). In that play the character Experience, pointing to a "figure" (either a world map or a globe) is made to say:

> This sayde north parte is callyd Europa
> And this south parte callyd Affrica
> This eest parte is callyd Ynde
> But this Newe Landes founde lately
> Ben callyd America bycause only
> Americus dyd furst them fynde.[14]

Europe to the north, Africa to the south, India to the east, and America to the ——; Rastell does everything short of actually saying the word "west." And America is made one of four parts of the earth, all referred to in terms that are identical except for this one omission and the addition of the derivation of the name. Furthermore, that addition indicates an acquaintance with Waldseemüller's cosmography, where South America (or part of it) is called America and characterized as the fourth part of the earth. The implication that Rastell looked upon "America" in this light is very strong indeed. It is entirely probable that Rastell meant both North America and South America, since his description of the new land in other passages of the interlude concentrates on North

America rather than its southern neighbor. Thomas More was clearly exposed to the weaker form of the concept, the identification of the new land with continent without reference to it as the fourth part of the earth, for the Soderini letter was the origin of the setting for his *Utopia* (1516 or 1517).[15] If he read the Latin version attached to Waldseemüller's cosmography, which is quite possible, then he was also exposed to the stronger statement found in the cosmography.

It is hardly surprising that informed, scholarly Englishmen like Rastell and Eden may have looked upon North America as a part of the fourth part of the earth. John Cabot, the Genoese who sailed for England, seems to have believed that he had found one of the Western Islands and the mainland of Asia too, when he reached its shores in 1497, thus taking the first two steps in the discovery of America the continent at a single bound. During the first five years of the sixteenth century his find was still being referred to in England as both island and land (mainland). The adjective "new" appears frequently in these early references, suggesting that the third step in the discovery of America the continent had taken place in England by 1505. But "new" was till used so loosely that we cannot be sure. The eastern seaboard had not yet been carefully explored nor the matter of the middle and northwest passages to Asia settled. By 1509 Sebastian Cabot had sailed along most of the coast of North America, thus proving it mainland, and since he had set out to search for the supposed northwest passage, he must have known it was not Asia before he started. By the date of Rastell's play, about 1519, the Spanish had gone a long way toward disproving the existence of a middle passage. If North America was mainland that was not Asia and was connected to South America, then it might reasonably be considered a part of the fourth part of the earth. That it is in reality a separate continent and the fifth part could not be appreciated until some notion of its shape and great areal extent had been obtained.

Proper understanding of the early steps in the discovery of North America, the mainland that was not Asia, necessitates a somewhat detailed examination of the activities of English mariners during the later years of the reign of Henry VII, with particular attention to two voyages by John Cabot, one in 1497 and the other in 1498, and one by his son Sebastian in the spring of 1509. In the past there has been much confusion of thought about the early voyages to North America by these two men, due largely to the meager character of the official record, which has had to be supplemented by information from secondary sources, some of it conflicting. Unsettled problems still plague the investigator, but the recent work of Williamson [16] presents convincing proof of these three voyages in the years indicated. He has made available in transcription the most important evidence, both primary and secondary.

The search for the island of Brazil, said by William of Worcester to have been undertaken by Bristol mariners as early as 1480, was continued by them before and after Columbus' first voyage to America, if we can believe Pedro de Ayala, temporary Spanish ambassador to England in 1498. Writing to Ferdinand and Isabella on July 25 of that year, he reported: "For the last seven years the people of Bristol have equipped two, three [and] four caravels to go in search of the island of Brazil and the Seven Cities according to the fancy of this Genoese." [17] That John Cabot was the Genoese referred to is indicated by the rest of the letter. This seems to show that he was looking for Brazil and the Island of the Seven Cities when he embarked on the voyage of 1497 that was to take him to North America. Upon his return, contemporary letters written by Italians in England to friends or relatives in Venice and Milan reported [18] that he had reached the Island of the Seven Cities and the mainland of Asia.

This voyage to "Asia" and the "Island of the Seven Cities" seems to have aroused considerable popular enthusiasm in England, for Lorenzo Pasqualigo reported on August 23, 1497, to his brothers in Venice that "these English run after him [John Cabot] like mad, and indeed he can enlist as many of them as he pleases, and a number of our rogues as well." [19] Cabot's achievement had already received official recognition, for a royal grant of ten pounds was made to him on August 10, 1497, "to hym that founde the new Isle," [20] and on February 3, 1498, supplementary letters patent were granted, authorizing him to requisition six ships for another voyage, to "convey and lede to the londe and Iles of late founde by the seid John." [21] The term "new" is probably used here in its general sense, which could include Western Islands and Asia as well as America.

In view of the favorable reception of the first voyage, it is remarkable that so little is known of the second. There is no official English record of it, perhaps because the record has been lost. That John Cabot did sail from England in 1498 is all that we can be sure of, and for this information we are indebted once more to the Spanish ambassador, Pedro de Ayala.[22] Presumably he sailed again to "Asia" and the "Island of the Seven Cities." We are not sure that he ever returned to Europe. The best evidence of his return is suggestive and inferential only, the appearance of mainland north and northeast of the West Indies on the La Cosa map of 1500, there ascribed to English discovery. Williamson apparently assumes that the information set down is too extensive to have been acquired on the voyage of 1497, but this is not necessarily so. The mainland shown, which curves to the south on the west side of Cuba, is continuous with that of South America except in the latitude of the Indies, where it is broken by a picture of St. Christopher. La Cosa must have been calling on the patron saint of the sailor to save him from deciding whether Cabot's land was joined to that discovered by Spain. Nevertheless, he visualized Cabot's land as mainland, and if he got his information from a map drawn by Cabot and now lost, as is generally supposed, then Cabot probably so regarded it. There is no evidence, however, to indicate that either Cabot or La Cosa looked upon it as other than the mainland of Asia.

During the years 1501–1505 some money was granted by the English government to mariners returning from North America, and the phraseology of the grants shows [23] that there was still some confusion of thought about the nature of the land visited. In September, 1502, small pensions or sums of money were allowed to certain Bristol merchants and Azores mariners for sailing to the "newe founde lande" or "newe founde Launde." In 1502, 1503, 1504, and 1505 small payments were made to men who had been to the "newe founde Launde," "Newfounded Island," "new Ilande," and "Newfound Island." Apparently there was still doubt as to whether North America was mainland or island. The increasing occurrence of "found" with "new" indicates a trend which eventually led to the adoption of the name Newfoundland for the very large island off the shores of North America visited by so many of the early English voyagers. However Sebastian Cabot and his English backers may have characterized North America, by 1509 they must have been convinced that the land was not Asia, else Sebastian would not have sailed that year in search of the supposed northwest passage to Asia.

Official evidence for a voyage by Sebastian Cabot in 1509 is completely lacking. The secondary evidence, fully presented in transcript and carefully analyzed by Williamson,[24] is in part ambiguous, but there is ample evidence of the voyage from a number of reliable sources. Peter Martyr, an intimate as well as a contemporary of Sebastian Cabot, refers to it in his *Decades* (1516, 1530). There was a contemporary investigation of the activities of Sebastian Cabot by the Venetian senate, and the report (1536) of that investigation also refers to it. The English voyagers Humphrey Gilbert and George Best, who was one of Frobisher's captains, and such reputable sixteenth century historians as Ramusio, Gomara, Thevet, Galvana, and Richard Willes all accepted it.

These various accounts, when put together, indicate that Sebastian Cabot sailed toward the northwest with two ships in the spring of 1509, perhaps as far north as 67½ degrees north latitude. Sea continued to stretch ahead of him, but his crew, dismayed by the extreme cold and the great quantity of ice, refused to proceed. Thus balked in his search for a passage to Cathay, he turned about and coasted south, perhaps to 38 degrees north latitude (Virginia), perhaps as far south as 25 degrees north latitude (southern tip of Florida), before sailing again for England. Cabot reached England to find that a new era had already begun there. Henry VII had died on April 21, 1509, while he was on the high seas, and presumably no one in the new administration was sufficiently interested in his voyage to reward him upon his return or even to record his arrival.

CHAPTER IV

English Voyages to America, 1509–1547

ENGLISH INTEREST in America was at low ebb during the reign of Henry VIII (1509–1547) and with good reason. It became increasingly apparent in that time that America was not Asia but a new land or lands of vast extent. This realization, when the last faint doubt had been dispelled, required a major change of view. The riches of eastern Asia were not within easy reach by direct westward voyage from England, as had been at first supposed. Attention was bound to focus on Spanish America, where so much gold was reported to be found, and to a lesser extent on Portuguese America, where the product of principal value was brazilwood, a much less exciting commodity. It was bound to shift away from a "new found land" which had only codfish and timber to offer, products readily obtainable elsewhere and consequently not especially valuable or profitable. Furthermore, this "new found land" was worse than a region limited as to profit; it was an obstacle on the western approach to Cathay, Tartary, and the Spice Islands, the regions in eastern Asia of particular interest to Englishmen. There was little reason to explore this cold, inhospitable, and unattractive land except to search for a passage that could lead to the wealth beyond.

The information which made possible this change of view probably circulated in English ports and no doubt was available at the English court. Some of it could be had by the English scholar, particularly through Martyr's *Decades*. It was not available to the ordinary English layman.

Detailed information about Spanish America was first made

available in print by Peter Martyr, an Italian scholar living in Spain. His *De orbe novo*, better known simply as his *Decades*, began as a series of letters to friends in Italy. Some of the information contained was printed in pirated form in 1504. The *First Decade*—and the name is fitting since each "decade" contains ten books—was printed in 1511. The *Three Decades*, covering Spanish exploration and settlement in America during the years 1492–1516, appeared in 1516. The *Fourth Decade*, concerned largely with the beginning of the conquest of Mexico, appeared in 1520. The *Eight Decades*, the complete work, was first published in 1530. Many of the Spanish voyagers to America, distinguished Italians like Vespucci and Sebastian Cabot as well as native Spaniards, were friends of Peter Martyr and he drew heavily on them for information. Sound scholarship, vivid narration, early date of publication, and an abundance of essentially correct information combined to make Martyr's *Decades* for many years the most important single source of information about America. Though a great variety of matter was included, it was essentially the record of one of the greatest and longest gold rushes in history, and for the sixteenth century reader that must have been its principal attraction.

There is little evidence that this valuable work was widely read in England in the reign of Henry VIII, so that even the scholar may not have made much use of it. No Latin edition appeared in England until much later. Only by stumbling onto a chance remark [1] like that made by Eden in the dedication of his translation of part of the fifth chapter of Münster's cosmography, published in 1553, that he had read Martyr's *Decades* in his youth, can we be sure that it was known to the English scholar at all. The English layman could not know it until 1555, when Eden published his translation of the first half of the work.

However soon any Englishman might become interested in Spanish America or Portuguese America, there was little he could do about either at this time without grave risk. Before the beginning of the sixteenth century Spain and Portugal had divided

America between them and established trade monopolies with their respective holdings. Official England was in neither the mood nor the position to challenge either the partition or the monopolies. Henry VIII was preoccupied with affairs at home and on the continent of Europe. He was also on relatively good terms with Spain and Portugal through much of his reign. Had he been in a challenging mood, he would have found his naval power no match for that of either nation. If private English ships ignored the monopolies, they were liable to capture and confiscation by the government involved, and the owners ran the further risk of incurring the displeasure of their own government.

In view of these circumstances, it would not be surprising had there been no English voyages to Spanish America and Portuguese America in the reign of Henry VIII. Yet there were several. At least six trading voyages were made to Portuguese America (Brazil) in English ships between 1530 and 1542, and the record implies that there were others. Apparently no comparable voyages were made to Spanish America, but there is evidence of less direct contact there. Two Englishmen sailed in 1526 with a Spanish expedition to the Plata River. An English ship put into the harbor of Santo Domingo (Ciudad Trujillo) in distress in 1527. Another English ship captured a Spanish vessel off the island of Hispaniola in 1540 while returning from Brazil to England.

Three expeditions left England for the "new found land" between 1517 and 1536. Their objectives have been obscured by the passage of time. The first expedition seems to have been bent on exploration with a view to colonization. If this is true, then it was nearly seventy years ahead of its time. The second was looking for a north or northwest passage to Asia. The third may have had same vague notion of "exploration" but seems to have been concerned with nothing more important than adventure.

English Voyages to Brazil and Spanish America

Three voyages were made to Brazil between 1530 and 1532 by William Hawkins, "Olde M. William Haukins of Plimmouth," [2] father of the redoubtable John. The account, though brief, is particularly interesting because it suggests that William was already using a technique which John was to adopt in slightly modified form in trading at a later date with Spanish America. William touched first at Guinea, where he picked up ivory "and other commodities which that place yeeldeth," [3] then went on to Brazil where he traded with the natives, perhaps for brazilwood, cotton, monkeys, popinjays (parrots), or low-grade pepper, the then common commodities of the country. John, in his turn, was to stop first at Guinea, but he picked up Negroes instead of ivory for trade with the Spaniards. William made friends with the Indians. He took with him to England a native chief, who came of his own accord on promise of a safe return and the deposit of a hostage, and presented him to Henry VIII and the court at Whitehall. After the lapse of nearly a year, William carried him back to Brazil as he had promised. The chief died at sea, but his people, aware that William had acted in good faith, returned the hostage and once more loaded his ship with goods. John had no occasion to make friends with the Indians.

Two similar voyages were made about ten years later, one by Reniger and Borey in 1540 and the other by Pudsey in 1542, both out of Southampton. Hakluyt says little about either beyond pointing to their gainful character and indicating that they were representative of a number of such voyages.[4]

The sixth voyage to Brazil, though in some measure a trading voyage, was in essence quite different in character. Among the papers of the High Court of Admiralty are depositions, apparently overlooked by Hakluyt, which relate to the American voyage of the *Barbara* of London in 1540. She left Portsmouth for "the Ile of Brasell," [5] which suggests that some Englishmen had by this time come to regard Brazil, the region on the continent of America, as identical with the legendary island of that name which had so long been sought in vain. Though her commission from the mayor of Portsmouth specifically enjoined against "robery," [6] the *Barbara* captured two Spanish ships before reaching the Canaries.

Once off the coast of Brazil, she did some desultory trading in the vicinity of Cape San Roque, then sailed up the coast in search of the area producing brazilwood. This she seems not to have found but did secure cotton, popinjays, and monkeys. Encountering local opposition from Portuguese, French, and Indians, she sailed home by way of the West Indies. Off the island of Hispaniola she captured a galleon of Seville loaded with sugar and hides. Here the *Barbara*, leaking badly, was abandoned, and her crew sailed for England in the captured Spanish vessel. Criminal action against ship and crew was instituted by the Lord High Admiral at the instigation of the Spanish ambassador.

Among the English merchants residing in Seville during the reign of Henry VIII was a patriotic young man named Robert Thorne, who was eager to see England share in the lucrative trade with the "Spiceries" or Spice Islands, then divided between Portugal and Spain. Portugal controlled the trade route to the east and Spain, by virtue of Magellan's voyage (1519–1522), that to the west. Thorne believed that a third sea route, shorter than either of the others, could be located over the North Pole. When, therefore, he heard of an expedition which was preparing to sail from Spain in the spring of 1526 under the leadership of Sebastian Cabot, bound ostensibly for the Spice Islands, he eagerly subscribed. No doubt he anticipated a profit, but more important than that was the privilege acquired of sending along two Englishmen, Roger Barlow and Henry Latimer, to gather information about the location and nature of the islands and the navigation of the surrounding waters, all of which might help promote his pet project. Thorne speaks of this in the "booke" he prepared in 1527 for Dr. Lee, English ambassador to Spain, enlarging on his plan.[7]

The fleet left as scheduled, but instead of proceeding to the Spice Islands it explored the Plata River and vicinity, the mouth of which a Spanish expedition under Juan Diaz de Solis had entered in 1515. Barlow gathered information about America with the same care he would have exercised on the Spice Islands. It was incorporated in a treatise called *A brief summe of Geogra-*

phie which he prepared in 1540–1541 for the double purpose of reviving Thorne's plan and stimulating in Englishmen a greater interest in voyaging. The work was presented to Henry VIII, and in his address to the king Barlow expressed [8] the desire that the work be printed in order to further his second objective. Despite this plea it remained in manuscript until 1932, when it was published by the Hakluyt Society. The loss to the English layman and English voyaging was very considerable, for this work, an expansion of Enciso's *Summa de geographia*, covered the entire earth.

Barlow's narrative is as fresh and graphic today as when it was written and includes a variety of subject matter. It contains detailed reference to the physical appearance, customs, and habits of the Indians, with special attention to the practice of cannibalism by the Guaraní, a subject which had a special fascination for Europeans. Several species of fish are described. Barlow enlivens this passage by explaining that if the Spaniards caught a shark alive, they sometimes put a stake through its tail and cast it back into the sea, "and there he will plonge up and downe in the water and a grete nombre of fysshe will be about him other to wonder at him or to devoure him, but it is a pastyme to beholde." [9] Several species of birds are described, including the hummingbird, which was new to him and indeed new to all Europeans, hummingbirds being "byrdes which be no bigger of bodie then the toppe of a mans thombe but thei have the goodliest colored fethers that ever man might se, the colours wold chaunge in moving of them as it were chaungeable silke." [10]

Apparently Barlow saw no gold in the vicinity of the Plata River but he did hear of it, for he mentions the report that in the mountains toward the west lived a king with so much gold and silver that he had vessels, stools, and ornaments made of them. Furthermore, Barlow knew by 1540–1541 that this seemingly fabulous kingdom was to be identified with the real Perú, for he comments: "This lond and the lond of pirro, which is in the southside that the spaniards have dyscouered of late, is all one lond, wheras thei had so grete riches of gold and sylver." [11]

The visit of an English ship to the West Indies in 1527 was accidental, and the circumstances attendant upon it have some of the broad humor of good comic opera. Contemporary Spanish documents,[12] principally depositions taken on the spot, show that on November 25, 1527, to the considerable astonishment of the local Spanish inhabitants, a large, three-masted English ship appeared off the harbor of Santo Domingo. The master and some of his crew came ashore in the ship's boat. They told the inhabitants that this was one of two ships which had cleared England about nine months before on order of Henry VIII to search between Labrador (Greenland) and the "Newfound Land" for a passage to Tartary. They said that they had sailed north beyond fifty degrees north latitude and that during this part of the voyage the pilot had died, others had died of cold, and one of the vessels had been lost. Their ship carried linens, woolens, and other goods for barter but was short of food and water. They asked safe conduct into the port in order to replenish these supplies. This request was granted and the port pilots brought the ship into the harbor the next morning. No sooner had she dropped anchor than a gun, loaded with stone, was fired from the fortress nearby, the shot passing very close to the poop of the ship. The master, fearing a plot to take his ship, put the two pilots over the side, despite their protestations that this was merely a salute of welcome, and sailed away.

The local Spanish officials were distressed. The commander of the harbor fortress protested that he had not been informed that the ship had permission to enter the harbor and had ordered the cannon fired as a warning, a customary signal in such cases. Clearly there had been a misunderstanding all around, as a result of which the English ship had been scared off. The local officials, fearing a reprimand from Spain for offending a friendly power, took depositions immediately (November 26–December 9) so as to record all pertinent facts while they were still fresh in mind, just in case they needed to defend their actions. Eventually a reprimand did come from Spain—not for offending England, however, but for failing to hold a foreign ship whose crew had now a considerable knowledge of the most important Spanish harbor in the West Indies.

We cannot be absolutely sure what ship this was, but it seems quite likely that it was either the *Mary Guilford*, commanded by John Rut, or the *Sampson*, which had sailed west together from Plymouth on June 10, 1527. The information in the Spanish documents tallies closely with that contained in a letter [13] sent by Rut to Henry VIII on August 3 of that year.

English Voyages to the New Found Land

Three expeditions, attracted by something other than codfishing, left England for the "new found land" in the reign of Henry VIII. There may have been others, but these are a matter of record and constitute a known minimum. The first, apparently fitted out for both discovery and colonization, sailed in 1517. Internal dissension prevented it from getting beyond Ireland. The second left England in 1527 in search of a north or northwest passage to Asia. Though it necessarily failed of this objective, it did reach America and at least one of its two ships returned to England either late that year or early the next. The third, seemingly bent on little more than travel and adventure, reached "Newfoundland" in 1536 and returned the same year under rather extraordinary circumstances.

Letters of recommendation [14] were granted in 1517 to John Rastell and others for a contemplated voyage to distant parts. Since this is the only official notice of the voyage, we should know nothing more were it not for reference to it in Rastell's play, the *Interlude of the Four Elements*, and the court record,[15] first published by A. W. Reed in 1923, of legal proceedings instituted by Rastell against John Ravyn for the value of certain specified goods. The court record shows that an expedition of several ships actually left England in 1517 but did not get beyond Ireland because of the disaffection of Ravyn, purser of the *Barbara*, and others. The dissidents put Rastell and the other initiators of the voyage ashore, either at Waterford or Cork, and sailed to Bordeaux, where they seem to have sold the goods and supplies aboard for their own profit.

Neither the land sought nor the object in seeking it is apparent from the letters of recommendation. Certain descriptive passages [16] in the play indicate, however, that the land was the "new found land." The goods stolen, for which Rastell demanded indemnity, included white flour, salt, mercers' goods, salt hides, tallow, and such household stuff as feather beds and pots and pans. It may be that this was all trade goods, but the character of some of it, especially the feather beds, suggests that it was meant to be used by the voyagers themselves, which implies settlement as well as exploration. The sentiments expressed by Rastell in his play seem to confirm this diagnosis.[17]

A letter [18] from John Rut to Henry VIII, dated August 3, 1527, together with a note by Purchas, shows that two ships, the *Mary Guilford* and the *Sampson*, sailed from Plymouth on June 10, 1527, and reached the "New-found Land" on July 21. Thence they sailed northward to 53 degrees north latitude, where they ran into islands of ice and water too deep for sounding. Scared by the ice, they turned south until they reached a wooded, uninhabited mainland. There, says Rut, master of the *Mary Guilford*, a storm separated his ship from the *Sampson*, which he has not seen since. Rut then sailed south to the harbor of St. John (in modern Newfoundland) where he found fourteen fishing boats, eleven from Normandy, two from Portugal, and one from Brittany. There he wrote his letter, which he apparently dispatched to England by one of the fishing boats. Just when he returned to England is not known, but Rut and his ship survived the return voyage to participate in the wine trade between France and England in 1528.[19]

It seems clear enough from this letter that Rut was seeking a passage to Asia, even though that objective is not specifically stated. Whether he was seeking it to the north or to the northwest is not so evident.

Thorne's plan advocating search for a passage to the Spice Islands, and also to Tartary, "between our New found lands or Norway, or Island," [20] was elaborated for Dr. Lee in February or March, 1527.[21] Rut sailed on June 10 of that year. Whether there was any connection between plan and voyage remains a matter of conjecture. Their common objective, the location of a passage to Asia, suggests that there was. Their time relationship does not destroy the possibility. The plan preceded the voyage by perhaps as much as three months, and that was time enough to get the paper to England by special courier and fit out two ships if the king wanted it done. It is true that Rut sailed west to America before he sailed north, which seems to point to search for a northwest passage, yet this course does not necessarily eliminate the other possibility. Indeed, Thorne specifically recommended sailing to the "New found lands" before sailing "Northward and passing the Pole." [22] On the other hand, the crew of the English ship entering the harbor of Santo Domingo on November 26, 1527, told the Spaniards of instructions to search between Greenland and the "Newfound Land" for a passage to Tartary, clearly a northwest passage.

Such a passage seems to have been shown on a map by Verrazzano, though that map is now lost and must be reconstructed from others based upon it, together with a narrow isthmus in 40 degrees north latitude (the vicinity of Philadelphia), across which the South Sea (Pacific Ocean) could be seen. E. G. R. Taylor believes that the *Sampson* looked first for the one and then for the other, basing her conclusion on the probable availability of the map and the presence of an English ship as far south as the island of Hispaniola on the date specified; she feels that the ship involved was the *Sampson* rather than the *Mary Guilford* because Rut makes no mention of having lost any men. Rut's course after writing the letter to Henry VIII is not discussed. Taylor's explanation, tempting in spite of being incomplete, would eliminate possibility of reliance on the Thorne plan.[23]

The established facts are so few that no explanation of Rut's

objective or the identity of the ship which reached the harbor of
Santo Domingo is entirely satisfactory. Both must remain open
questions until more facts are turned up. It seems certain only
that he sailed in search of a passage to Asia and probable that one
of his two ships established fleeting contact with Spanish America.

The expressed purpose of the third expedition, "discoverie upon
the Northwest parts of America," [24] was a serious one. The elder
Hakluyt, cousin to the editor of the *Principall Navigations*, refers
to their leader, Master Hore of London, as a man of courage and
one given to the study of cosmography. Despite such good omens
the voyage itself was a harum-scarum one. It illustrates the risks
inherent in recruiting a following from young gentlemen "desir-
ous to see the strange things of the world." [25]

The expedition left Gravesend at the end of April, 1536, in
two ships, the *Trinity* and the *Minion*, and included among its
number such men as Master Weekes, "a gentleman of the West
countrey of five hundred markes by the yeere living," Master
Armigal Wade, afterward Clerk of the Councils of Henry VIII
and Edward VI, and Master John Rastell, son of the author of
the *Interlude of the Four Elements*. The gentlemen constituted
a fourth of the entire personnel of about 120 men, an unusually
high and, as it proved, dangerous proportion. The ships came
first to "Cape Briton" (probably Cape Breton Island), then shaped
their course northeastward to an island which is referred to as
the "Island of Penguin." [26] There they saw a great many gray
and white birds the size of geese and an enormous number of eggs.
They killed many of the birds, some of which they ate, and collected some of the eggs. They also killed and ate some bears, both
black and white.

This island was apparently a recognized landmark off Newfoundland, though the name may have been applied to more than
one island used as a nesting ground by the great auk. Edward Hay
and Steven Parmenius, members of Gilbert's expedition of 1583,
both refer to it.[27] The name Penguin was supposed to be old.
George Peckham, one of their contemporaries, points out that it

is Welsh and adds that it was given to the island about the year 1170 by a Welsh colonist said to be descended from the royal line of Madock ap Owen Gwyneth.[28] The island cannot be positively identified today. The name Penguin Islands has been attached to a group of small islands lying off the southern coast of Newfoundland between 47 and 48 degrees north latitude. It is possible that this group is the "Island of Penguin," but both Hay and Parmenius put their island farther north, at about 50 degrees north latitude. The younger Hakluyt, in a note to the account of Master Hore's voyage, locates the island at about 30 degrees, an obvious misprint since that is the latitude of St. Augustine, Florida.[29]

As the ships of Master Hore lay at anchor "in Newfoundland," one of the gentlemen glanced up from the hatches one day to see a boatload of natives rowing down the bay to have a look at the ship. He called to his shipmates, and they lowered a boat to intercept and capture them. In this they failed, for the natives turned toward land and escaped.

The Englishmen soon ran short of food and were reduced to digging roots, gathering herbs, and robbing the nest of an osprey of the fish it brought hourly to its young. So desperate did they become that they even began to eat one another on the sly. A man would be reported missing, killed by natives or wild beasts, when in reality he had been killed by a comrade in arms, who had broiled his flesh over a small fire and eaten him. In time this became known to "the Captaine," who made a speech to the men, exhorting them to endure their distress and trust in God rather than to condemn body and soul to hell by such a practice. As their circumstances grew progressively worse, however, they agreed to cast lots to determine who should be killed, so that some might have a chance to live. That very night a well-furnished French ship arrived. Looking upon this as a direct answer to prayer, the Englishmen, or as many of them as were left, captured it, turned out the Frenchmen, and sailed in it for home, arriving in Cornwall about the end of October.

The story has a sequel. The Frenchmen, in spite of their predicament, eventually reached Europe again and complained of their treatment to Henry VIII. He was so moved with pity for the distress of his subjects that he refrained from punishing them and indemnified the Frenchmen out of the royal treasury.

A large portion of the blame for the failure of the voyage must be borne by the gentlemen adventurers. Whether they shared in the practice of cannibalism we do not know. The account indicates only that the "officers" did not. Inadequate preparation must be laid at the door of Master Hore, particularly in the matter of basic food supplies. Inability to live off the land in a region teeming with fish and game seems to have been common to all. But discipline and morale, which at this time depended largely on the consent and cooperation of the gentlemen adventurers,[30] were the real keys to the success of the voyage, and these virtues seem to have been conspicuous by their absence.

CHAPTER V

America in Imaginative English Literature
Before 1550

BEFORE 1550 America, then, had a negative rather than a positive significance for Englishmen. To be sure the voyage of John Cabot in 1497 had momentarily awakened great hopes, but subsequent voyages to that part of America north of Mexico, except those concerned solely with the Newfoundland fishing, had ended in failure and produced only disappointment and bitterness. The land was cold and forbidding and its products were of little value. Furthermore, it stood athwart the western route to the rich and still mysterious East—Tartary, Cathay, the Spice Islands, and India. The rest of America possessed a mild climate and wealth in abundance, but it was prohibited territory. Englishmen who coveted either the land or its gold, and that was the product which particularly attracted them, had to choose between braving the wrath of Spain or Portugal and nursing their desires by the family hearth, and the great majority elected the latter course.

We could hardly expect Englishmen to celebrate America in song or story under such adverse circumstances. Indeed we should not be surprised had they been completely inarticulate on the subject. Yet there is some mention of America in the imaginative literature of the period, always collateral or secondary or indirect or for purposes of illustration. A Devonshire priest wrote a group of poems, in one of which he used the discovery of America as evidence to support his belief that the study of geography is a limitless and consequently a vain pursuit. The greatest Englishman of his day, a statesman who was also a man of letters, composed a prose tale about an ideal commonwealth, which he located in America. An eminent printer-playwright, the brother-in-law of the statesman, expressed in a play primarily concerned with the four Greek elements his outraged feelings at the failure of a projected voyage to America in which he was to have had a large share. An unnamed author wrote a play in which he referred to the "new founde land" as a place where a condemned man might make a new start.

The Poem

In the year 1509 there appeared in London a curious work called *The shyp of folys of the worlde* . . . , today simply *The Ship of Fools*, a collection of satirical poems by Alexander Barclay, a Devonshire priest. Its professed purpose was to deride the follies of mankind, its device a ship filled with as many different species of fool as the author could crowd aboard. The modern reader, aware that Englishmen were a bit laggard in exploration and voyaging at this time, would not be surprised to find in the collection a poem chiding them for this failure, for Barclay was writing for Englishmen. But it is something of a shock to discover instead one entitled "Of the folysshe descripcion and inquisicion of dyuers contrees and regyons" which takes the opposite line and reproves those who would search out and seek to know the regions of the earth.

The attitude revealed in this poem was not entirely original with Barclay. He borrowed it in some measure from Sebastian Brant. In fact the *Narrenschiff* of Brant, published at Basel in 1494, furnished the plan and subject matter for Barclay's entire collection. But Barclay adapted Brant's material to his own needs, and the two works show marked differences in humor, moral teaching, and poetic skill. These differences are to be seen in this particular poem which shows, in addition, a considerable difference in knowledge of the regions of the earth, in understanding of various geographical problems, and in attitude toward the new land.

Sebastian Brant was a man learned in civil and canon law who also had broad interests in art and science, as he himself declares in the first satire of the *Narrenschiff*. A sense of humor, which he does not mention, is also plainly evident there, for this same poem is devoted to satirizing his inordinate fondness for books. A man who could thus point up his own favorite weakness was also capable of laughing at or with the foibles of others, as the situation demanded. The light touch is evident throughout the collection, yet the principal purpose of the book was to teach rather than to entertain. Brant, apparently aware that many men shy away from the moral teachings of such avowedly didactic works as the Bible and accounts of the lives of the saints, conceived the idea of disguising his with satirical allegory. He invented an imaginary ship which he filled with all manner of fools, hoping, as he says in the prologue to the *Narrenschiff*, to arouse men by this device to the need for curing their folly. Each poem is devoted to a particular type of fool, who is treated savagely or with humor as the case seems to warrant. Each poem is illustrated by a woodcut, its satire as trenchant as that of the verse.

The sixty-sixth poem is devoted to the man who would measure and understand the earth and its regions. The following translation, made by Edwin H. Zeydel from the vernacular German in which the poem was first written, retains the four-foot, iambic couplets of the original and manages to catch its vigor and humor as well as the quality of its moral teaching.

66. OF EXPERIENCE OF ALL LANDS

I do not deem him very wise
Who energetically tries
To probe all cities, every land,
And takes the circle well in hand
That thereby he may well decide
How broad the earth, how long and wide,
How deep and large the seas expand,

What holds th'extremest sphere of land,
And how at ends of earth the sea
Clings tight to its extremity,
If round the earth a man can fare,
What men live here, what men live there,
If underneath our feet below
Men walk the nether earth or no,
And how they hold their ground down there,
That they fall not into the air,
And how with rule and compass you
May cut the whole great world in two.
Archimedes, too, who knew a lot,
Drew circle in the sand, and dot,
That many things he might compute,
But all the while he played the mute,
He feared he'd blow the sand away
And all the circles might not stay.
Before he'd speak, he'd suffer pain
And let himself be foully slain.
His skill was in geometry,
His death, though, he could not foresee.
With ardor Dicearchus tried
To measure every mountainside,
Mount Pelion, he then confessed,
Loomed up, the highest mountain crest.
He never measured with his hand
The Alps in mountainous Switzerland,
Nor measured he how deep is hell,
To where he went and still must dwell.
And Ptolemy described the girth,
The length and breadth of all the earth,
He drew the length from Orient
And ended it in Occident,
Degrees one hundred eighty he
Set down, toward midnight sixty-three,
The breadth from equinoctial ran.
Toward midday 't has a narrower span,
While twenty-five degrees are shown

Of land, as far as now is known.
Then Pliny figured that in paces,
Strabo used miles to measure places.
Since then more countries far away
We've found past Thule, past Norway,
As Iceland and Pilappenland,
Which ancient writers never scanned.
They've found in Portugal since then
And in Hispania naked men,
And sparkling gold and islands too
Whereof no mortal ever knew.
Marinus failed most grievously,
To figure earth by means of sea.
The master Pliny once did say
That vain it is in every way
To measure out the world's expanse
And then to cast a further glance
Beyond the earth, beyond the sea;
In this all men err grievously,
Into these problems each would delve,
Yet can he understand himself?
In knowledge many will persist
Of matters e'en that don't exist.
Once Hercules set in the sea
Two brazen pillars plain to see,
The tip of Africa is one,
By the other Europe is begun.
To ends of earth he paid much heed,
But his own fate he would not read:
For all his deeds of bravery
He died by woman's treachery.

   .   .   .   .

Why should we humans seek to be
More than we are in verity?
We never know what gain it brings
To study many lofty things,
No one his hour of dying knows,
Which like a shadow comes and goes.

Although his arts are great, no doubt,
He's but a mad and foolish lout
Who rates this lightly in his mind:
That toward himself he's always blind
And puzzling problems would dissect
Quite alien, then himself neglect.
Self-knowledge never was his aim,
He strives for honor and for fame
And thinks of no eternal life,
How spacious 'tis, with beauty rife,
Where live the souls of sterling worth.
Blind fools can only see this earth
And find their joys and pleasures vain
Which bring more injury than gain.
Some have explored a foreign land
But not themselves can understand.
If like Ulysses men got wise,
As when he fared 'neath foreign skies
And saw new lands, men, towns, and sea,
Acquiring new sagacity;
If they were like Pythagoras—
Of Memphis he a native was—
And Plato Egypt once did see
And also went to Italy
With hope of learning ever more
And making rich his wisdom's store;
Appolonius went to every place
Where'er he found a wise man's trace,
He followed it without surcease,
His skill and knowledge would increase,
And everywhere he learned new lore
Of things he'd never heard before.
He who would take such trips as these,
That e'er his wisdom might increase,
He could be pardoned one sole vice,
Though even that would not suffice.
For those ay longing to depart
Cannot serve God with all their heart.[1]

Thus Brant stresses man's folly in trying to know so large a subject as the earth when he can hardly know himself. Better that the voyagers should think upon the lasting joys of eternal life than the passing glory and fame incident to the discovery of new lands. And he satirizes the study of geography and the act of voyaging to foreign lands with equal zest. Brant's attitude was not original in any sense but reflected that of the medieval church which stressed self-knowledge and the knowledge of God, both through inward contemplation, even to complete retreat from the world to a monastery. Such doctrine, balanced only in part by the missionary zeal of the church, must have deterred many who might otherwise have been interested in the study of geography and in voyaging too. Brant, however, was not as defeatist as he sounds. His evident relish for the matter satirized is indicated both by the light way in which he refers to it and the scope and accuracy of his own knowledge. Furthermore, he would make an exception of those who journeyed in search of knowledge and wisdom rather than glory and fame, though he feels that the insistent, gnawing "longing to depart," if present, might interfere with service to God. Clearly Brant would have approved of the modern scientific expedition with the reservation just named. In practice today the "longing to depart" is so widespread among geographers as to constitute an occupational disease, yet no one suggests that it necessarily interferes with service to God, which has taken on new content and meaning since Brant's day.

The earth revealed in Brant's poem is a combination of the static and changing earths similar to that already noted in Waldseemüller's cosmography, which was published thirteen years later. Brant's earth, as shown by the woodcut which accompanies his text, is the ancient Greek earth, surrounded by the other elements water, air, and fire in homocentric shells. Most of his illustrations and examples are drawn from the static earth. Furthermore, such problems as the size of the earth, the depth of the sea, the proportion of land to sea, and the possible existence of antipodean peoples—all mentioned in this poem—are drawn from that

Who measures heaven, earth, and sea,
Thus seeking love or gaiety
Let him beware a fool to be.

WOODCUT ACCOMPANYING SEBASTIAN BRANT'S SATIRE ON GEOGRAPHY
IN *Das Narrenschiff*

same ancient earth. Information about Iceland and Pilappenland (probably Lapland), on the other hand, has been drawn from the changing earth. Brant's Thule, by the way, must have been either the Shetlands or the Faroes rather than Iceland, since he says that Iceland is past Thule. On this point he differs from Dicuil, the ninth-century Irish geographer, for whom Thule was Iceland. From the same expanding earth, and more up-to-date still, is Brant's reference to the naked men, sparkling gold, and islands found in Portugal and Spain, an obvious reference to recent Portuguese discoveries and the brand new voyage of Columbus.

How Brant learned of the Portuguese discoveries we do not know, but Zeydel has shown [2] that the letter Columbus wrote in 1493 describing his first voyage to the "Indies" was probably the source of Brant's knowledge of the Spanish discovery. In 1494 Bergmann von Olpe, Brant's publisher and close friend, published that letter and the *Narrenschiff*. They appeared separately, the letter in an appendix to a work on the conquest of Granada, which also contained a short poem by Brant praising the conquest. The close personal relationship of the two men, Brant's professed interest in science, and the appearance of the letter in the same volume that contained Brant's poem all suggest that Brant had read the letter, quite apart from the internal evidence of the satire itself.

The reference to Portuguese and Spanish discoveries is followed directly by the remark that Marinus failed to measure the earth by means of the sea. This remark is somewhat ambiguous, but it probably means that the figure given by Marinus of Tyre for the width of the ocean had been shown by the voyage of Columbus to be much too high. That figure was 135 degrees, and Columbus had found the "Indies" by sailing west about 61 degrees. Columbus gave no figures for the width of the ocean in the letter of 1493, but he did say he was 33 days on the way out and 28 days on the way back, and anyone with an elementary knowledge of the distance usually sailed in a day could determine that Columbus had sailed much less than 135 degrees. It may be that perusal of

the letter of Columbus, calling this and other geographical problems to Brant's attention, was the spark that touched off this
particular satire.

Alexander Barclay, chaplain of the College of Ottery St. Mary
in Devonshire, speaks of his *Ship of Fools*, published by Pynson in
1509, as a "translacion," but it is actually an adaptation. Moreover,
it is an adaptation made from French and Latin works, themselves
adaptations from the original German of Brant. All three adapters
made changes and additions, but it hardly seems necessary here
to point out those for which Barclay alone was responsible. For
our purposes it is chiefly important to remember that Barclay's
Ship of Fools represents his own point of view and his own knowledge of the earth in 1509 and to compare these with those of
Brant.

Most of the changes evident in Barclay's *Ship of Fools* are for
the worse. For the vigorous, four-foot couplets of Brant, Barclay
substituted the bulky, five-foot, seven-line rhyme royal with its
relatively complicated rhyme scheme, a form admirably suited
to storytelling in a long poem, as Chaucer had already demonstrated, but ill-suited to satire. Barclay's contemporary John
Skelton would have known better. The French adaptation from
which Barclay worked retained the metrical scheme of the original, and he could have chosen it if he would. The changes in
subject matter are as unfortunate as this change in form, for they
tend to play down the humor and play up the moral teaching to
the real detriment of the latter.

These changes are well illustrated by the poem entitled "Of
the folysshe descripcion and inquisicion of dyuers contrees and
regyons," Barclay's adaptation of Brant's poem, "Of Experience
of All Lands."

OF THE FOLYSSHE DESCRIPCION AND INQUISICION OF
DYUERS CONTREES AND REGYONS

Who that is besy to mesure and compace
The heuyn and erth and all the worlde large

Describynge the clymatis and folke of euery place
He is a fole and hath a greuous charge
Without auauntage, wherfore let hym discharge
Hym selfe, of that fole whiche in his necke doth syt
About suche folyes dullynge his mind and wyt.

That fole, of wysdome and reason doth fayle
And also discression labowrynge for nought.
And in this shyp shall helpe to drawe the sayle
Which day and nyght infixeth all his thought
To haue the hole worlde within his body brought
Mesurynge the costes of euery royalme and lande
And clymatis, with his compace, in his hande

He coueytyth to knowe, and compryse in his mynde
Euery regyon and euery sundry place
Which ar nat knowen to any of mankynde
And neuer shall be without a specyall grace
Yet such folys take pleasour and solace
The length and brede of the worlde to mesure
In vayle besynes, takynge great charge and cure

They set great stody labour and besynes
To knowe the people that in the east abyde
And by and by theyr mesures after dres
To knowe what folke the west and north part gyde
And who the sowth, thus all the worlde wyde
By these folys is meated by ieometry
Yet knowe they scant theyr owne vnwyse body

Another labours to knowe the nacions wylde
Inhabytynge the worlde in the North plage and syde
Metynge by mesure, countrees both fyers and mylde
Vnder euery planete, where men sayle go or ryde
And so this fole castyth his wyt so wyde
To knowe eche londe vnder the fyrmament
That therabout in vayne his tyme is spent

Than with his compace drawyth he about
Europe, and Asye, to knowe howe they stande
And of theyr regyons nat to be in dout
Another with Grece and Cesyll is in honde
With Apuly, Afryke and the newe fonde londe
With Numydy and, where the Moryans do dwell
And other londes whose namys none can tell

He mesureth Athlant, calpe, and cappadoce
The see of Hercules garnado and Spayne
The yles there aboute shewynge all in groce
Throwynge his mesure to Fraunce and to Brytayne
The more and lesse, to Flaundres and almayne
There is no yle so lytell that hath name
But that these Folys in hande ar with the same

And regyons that ar compasyd with the se
They besely labour to knowe and understande
And by what cause, nature or propertye
These doth flowe, nat ouercouerynge the londe
So he descrybyth his cercle in his honde
The hole worlde: leuynge no thynge behynde
As in the Doctrynes of Strabo he doth fynde

Which wrote in bokes makynge declaracion
Somtyme hym groundynge vpon auctoryte
Howe eche Royalme and londe had sytuacion
Some in brode feldes some closyd with the see
But ye geometryans that of this purpose be
Ye ar but folys to take suche cure and payne
Aboute a thynge whiche is fruteles and vayne

It passyth your reason the hole worlde to discus
And knowe euery londe and countrey of the grounde
For though that the noble actour plinius
The same purposyd, yet fawty is he founde
And in Tholomeus great errours doth habounde
Thoughe he by auctoryte makyth mencyon
Of the descripcion of euery regyon

Syne these actours so excellent of name
Hath bokes composyd of this facultye
And neuer coude parfytely perfourme the same
Forsoth it is great foly vnto the
To labour about suche folysshe vanyte
It is a furour also one to take payne
In suche thynges as prouyd ar vncertayne

For nowe of late hath large londe and grounde
Ben founde by maryners and crafty gouernours
The which londes were neuer knowen nor founde
Byfore our tyme by our predecessours
And here after shall by our successours
Parchaunce mo be founde, wherin men dwell
Of whome we neuer before this same harde tell

Ferdynandus that late was kynge of spayne
Of londe and people hath founde plenty and store
Of whome the bydynge to vs was uncertayne
No christen man of them harde tell before
Thus is it foly to tende vnto the lore
And vnsure science of vayne geometry
Syns none can knowe all the worlde perfytely

THENUOY OF BARKLAY

Ye people that labour the worlde to mesure
Therby to knowe the regyons of the same
Knowe firste your self, that knowledge is moste sure
For certaynly it is rebuke and shame
For man to labour. onely for a name
To knowe the compasse of all the worlde wyde
Nat knowynge hym selfe, nor howe he sholde hym gyde [3]

Gone are the illustrations from the lives of Archimedes, Dicearchus, Hercules, Ulysses, and Appolonius, which had given life
to Brant's moral teaching, and with them all trace of the humor
which had given it zest. Gone, too, are the expressions of belief

that concentration on earthly matters might detract from the contemplation of heaven, that actual voyaging, particularly when accompanied by the "longing to depart," might interfere with service to God. Barclay directs his satire solely against man's search for earth-knowledge, and his reason for disapproving that pursuit is significantly different from that of Brant. Such a search is foolish, he says, not because it might divert man from service to God but because recent discoveries have shown that it has no foreseeable end and is therefore incapable of fulfillment.

Barclay on the whole lacked Brant's interest in and knowledge of geography. In place of Brant's lucid statement of specific geographical problems he used vague generalizations, and his geographical names appear to have been picked at random, perhaps from hearsay. Yet one item of knowledge he seems to have had that Brant lacked, namely an awareness that the new land was "new" in the sense that it had not been visited by Europeans within the memory of living man or, so far as he knew, at all. His use of the phrase "newe fonde londe," so common an English reference to America, suggests this. His complaint that the new discoveries had proved geometry (geography) an uncertain, and consequently vain, science makes such a conclusion almost inescapable. In 1494 Brant could hardly have been aware that the new land was new in any sense except that it was the "Indies" discovered from another direction. By 1509 Barclay could have and almost certainly had learned that it was an addition to the familiar, safe, three-part, classical earth.

The Prose Tale

In *Utopia*, written in Latin and first printed at Louvain either late in 1516 or early in 1517, Thomas More presented his concept of an ideal commonwealth. His chief aim was to help Englishmen solve certain grave social and economic problems by showing how the hypothetical Utopians had handled them. Because of these implications the work is not ordinarily considered a prose tale, yet it is nonetheless the tale of a visit to the island of Utopia told by Raphael Hythloday, the place, the journey, and the man all imaginary. The new land served as a convenient place off whose shores to locate this island, and for More the new land meant South America, though he does not mention it by name.

More needed a literary device which would enable him to tie Utopia to earth, to vest it with a sense of reality that it could not possess as a confessedly imaginary place. Such a problem is not an uncommon one in literature, but writers of romance have been confronted with it more often than writers on social and economic theory. Thomas More raised the problem by putting his theory in the form of a prose tale. Writers of romance have, in the past, chafed at the shackles imposed on the imagination by a real place that could be readily identified and perhaps visited by their readers. They have wanted to invent persons, situations, or events a bit out of the ordinary, yet not so strange as to be utterly incredible, a task requiring either an imaginary place somehow made real or a real place off the beaten track.

Philip Sidney, writing about sixty years after More, solved this problem in his pastoral romance *Arcadia* by placing his characters in a spot that was real but remote, a Greek province named Arcadia, ideally suited to his purpose because relatively inaccessible, an inland area surrounded by mountains, in Sidney's day inhabited principally by shepherds. No Elizabethan Englishman was likely to visit it. In our own day James Branch Cabell has achieved a similar result in a slightly different way. Instead of selecting a real, remote, and contemporary place, he has invented a kingdom, Poictesme, that pretends to be real, accessible, and medieval. It purports to be located in medieval Europe but is actually imaginary. No one can get there save through the doors that Cabell opens.

Plato let his republic take form gradually as a set of principles, evolved through the clashing arguments among a small group of men, so he was not faced with such a problem. As More set up his tale, however, he needed a place and a person. He needed a real place, so remote from Europe that it could not be readily visited, and at least one person, either a Utopian who would come to Europe and talk about the differences in custom and government between Utopia and the European nations or a sympathetic European who had visited Utopia and was able and willing to do the same thing.

Let us imagine that More was in just this frame of mind when the Soderini letter came to hand and he read, in the account of the supposed fourth voyage:

We sailed 260 leagues farther until we reached a harbor where we decided to build a fort. We did so, and left in it 24 Christian [men] who were aboard my consort, and whom she had received from the wrecked flag-ship. In that harbor, we stayed full five months, building the fort and loading our ships with brazil wood; for we could not go farther, because we had no crews and I lacked much gear. When this was accomplished, we decided (fol. 25v, M) to return to Portugal, which was on our course between north and northeast. We left the 24 men who remained in the fort [with] supplies for six months, 12 mortars, and many other weapons. We pacified all the natives, of whom I have made no mention in this voyage, not because we did not see and associate with countless natives; because full 30 of us men went inland 40 leagues, where I saw so many things that I refrain from telling them, reserving them for my Four Journeys. This land is 18 degrees south of the equator, and 35 degrees west of the longitude of Lisbon, as our instruments showed. And when all this was done, we took leave of the Christians and the land.[4]

Here was a place made-to-order for his purpose, a place both real and remote. To make doubly sure that no one could check on his Utopia, however, More located it on an imaginary island in the vicinity of Vespucci's new land, without, of course, mentioning that it was imaginary. Then he invented Raphael Hythloday, a European who had visited Utopia, and nothing remained but to introduce Hythloday to his readers. This he does through the mouth of his friend Peter Giles:

"For thys same Raphaell Hythlodaye (for thys ys hys name) is verye well lerned in the Latyne tonge; but profounde and excellent in the greke tonge, wherein he euer bestowed more studye than in the lattyne, because he had geuen hym selfe holye to the studye of Phylosophy. Wherof he knewe that there ys nothinge extante in the lattyne tonge, that is to anny purpose, sauynge a few of Senecaes and Ciceroes doinges. His patrymonye that he was borne vnto he lefte to his bretherne (for he is a Portugalle borne); and for the desyre that he hadde to see and knowe the farre contreys of the worlde, he joyned him selfe in company wyth Amerike vespuce, and in the .iii. laste voyages of thoes .iiii., that be nowe in prynte and abrode in euerye mans handes, he contynued styll in hys companye; sauynge that in te [the] laste voyage he came not home again wyth hym. For he made suche meanes and shyfte, what by intreataunce and what by importune sute, that he gotte lycence of mayster Amerycke (thoughe it were sore agaynst his will) to be one of the .xxiiii. whyche in the ende of the laste voyage were lefte in the countrye of Gulike. He was therefore lefte behynde for hys mindes sake, as one that toke more thoughte and care for trauaylyng then dyinge; hauynge customablye in hys mouthe theis sayinges: He that hathe no graue ys couered wyth the skie; and, The way to heauen owte of all places is of like lenghth and distance. Which fantasye of his (if God had not bene his better frende) he hadde suerlye bought full deere.

"But after the departynge of Mayster vespuce, when he hadde trauayled thoroughe and abowte manye contreis, with v. of his companyons Gulykyans, at the laste by maruelous chaunce he arryued in Taprobane, from whens he wente to Calyquit, where he chaunced to fynde certeyne of hys contrey shyppes, wherin he retorned again into hys countreye, nothynge lesse then lokyd for." [5]

There can be no reasonable doubt that the "countreye of Gulike" was located on the eastern shores of Vespucci's new continent, though the name Gulike, as Lupton points out,[6] was one which Robynson, who translated *Utopia* into English in 1551, read into the Latin text. The text of *Utopia* shows clearly that the Soderini letter inspired More to make Hythloday one of the twenty-four mentioned there. That letter located the land 18 degrees south of the equator and 35 degrees west of Lisbon, a point in eastern Brazil near the present town of Diamantina, about 300 miles north of Rio de Janeiro and an equal distance inland. The position of Utopia is not so easily determined.

Locating Utopia has been a favorite pastime with readers of the work, seriously or in jest, since the time it first appeared. More's intent is plain enough from the name itself, which means "nowhere." More, with a twinkle in his eye, reminded Peter Giles in the dedicatory letter addressed to him that they had forgotten to ask Hythloday in what part of the new world Utopia lay, a matter which he hoped Giles would soon remedy as he knew a preacher who wanted to go to Utopia as a missionary.[7] Budé, the eminent French humanist, wrote Thomas Lupset in the same high good humor that he thought Utopia lay quite outside the known world, implying that it was too good for this earth: "But in truth I have ascertained by full inquiry, that Utopia lies outside the bounds of the known world. It is in fact one of the Fortunate Isles, perhaps very close to the Elysian Fields; for More himself testifies that Hythloday has not yet stated its position definitely.[8] The question is still an open one, and Arthur E. Morgan, in a book aptly called *Nowhere was Somewhere* (1946), is the latest to speak of it. He thinks Utopia was Perú.

Morgan is driven to this identification by the similarity between the social and economic orders in Utopia and Perú, and he presses his argument by quoting parallel passages [9] from More's *Utopia* on the one hand and Prescott's *Conquest of Peru* [10] and Means' *Ancient Civilizations of the Andes* [11] on the other. The degree of similarity between the two orders with respect to such matters as family, labor, agriculture, money, and laws is impressively high. Once convinced, Morgan concludes that Raphael Hythloday was a real person who had traveled from the Brazilian coast along a Guaraní Indian trade route to Lake Titicaca in Perú and later returned to Europe, where he met More and told him of what he had seen, much as More relates the incident.

The chief difficulty attendant upon identifying Utopia with Perú and Hythloday with a real person, apart from More's own attitude, is the time element involved. Pizarro conquered the city of Cuzco in 1533. Before 1531, when Pizarro set out to conquer Perú, the number of Europeans who had visited there was small indeed. The earliest visitors mentioned by Morgan,[12] survivors of the expedition of Juan Diaz de Solis to the Plata River in 1515–1516, did not return to Europe until after *Utopia* was published. He must rely, then, on a hypothetical earlier traveler, a remote possibility. There can be little question that the Guaraní Indians, who lived along the eastern coast of South America in what is now Brazil, Uruguay, and Argentina, had established contact with Perú before the white man visited them and that they mentioned the land to the west to early voyagers, who in turn carried the word back to Europe before More wrote *Utopia*. But they probably mentioned it in response to inquiries about gold, and it is hardly likely that they discussed in detail the social and economic order there assuming that they were able. The rumor Barlow picked up in the vicinity of the Plata River shortly before Pizarro's conquest of Perú suggests the pattern.[13]

Though it seems unlikely, in view of this difficulty, that More had a detailed knowledge of Perú when he wrote *Utopia*, there is a good possibility that he had read Peter Martyr's account of other parts of America by that time and drew on it. Hythloday emphasizes the low regard Utopians had for gold and silver and their high regard for iron, saying:

In the meane tyme golde and syluer, whereof moneye ys made, they doo soo vse, as none of them dothe more estyme yt, then the verye nature of the thynge deseruethe. And then who dothe not playnlye see howe farre yt ys vnder Iron? as wythoute the whyche men canne no better lyue then withowte fyere and water; whereas to golde and syluer nature hathe geuen no vse that we may not wel lacke, yf that the folly of men hadde not sette it in hygher estymacyon for the rarenes sake. . . . For where as they eate and drincke in earthen and glasse vesselles, which in dede be curiously and properlie made, and yet be of very small value; of gold and siluer they make commonlye chamber pottes, and other like vesselles that serue for moste vile vses, not only in their common halles, but in euery mans priuate house.[14]

More could have borrowed the concept of disdain for gold from the Soderini letter, where he read: "The wealth which we affect in this our Europe and elsewhere, such as gold, jewels, pearls, and other riches, they hold of no value at all; and although they have them in their lands they do not work to get them, nor do they care for them." [15] There is a closer parallelism, however, between the passage from *Utopia* just quoted and two from Martyr's *Three Decades* (1516). Both passages refer to the adventures of Balboa in Veragua before 1514.

In the third book of the *Second Decade* Martyr speaks briefly of an encounter between the Spaniards and the eldest son of King Comogre, a local cacique, which savors of the experience Christ had with the money-changers in the temple. Comogre, following a mistaken policy of appeasement, sought to win the friendship of the Spaniards with a gift of 4,000 "drachmas" of gold. On the porch of the palace the Spaniards weighed up the gold and separated the fifth part due the king of Spain. Then they fell to quarreling among themselves over the division of the remainder. At this, the eldest son of King Comogre angrily struck the balances with his first, so that the gold was scattered about the porch, and rebuked the Spaniards, in part for their greed, in part for sacrificing their peace of mind for so small a quantity of the stuff. Then, adds the chronicler:

Such was his speech, and he added that the cacique Tumanama, and all the other mountaineers living on the other slope of the mountain, used kitchen and other common utensils made of gold; "for gold," he said, "has no more value among them than iron among you." [16]

In the third book of the *Third Decade* Martyr tells of a somewhat less dramatic encounter between the Spaniards and a delegation from King Chiorisos, another local cacique. The spokesman for the Indians presented Balboa with thirty plates of gold in token of friendship and asked his aid against a neighboring and hostile cacique. The chronicler says:

Vasco encouraged their hopes and sent them away satisfied. In exchange for their presents he gave them some iron hatchets, which they prize more than heaps of gold. For as they have no money—that source of all evils—they do not need gold. The owner of one single hatchet feels himself richer than Crassus. These natives believe that hatchets may serve a thousand purposes of daily life, while gold is only sought to satisfy vain desires, without which one would be better off.[17]

The *Three Decades* did not appear in print until November 9, 1516, probably too late to have been of use to More, since letters of the period indicate [18] that *Utopia* was in the printer's hands by November 19, 1516. Nothing short of a miracle would have permitted More to receive Martyr's work and read it, then revise his own and get it to the printer in that ten-day period. But Martyr's *Decades* was written on the installment plan as letters to friends in Italy, the part in question addressed to Pope Leo X. Copies of these letters circulated before the *Three Decades* was published. It is not beyond the realm of possibility to suppose that More saw copies before he wrote *Utopia*. They could have come from the Pope, since Henry VIII was still a good Catholic in 1516. They could also have come directly from Spain, since Henry VIII was still married to Catherine of Aragon and on good terms with her father Ferdinand in 1515-1516, the period in which *Utopia* was written. If they came, the rising young statesman who was to become Lord Chancellor in 1529 stood a good chance of seeing them, and the scholar More would have had no trouble with Martyr's Latin.

The Two Plays

While More was writing *Utopia*, or soon after, his brother-in-law John Rastell became interested in explaining the Greek universe to the English reader. About 1519 he published in London his play called *A new Interlude and a mery of the Nature of the iiij Elementes*, more commonly referred to today as the *Interlude of the Four Elements*. As the title indicates, attention was directed primarily to the lower part of that universe, the under-world, to the ancient elements earth, water, air, and fire. The title does not, however, prepare the reader for the disproportionate emphasis on the element earth nor for the very considerable attention devoted to America, a region of the earth unknown to the Greeks.

In the first quarter of the sixteenth century English drama was undergoing a marked change. The morality play was giving ground to the interlude which, in turn, was to be supplanted in the public favor by the farces of John Heywood and they, shortly after the middle of the century, by the earliest examples of English comedy in the modern sense. The emphasis the morality play had placed on abstractions was retained in the interlude but shifted by degrees from moral to intellectual abstractions. The actors were not yet persons—that development had to wait until later —but the Vices and Virtues were opening their ranks to Nature, Wit, Science, Reason, and other intellectual abstractions. Such abstractions, intellectual as well as moral, have always lacked dramatic interest save as they took on the attributes of human beings. Furthermore, considered solely as subject matter rather than actors, natural science, logic, and philosophy hardly seem suited for dramatic presentation. Nevertheless, John Rastell thought to try his hand at giving the subject of natural science the center of the stage in his *Interlude of the Four Elements*, and his experiment has preserved for us an unusually enlightened combination of the static and the changing earths together with a description of part of North America. It is unfortunate that the play has come down to us through a single imperfect copy, which lacks the conclusion and eight pages near the middle.

The universe presented by John Rastell is the Greek universe which we have come to regard as standard for England in the Middle Ages. The actor Nature describes it in considerable detail, concentrating of course on the nature of the four elements rather than that of the ethereal region or over-world. The proofs for a round earth seem to have had a particular attraction for Rastell, for he included four of the important ones, omitting only reference to the round shadow of the earth on the moon at the time of a lunar eclipse. Two actors, Humanity and Studious Desire, work out two of them, the significance of the rising of the sun in the east and its setting in the west and the significance of the progressive appearance of an eclipse in different parts of the earth. Another actor, Experience, later adds two others, that the farther north a man goes the higher the Pole Star rises and that the sailor on the mast of a ship sees land before his mate on deck.

Rastell's attitude toward the known, inhabited earth is surprisingly flexible, despite his reliance on a Greek universe. His Asia and Africa do belong to the static earth. His Europe belongs there, too, but shows additions from the changing earth comparable to those found in the works of Bartholomew and Higden. His America, however, belongs entirely to the changing earth—it has picked up no legends from the other—and he gives it more attention than any other region of the earth, thus indicating his special interest in it, speaking through Experience, who instructs Studious Desire in these matters as they stand before a "figure" (either a world map or a globe):

> *Experyence:* Westwarde be founde new landes
> That we never harde tell of before this
> By wrytynge nor other meanys
> Yet many nowe have ben there
> And that contrey is so large of rome
> Muche lenger than all Cristendome
> Without fable or gyle
> For dyvers maryners have it tryed
> And sayled streyght by the coste syde
> Above v. thousand myle [19]

North America does not present five thousand miles of continuous shoreline between Newfoundland and the southern tip of Florida, that part of her eastern coast along which Englishmen and Portuguese might have sailed before 1519, unless you circle the Great Lakes. Of the several mariners who had sailed along the eastern coast of South America by that date, Vespucci was probably the only one who had seen more than five thousand miles of continuous shoreline there. Rastell may have been referring to Vespucci's voyages or lumping together the overlapping voyages of several mariners. He may simply have been looking at either

North or South America or both on the map or globe before him
and miscalculating distances. However that may be, he had certainly grasped two important facts about some portion of that
shoreline, namely, its continuity and its continental extent. Experience continues:

> But what commodytes be within
> No man can tell nor well Imagin
> But yet not long ago
> Some men of this contrey went
> By the kynges noble consent
> It for to serche to that entent
> And coude not be brought therto
> But they that were they venteres
> Have cause to curse their maryners
> Fals of promys and dissemblers
> That falsly them betrayed
> Whiche wolde take no paine to saile farther
> Than their owne lyst and pleasure
> Wherfore that vyage and dyvers other
> Suche kaytyffes have distroyed
> O what a thynge had be than
> Yf that they that be Englyshe men
> Myght have ben the furst of all
> That there shulde have take possessyon
> And made furst buyldynge and habytacion
> A memory perpetuall
> And also what an honorable thynge
> Bothe to the realme and to the kynge
> To have had his domynyon extendynge
> There into so farre a grounde
> Which the noble kynge of late memory
> The moste wyse prynce the vij. Herry
> Causyd furst to be founde
> And what a great meritoryouse dede
> It were to have the people instructed
> To lyve more vertously
> And to lerne to knowe of men the maner
> And also to knowe God theyr maker

Whiche as yet lyve all bestly
For they nother knowe God nor the devell
Nor never harde tell of hevyn nor hell
Wrytynge nor other scripture
But yet in the stede of God almyght
The honour the sone for his great lyggt
For that doth them great pleasure
Buyldynge nor house they have not at all
But wodes cotes and cavys small
No merveyle though it be so
For they use no maner of yron
Nother in tole nor other wepon
That shulde helpe them therto
Copper they have whiche is founde
In dyvers places above the grounde
Yet they dug not therfore
For as I sayd they have non yryn
Wherby they shuld in the yerth myne
To serche for any wore
Great habondance of woddes ther be
Moste parte vyr and pyne aple tre
Great ryches myght come therby
Both pyche and tarre and sope asshe
As they make in the eest landes
By brynnynge therof only
Fyshe they have so great plente
That in havyns take and slayne they be
With stavys withouten fayle
Nowe Frenchemen and other have founde the trade
That yerely of fyshe there they lade
Above an C. sayle
But in the south parte of that contrey
The people there go nakyd alway
The lande is of so great hete
And in the north parte all the clothes
That they were is but bestes skynnes
They have no nother fete
But howe the people furst began
In that countrey and whens they cam

> For clerkes it is a questyon
> Other thynges mo I have in store
> That I coude tel therof but now no more
> Tyll another season [20]

The "men of this contrey" were of course Rastell and his friends
and the "maryners fals of promys" Ravyn and his supporters.[21]
The three objectives given for the ill-fated voyage of 1517, extension of English territory by colonization, Christianization of the
natives, and search for commòdities coupled with possible exploita-
tion of timber and fishing, are presented in such a manner as to
stress the first two. Indeed the possibility of profit is simply
touched upon lightly in passing. It is quite likely that this represents the true emphasis, though it was the profit motive that
sparked most sixteenth century voyages. Thomas More was characterized by intense patriotism and deep religious feeling and his
brother-in-law may have shared in these emotions. This relative
emphasis strengthens the hypothesis that settlement was actually
intended, although such an objective would have been far in ad-
vance of its day. It could have provoked the break with the obviously greedy Ravyn. Specific reference to fir and pine and their
products and to fish shows that the land sought was the "new
found land." Over a hundred ships a year to the Newfoundland
fishing by about 1519 was, if true, a very considerable traffic.

The rest of the description of the new land mentioned in the
last three lines of the above passage is lost to us, perhaps through
the missing pages, though Rastell may have had no intention of
putting it into this play. This, however, does not conclude the
discussion of the regions of the earth. Experience, at the insistence
of Studious Desire, points out some regions not yet mentioned,
including a Turkey which belongs to the expanding earth and
an India which is still the land of Prester John, just as it was for
Sir John Mandeville. He says:

> Than wyl I torne agayne to my matter
> Of Cosmogryfy where I was ere
> Beholde take hede to this
> Loo estwarde beyonde the great occyan

> Here entereth the see callyd Mediterran
> Of ij. M. myle of lengthe
> The Soudans contrey lyeth hereby
> The great Turke on the north syde doth ly
> A man of merveylous strengthe
> This sayde north parte is callyd Europa
> And this south parte callyd Affrica
> This eest parte is callyd Ynde
> But this Newe Landes founde lately
> Ben callyd America bycause only
> Americus dyd furst them fynde
> Loo Ihrsin [Jerusalem] lyeth in this contrey
> And this beyonde is the Red See
> That Moyses maketh of mencyon
> This quarter is India minor
> And this quarter India Major
> The lande of Prester John
> But northwarde this way as ye se
> Many other straunge regions ther be
> And people that we not knowe
> But estwarde on the see syde
> A prynce there is that rulyth wyde
> Callyd the Cane of Catowe
> And this is called the great eest see
> Whiche goth all alonge this wey
> Towardes the newe landis agayne
> But whether that see go thyther dyrectly
> Or if any wyldernes bytwene them do ly
> No man knoweth for certeyne
> But these newe landes by all cosmografye
> Frome the Cane of Catous lande can not lye
> Lytell paste a thousand myle
> But from those new landes men may sayle playne
> Estwarde an cum to Englande againe
> Where we began ere whyle [22]

Having thus disposed of the known, inhabited earth, Experience begins to speculate upon that unknown portion to the south and the nature of its antipodean peoples, a trend of thought interrupted

by the return of the actor Humanity. He concludes his discourse
as follows:

> Lo all this parte of the yerth whiche I
> Have here discryvyd openly
> The north parte do it call
> But the south parte on the other syde
> Ys as large as this full and as wyde
> Whiche we knowe nothynge at all
> Nor whether the people that there be
> Be bestyall or connynge
> Nor whether they knowe God or us
> Nor howe they beleve nor what they do
> Of this we knowe nothynge
> Lo is not this a thynge woonderfull
> How that—
> > *Et subito* Studyouse Desire *dicat*
> Pese syr no more of this matter
> Beholde where Humanyte commeth here [23]

It seems quite likely that Experience is not speaking for John
Rastell in thus disclaiming all knowledge of antipodean regions.
Thomas More, speaking through Raphael Hythloday in *Utopia*
had already referred to that account of Vespucci's purported four
voyages now known as the Soderini letter as being "abrode in
euerye mans handes," [24] and if More had read it the chances are
that Rastell had too, for the two men were intimates at this period
as well as brothers-in-law. It contains a somewhat extended description of the "south parte" of the earth and its inhabitants.
Rastell's use of the name America suggests that he had read the
Soderini letter in Waldseemüller's cosmography or talked to
somebody who had.

Morality plays continued to be written and produced in England during the second quarter of the sixteenth century, and one
of the examples remaining today is a fragment owned by Professor
Ray Nash of Dartmouth College, preserved through the accident
of having been made a part of the cover of another book. Neither

the title of the play nor the name of the author has come down to us. Frost and Nash have, however, dubbed the play "Good Order" after one of the characters and deduced from internal evidence that John Skelton may have been the author.[25] The text of the play presents two Vices, Riot and Gluttony, brought to trial by one of the Virtues, Good Order, before his master Old Christmas. Riot and Gluttony there turn against each other with mutual recriminations. Both are proclaimed traitors and sentenced to be banished from England forever. Riot then turns to Gluttony and says, "Alas Glotony what shall we than do." Gluttony replies:

> In fayth to the new founde land let vs go
> For in englond there is no remedy.[26]

We have no way of knowing what the author meant by "new founde land" since we know neither his name nor the date of composition of the play. If he wrote it before 1504 we might doubt that the reference is to America. Though we do not know these things, we do know that the play was printed by William Rastell, the son of John Rastell, in 1533 because the last page carries his colophon. By this date "new founde land" for many Englishmen meant something more than known land discovered from a different direction, and this must have been particularly true of William Rastell. Had not his uncle written a prose tale set in America? His father planned and almost executed a voyage there? And was not his brother to sail there and back in 1536? It is nothing short of astonishing how the "matter of America" kept gravitating to the More-Rastell family during the first half of the sixteenth century. It is difficult to imagine William Rastell printing a play in which "new founde land" meant something other than America. And even if he had, many of his readers would have read that meaning into it. The most significant aspect of the use of the phrase here, however, is the concept of America as a place where a condemned man might make a new start. This is very early for Englishmen, even characters in a play and desperate and disreputable ones at that, to consider going to America to live.

CHAPTER VI

Expansion of English Interest in Voyaging, 1547–1558

IN THE DISTURBED years between the reign of Henry VIII and the reign of Elizabeth, in the short reigns of two weak rulers, Edward VI and Mary Tudor, the spirit of voyaging throve and grew strong in England. It was high time. The period of incubation had been so much longer there than in Spain, Portugal, or even France that these countries were already far ahead of England in their knowledge of a rapidly expanding earth. Out of this growing interest in voyaging there was eventually to come a real and widespread interest in America. But the English discovery of America was, at this time, only a small, relatively unimportant part of the English discovery of the earth and inseparable from it. For fuller understanding of the lesser discovery, our principal interest, some attention must be given to the English discovery of other regions of the earth too.

The probable establishment of trade with Barbary between 1546 and 1552 constitutes the first tangible sign of enhanced English interest in voyaging. Additional signs appeared in 1553. In that memorable year the Willoughby expedition sailed in search of a northeast passage to Asia and found access to Russia by the White Sea; Thomas Wyndham sailed on a trading expedition to Guinea; and Richard Eden published *A Treatyse of the newe India* . . . , his translation of part of the fifth book of Sebastian Münster's cosmography. The voyages opened up two new regions to the English and stimulated other voyages to both of them. The book called attention to the axiom, previously ignored by the vast majority of Englishmen, that the easy avenue to knowledge of the regions of the earth is the printed word. This earlier effort of Eden paved the way for the writing and publication of his *Decades*, a much sounder work, which made available in English a large quantity of information about America, Russia, Guinea, and other regions then in the public eye.

Search for a Northeast Passage to Asia and Establishment of Trade with Russia

The undercurrent of expanding interest in voyaging showed itself early in the reign of Edward VI by a variety of small signs which did not immediately lead to voyages to these distant and little known places. In May, 1547, John Dee, who was to be one of the important technical advisers of the Elizabethan voyagers, went from England to the University of Louvain to study under Gemma Phrysius, the great Flemish mathematician, cosmographer, and cartographer. In 1548 Sebastian Cabot was recalled to England from Spain, presumably by official request, since he was granted an annual pension commencing in that year. In 1549 John Dudley, then Earl of Warwick, created Duke of Northumberland in October, 1551, was also Lord Admiral, a post more important to us than his other perquisites because it suggests his strong interest in voyaging. It was he, in fact, more than any other one person who at this time helped arouse official England to the need for promoting and supporting English voyages to distant regions. In November, 1549, he appointed Roger Barlow Vice-Admiral of the coast of Pembrokeshire, an act probably designed to capitalize on Barlow's experience and knowledge as a mariner and also make him readily available for consultation on projected voyages to Asia and America. In 1551 Richard Chancellor, the navigator who was to have so large a share in opening up trade with Russia, was learning his craft under Roger Bodenham in the bark *Aucher* on a voyage to the islands of Chios and Candia (Crete), important outlets for the Levant trade.

What plans for voyaging were under consideration in these early years must remain in large measure a matter of conjecture. That there were such plans can hardly be doubted. Northumberland pumped Cabot for information about Perú and discussed with him a tentative plan for raiding that fabulously wealthy Spanish possession from the east by sending a large company of men up the Amazon River in small boats. Such a trip was not beyond the realm of possibility since the Spaniard Orellana had made it downstream in 1541, but the much slower journey upstream, giving fever and hostile Indians opportunity for their deadly work, would almost certainly have been doomed to failure. It was made for the first time in 1638 by a Portuguese. But the plan was considered, and others, too. Rumors of plans were afloat among the diplomatic set in England [1] —for an expedition against France or Scotland, for a voyage to the east, for a voyage utilizing the services of Jean Ribault, for a voyage to the north past Iceland. It is quite possible that Northumberland was considering the northern route proposed by Thorne and Barlow, using either Cabot or Ribault as pilot. At least Barlow was at hand, and Northumberland had seen to it that Ribault found employment with his cousin, Vice-Admiral Sir Henry Dudley, where the French pilot, too, could be found if his services were needed.

The project that finally crystallized in this broth of rumor and tentative plan was a voyage of discovery to the *northeast*. Not the north or the northwest, the expectable directions, but the northeast, and the reasons for seeking a passage to Asia there are somewhat obscure.

The reasons for seeking a passage somewhere at this time seem clear enough. The very good contemporary account by Clement Adams, written in Latin, indicates that the London merchants were the driving force behind the voyage. He says [2] they had watched with alarm the decline of English goods abroad, both in demand and price. They had come to envy the wealth flowing to Portugal and Spain from India, the Spice Islands, Africa, and America. Resolving to repair their declining fortunes by tapping some of that wealth, they joined, sometime before May, 1553, with courtiers and other interested persons in forming a stock company, capitalized for 6,000 pounds, to explore northern regions and open a passage to new kingdoms, presumably Tartary as well as Cathay and the Spice Islands since two Tartars then in England were consulted. It is quite possible that the Duke of Northumberland was a principal backer, though none of the documents which might prove this exist today.

Whether the plan for this voyage was, in any real sense, based on the old Thorne-Barlow plan we do not know. It does seem to have had at least one of the elements of that plan, trade with Tartary. Yet Sebastian Cabot, not Barlow, was chief technical adviser. As such, responsibility for choosing the direction in which the expedition would sail was likely to rest, in the last analysis, with him. It is not difficult to imagine Cabot throwing his weight against an attack on Spanish possessions, whether Perú or the vicinity of the Plata River, because of personal knowledge of the hazards involved, gained through long service with Spain. Once the objective, eastern Asia, had been fixed upon, he was faced with the choice of direction. There was very little information available to help him decide which northern route to take—and it had to be northern because Portugal and Spain had monopolies on the sea routes in other directions. So little, indeed, was then known about the extent and shape of northern lands, even to Cabot, that he may have sent the expedition northeast instead of northwest simply because that direction had not yet been tried, northeast instead of north because the expedition could remain longer in sight of land in that direction.

On May 10, 1553, the planning over, an expedition of three ships, the *Bona Esperanza* carrying Willoughby, captain general of the expedition, the *Edward Bonaventure* with Richard Chancellor, pilot major, aboard, and the *Bona Confidentia*, sailed from Ratcliff on what proved to be a search for a northeast passage to eastern Asia. Sebastian Cabot was by this time too old for active service and stayed in England. Northward the fleet followed an old Norse route, coasting along the eastern shores of England and Scotland, thence proceeding northeast past the Orkneys and Shetlands to the west coast of Norway. It then moved slowly northward, always within sight of land, occasionally sending out a pinnace to make contact with some of the islands passed. On August 2 the fleet anchored off the island of Senja, which is north of the Arctic Circle, just under 70 degrees north latitude. Here the weather must have begun to thicken up a bit, for, at the conference of the chief men, it was agreed that in case the ships became separated by storm, each would make for the harbor of Vardo on the other side of the North Cape. Beyond Vardo lay the great unknown. That night the anticipated storm struck with great force, separating the *Bonaventure* from the other two ships. When the storm eased, both Willoughby and Chancellor, from their separate positions, sailed for Vardo as agreed. Willoughby, however, made the mistake of relying on his globe,³ which proved inaccurate in this latitude. Before he realized his mistake, he had sailed so far north and east that he missed the North Cape entirely, reaching uninhabited land on the far side of the White Sea. There the early northern winter caught his two ships, and every man jack of the two crews perished before spring. Chancellor had better luck. The *Bonaventure* made Vardo in good season.

Vardo was not the end of the voyage for the *Bonaventure*. After lingering there seven days Chancellor and the crew, regretfully and with some misgivings, decided to push east without further delay. They continued to skirt the shore, passed the estuary that now leads to the town of Murmansk, and sailed along the shore of the Kola Peninsula until they entered the White Sea. There they found people, a discovery almost as significant for English trade as if they had reached Tartary or Cathay. They encountered a small fishing boat manned by Russians. This event changed their immediate objective from eastern Asia to the court of the Czar. It marks the beginning of friendly relations between England and Russia.

It is hard to say who were the more astonished at this meeting, the English or the Russians. The English, feeling their way gingerly into the unknown, had little expected to find Russia, and these Russians, for their part, had never seen a large ship on the White Sea and perhaps never a large ship. Chancellor said he and his crew had been sent by the English king to establish friendship and trade and asked to be taken to the Russian court. The local officials provided him with necessary supplies but otherwise put him off while they sent a secret messenger to the Czar Ivan (later called the Terrible), asking his pleasure in the matter. Ivan was pleased to hear of the arrival of the English, readily granted his subjects permission to trade with them, and invited them to visit him in Moscow if convenient. The messengers managed to lose their way on the return journey, and Chancellor, irked at the delay, threatened to proceed with the voyage as first planned. His irritation is understandable, for the delay must have been considerable, and winter was setting in. At this threat the local officials reluctantly set out for Moscow with Chancellor and some of his crew. When they had traveled most of the way, they encountered the wandering messengers, whose favorable report at once transformed local¹ reluctance to help strangers into a straining eagerness to carry out the wishes of the great Czar.

Chancellor and his men were not received by the Czar until twelve days after they had reached Moscow, a waiting period no doubt flattering to Ivan's ego but especially irksome to the English, already wearied by the previous delay. Nevertheless they managed to keep their tempers, and Chancellor, as spokesman, behaved with admirable restraint and tact. After the audience the Czar, who was favorably impressed, invited them to dinner and eventually sent them back to the *Bonaventure* with a letter to Edward VI promising free trade.

How long all this took is not certain, but it seems to have been a little over five months. The expedition probably reached the White Sea in the latter part of August, and the Czar's letter is dated the following February. This concession was a real triumph for the English, who for years had been trying without success to break the monopoly of the Hanseatic League on trade with Russia by way of the Baltic Sea. They now had another outlet for their woolen goods, which they could trade to the Russians for furs, hemp, flax, hides, tallow, wax, honey, and other products. Although Chancellor describes [4] in detail numerous gold vessels used at the Russian court and the cloth-of-gold worn extensively by the Russian courtiers, there seems to have been no intent to trade for gold.

The *Bonaventure* returned to England in the summer of 1554 without further attempt to search for a northeast passage. The Duke of Northumberland did not live to welcome her home. His overweening ambition had led him to attempt to change the royal succession, with results which were fatal to himself. In 1553 he obtained letters patent from the ailing young king, shifting the succession from Mary and Elizabeth Tudor to Lady Jane Grey, to whom, in furtherance of his plan, he had married one of his sons on May 21 of that year. Upon the death of Edward VI, on July 6, 1553, Northumberland proclaimed Lady Jane Grey queen. This obvious attempt to switch the succession to his own family was too much even for his own followers to swallow, and they rallied to Mary Tudor. Northumberland, taken into custody, was executed on August 22, 1553. On the scaffold he made a cringing and ignoble statement wrongly blaming others for his uncomfortable position, a poor showing for an able man, an ending that must have been a source of some embarrassment to his son, the Earl of Leicester and favorite of Queen Elizabeth, and to his grandson Philip Sidney.

With the return of the *Bonaventure*, English merchants, courtiers with money to invest, specialists in navigation, and other practical men-of-affairs rallied to the task of developing trade with Russia. The company which had sponsored the Willoughby expedition was reincorporated on February 6, 1555, and a new charter [5] was granted by Philip and Mary to replace that of Edward VI. Thereafter it was known as the Russia Company, for the new charter gave it a monopoly on trade with that country. The new company sent its first expedition to Russia in that same year, a second in 1556, and a third in 1557.

In 1555 Chancellor returned to Russia with two ships, the *Philip and Mary* and his faithful *Bonaventure*. When he arrived he learned that Willoughby's two ships, the *Esperanza* and the *Confidentia*, had been discovered intact by the Russians, and plans were made to put them in service again, plans which did not reach fruition until the fall of 1556. Chancellor sent his own ships, laden with Russian commodities, to England in the fall of 1555 and himself spent the winter in Russia. When these ships returned to Russia in May, 1556, they were accompanied by the pinnace *Serchthrift*, commanded by Stephen Borough, who had been master of the *Bonaventure* under Chancellor on the initial voyage of 1553, with orders to continue the search for a northeast passage.

Although the development of trade with Russia was still of paramount importance, Englishmen had not forgotten that the Willoughby expedition of 1553 had been undertaken solely for the purpose of seeking a northeast passage to Tartary, Cathay, and the Spice Islands. Stephen Borough was commissioned to continue that search east of the entrance to the White Sea. His account [6] of the voyage shows that bad weather kept him from getting very far. He rounded the peninsula now called Kaninskaya Zemlya and coasted east, delayed by rain and fog, as far as the small islands south of Novaya Zemlya. Here, on August 22, 1556, he turned back since the ice was increasing, the season was already late, and he was having trouble sailing into the prevailing northeast and northerly winds. He spent the winter at Colmogro, a port fifty miles up the Dvina River. There was no further attempt to push the search for a northeast passage until that made by Pet and Jackman in 1580, which was also unsuccessful.

In the fall of 1556 four ships, the *Bonaventure*, the *Philip and Mary*, and the renovated *Esperanza* and *Confidentia*, all laden with Russian goods, left Russia for England under the command of Chancellor.[7] In addition, a Russian ambassador for England was on board the *Bonaventure* with Chancellor. Bad luck sailed with them. Off Trondheim, on the Norwegian coast, a violent storm struck the fleet. The *Esperanza* simply disappeared. The *Confidentia* struck a rock and went down with all hands. The *Philip and Mary* limped into Trondheim harbor and spent the winter there. Only the sturdy *Bonaventure* was able to proceed, and she went down off the coast of Scotland, carrying with her Chancellor who perished in saving the life of the Russian ambassador, a great loss to English voyaging.

The Russia Company, however, soon recovered from this staggering loss of men and ships. In the spring of 1557 it sent [8] to Russia under the command of Anthony Jenkinson a fleet of four ships, three of which, the *Primrose*, the *Trinity*, and the *John Evangelist*, had previously made voyages to Guinea. This fleet reached Russia without mishap, and Jenkinson went on to Moscow where, on Christmas Day, he was presented to the Czar.

About a year later Jenkinson began a journey [9] to Boghar, now called Bukhara, word of which was to arouse some hope in London that the English might tap from Moscow the caravan trade between Cathay and the Mediterranean, a new angle on the English search for a passage to eastern Asia. Late in April, 1558, Jenkinson and several companions, bearing credentials from the Czar, embarked on a tributary of the Volga River. They sailed down the Volga to the Caspian Sea, then across the Caspian to the opposite shore where they deserted their boat for a camel train, proceeding overland through the land of the Tartars to Bukhara. They would have gone on to Cathay, says Jenkinson, had it not been for local wars, by reason of which no caravan had gone that way for three years.

On November 17, 1558, while Jenkinson was on the road to Bukhara, Mary Tudor died and her sister Elizabeth succeeded her on the throne of England.

Africa

The Portuguese had looked upon parts of Africa as their own private preserve ever since their capture in 1415 of the Moorish stronghold of Ceuta, situated on the south side of the Strait of Gibraltar, including land washed by the Atlantic Ocean as well as by the Mediterranean Sea. At first this proprietary feeling was directed principally toward Barbary (Morocco, Algeria, Tunisia, and Libya), but, as ships worked south along the west coast of Africa, it soon extended itself to Guinea (the west coast of Africa approximately 15 degrees north and 16 degrees south of the equator at the time of maximum extension). As the trade proved profitable, the Portuguese attempted to monopolize it, and though they exerted diplomatic pressure and resorted to force of arms they made little effort to colonize the country, the only basis on which a workable monopoly could be founded. English and French ships broke it repeatedly.

How early Englishmen engaged in trade with Barbary we do not know. Their ships may have stopped there occasionally throughout the late Middle Ages. Blake has gathered together documents [10] which give evidence of privateering off the coast in 1546 and of well-established trade beginning with 1548. Hakluyt mentions [11] one voyage to Morocco in 1551 and gives a short account [12] of another to the same place in 1552. The possibility of pre-sixteenth century trade with Barbary is suggested by known interest in sailing to Guinea, a much longer and more difficult voyage, as early as 1481–1482. Hakluyt records [13] a protest by the Portuguese against an English voyage in preparation that early. A similar voyage was planned in 1488 by a Portuguese political exile in conjunction with some English merchants, which again drew protests from the Portuguese government.[14] No similar activity is recorded between this proposed voyage and the one which "Olde M. William Haukins" made to Guinea and Brazil in 1530–1532. Hakluyt printed detailed and illuminating accounts [15] of five later Guinea voyages, one by Wyndham to Benin (1553), another by John Lok to Mina (1554–1555)—both accounts taken from Eden's *Decades*—and three by William Towerson to Mina (1555–1558).

About the beginning of May, 1552, three ships left Bristol for Morocco. One was the *Lion* of London, which had made the voyage the year before under Thomas Wyndham, who was again in command, and another was a Portuguese caravel purchased in Wales. They touched first at the Atlantic port of Zafia (Safia), where some merchandise was set ashore to be sent overland to the city of Morocco (Marrakech). The expedition then coasted a short distance south to the port of Santa Cruz (Agadir), where it exchanged the rest of its goods, linen and woolen cloth, coral, amber, and jet, for sugar, dates, almonds, and molasses. Soon after they had put to sea again the *Lion* sprang a leak, forcing them to drop anchor in the road between the islands of Lanzarote and Fuerteventura, two of the Canaries.

Their reception on Lanzarote, where they landed, was a hostile one. The Spaniards, believing that the caravel had been taken from the Portuguese by force, met them with drawn sword. A truce was soon arranged and the matter explained, but not before some lives had been lost and property damaged. This damage the Spanish king eventually made good.

The English mended their leak and left the road for England, just in the nick of time. As they moved out at one end, a Portuguese fleet of armed vessels moved in at the other "and shot off their great ordinance in our hearing." This voyage and the one made the previous year greatly offended the Portuguese, who sent word through their own merchants that "if they tooke us in those partes, they would use us as their mortall enemies, with great threates and menaces." [16]

It was almost inevitable that English merchants should extend their efforts to Guinea because of the greater value of the commodities to be found there, particularly pepper, ginger, ivory, and the irresistible gold. There is only slight evidence of English participation in the slave trade before 1562, when John Hawkins first carried Guinea slaves to Spanish America. It soon became customary to go to certain places in Guinea for particular products, to the Rio dos Sestos for melagueta pepper or ginger, then on to the Mina coast (the vicinity of Cape Three Points) for gold, stopping sometimes at intermediate stations for ivory. Benin, which was beyond the Mina coast, furnished the Ashanti or red pepper. The Portuguese, of course, objected violently to English participation in this trade, by force of arms as well as diplomatic protests, but the merchants persisted. Englishmen were beginning to resent the Portuguese assertion of dominion over half the earth, to feel strongly, as Eden said in 1555, against "such, as for the conquering of fortie or fiftie miles here and there, and erecting of certaine fortresses, thinke to be Lordes of halfe the world, envying that other should enjoy the commodities, which they themselves cannot wholy possesse." [17] The English passion for gold was soon to be transferred to America, and their feeling of resentment against the Portuguese was about to give place to a similar but more active feeling against the Spaniards, who considered themselves entitled to the other half of the earth.

Wyndham's voyage to Benin in 1553, graphically described by Eden,[18] was as melodramatic as if it had been concocted in Hollywood in our time. On August 12, 1553, a fleet of three ships, the *Lion*, the *Primrose*, and a pinnace named the *Moon*, sailed from Portsmouth for Guinea. Eden indicates that the command was shared jointly by Thomas Wyndham, who had just made two voyages to Morocco, and by Antonio Anes Pinteado, a Portuguese navigator who knew the coast. Pinteado had been wrongfully imprisoned by the Portuguese government on a false information. Upon his release he went to England where, in a spirit of revenge, he urged a Guinea voyage upon the English merchants, offering his services as pilot. The ships touched first at the Madeira, where they added a quantity of wine to their stores. There a Portuguese galleon, which had been sent to intercept them, thought better of it in view of their strength, and they passed on in peace.

Before they reached the Canaries, bad blood arose between Wyndham and Pinteado. Eden lays the blame on Wyndham, saying that he suddenly assumed sole command over the protests of the other merchants' factors. Thereafter Wyndham neglected Pinteado's advice, except with respect to technical problems of navigation, and abused him shamelessly, a course which eventually

cost many lives. Though Pinteado himself was not entirely blame-
less for what followed, he seems to have been more in the right
than Wyndham.

In due time the ships reached the Rio dos Sestos, where they
might have loaded "graines," a hot, unnamed spice (melagueta
pepper) which was said to command a ready market in cold
countries. However, at the insistence of Wyndham, who had
gold fever, they went on to Mina, where English goods were
traded for 150 "pounds weight" of gold. With some goods still
left, Wyndham, against the advice of Pinteado, pushed the fleet
on to Benin, near the delta of the Niger River, thinking to trade
the remainder of it for pepper (Ashanti pepper). Pinteado pointed
out that the season called the Rossia was approaching, marked by
a smothering, rotting heat which made it unhealthy to linger
near the equator. Wyndham only called him a "whoreson Jew"
for his pains and forced compliance by threatening to cut off his
ears and nail them to the mast if he failed to lead on.

As they approached their goal, the two large ships were left
at sea and Pinteado piloted the pinnace *Moon*, with several factors abroad, fifty or sixty leagues up the "river of Benin." At
that point they disembarked and traveled overland another ten
leagues to the court of the local chief, where they were courte-
ously received. A trade was soon arranged, English goods for
pepper, the pepper to be loaded within thirty days. By the end
of that period a large quantity of pepper had been gathered and
more was still coming in, but apparently none of it had been
loaded, even onto the *Moon*. Meanwhile the sailors on the *Lion*
and the *Primrose*, with time on their hands, were eating too much
fresh fruit, drinking too much palm wine, and bathing too often
under the hot sun, as a result of which combination they were
dying at the rate of three to five a day. Wyndham, fearful of soon
finding himself so short-handed that he could not sail, sent Pinteado a message to come away with all possible speed. Pinteado
replied that in his judgment they had best wait until all the
pepper was in. Wyndham threatened to leave them behind unless

they returned at once and sought to relieve his mounting rage by wrecking Pinteado's cabin and instruments. Pinteado was then already on his way down river to reason with Wyndham. By the time he reached the two ships Wyndham himself had fallen sick and died. So many men had died that those remaining sank the *Lion* for lack of hands to man her and, taking Pinteado aboard the *Primrose*, sailed for England, leaving behind the factors and, presumably, the pepper and the pinnace *Moon*, too. Pinteado died on the return voyage "for very pensivenesse & thought that stroke him to the heart." It was this *Primrose* that formed a part of the fleet Jenkinson took to Russia in 1557.

The next English voyage to Guinea, also recorded by Eden,[19] was less colorful and more successful than that of 1553. It produced nearly three times as much gold as that of Wyndham, besides melagueta pepper, a considerable quantity of ivory, and five Negroes. On October 11, 1554, a fleet of three ships and two pinnaces, including the *Trinity* and the *John Evangelist*, which were also to form a part of Jenkinson's fleet to Russia in 1557, sailed down the Thames under the command of John Lok. It reached the Rio dos Sestos on December 22, except for the loss of one pinnace, and spent a week there trading for melagueta pepper. Thence it proceeded slowly eastward along the coast, stopping some twenty leagues beyond Cape Palmas to pick up about 250 elephant tusks, then moving on to Mina for the gold, 400 "pound weight" of it, and the five Negroes. Apparently these men were not slaves in the usual sense but were taken to England to be taught the English language so that they could return as interpreters. At least this was Towerson's reply [20] to inquiries for them at Mina in January, 1556. At one trading station on the Mina coast Martin Frobisher, who had been on Wyndham's voyage to Guinea, was set ashore as a pledge of good faith. The Negroes themselves broke faith and turned him over to the Portuguese, who held him prisoner for about nine months.[21] On February 13, 1555, the fleet sailed from Mina for England, warned by Wyndham's fate not to go on to Benin for red pepper.

The wealth brought back by Lok, particularly the gold, stimulated other voyages to Guinea patterned after his. Only three of those made before 1559 have been described in any detail, three to Mina under William Towerson. Their record has been preserved by Hakluyt,[22] who apparently had access to Towerson's journals. The chronological arrangement and the emphasis on landmarks, distances, and depth of water near shore suggest this. More important for most modern readers are valuable references to the natives encountered, to their towns, weapons, language, customs, and behavior. The first two voyages were more successful than the third. This was late in starting, consequently its timing was off throughout the entire journey. French ships had secured most of the gold before the English reached Mina. English sailors fell sick because their ships were off the coast at the wrong season of the year. Three ships and a pinnace sailed from Plymouth on January 30, 1558. Only one, the *Minion*, returned to England, reaching the Isle of Wight on October 30, 1558. Portugal protested, as was her custom. Queen Mary had more than once lent a sympathetic ear to these protests, perhaps because her husband Philip feared that otherwise Englishmen would soon challenge his own trade monopoly in America. Things were to be different under Elizabeth.

The Early Writings of Richard Eden

While English merchants and mariners were thus busily engaged with voyages to Russia and Guinea, Richard Eden was making it possible for the stay-at-home Englishman, the average layman who relied for his information on English rather than on Latin or a modern romance language, to discover these and other regions of the earth through reading books. Eden translated into English certain important cosmographical works. *A Treatyse of the newe India* . . . ,[23] his translation of a part of the fifth book of Sebastian Münster's *Cosmographia vniversale*, appeared in 1553. In 1555 he published *The Decades of the newe worlde or west India* . . . ,[24] his translation of the first four decades of Peter Martyr and several other works bearing on voyaging and related subjects, a much more ambitious project than the other.

Eden was moved to translate part of the fifth book of Münster's cosmography by his desire to increase English interest in voyaging and cosmography, the science which made possible extended voyages, and by his awareness that English literature on the regions of the earth was very much out-of-date. So far as he knew there was only one work in English, a short one entitled "of the newe founde landes," referring to recent discoveries (apparently he was not familiar with the *Interlude of the Four Elements*) and he rightly considered it very inferior in quality. Speaking of it in the dedication of *A Treatyse of the newe India* . . . , he says,

The whyche tytle when I readde, as one not vtterlye ignoraunt hereof, hauynge before in my tyme readde *Decades*, and also the nauigations *de nouo orbe*, there seemed too me no lesse inequalitye betwene the tytle and the booke, then if a man woulde professe to wryte of Englande, and entreated onelye of Trumpington a vyllage wythin a myle of Cambrydge.[25]

If, as seems likely, the work referred to was one entitled *Of the newe landes* . . . ,[26] printed in Antwerp about 1511 by John of Doesborowe, then Eden was much too gentle in his criticism. This little tract is not merely inadequate; it is gravely misleading and was when it was written.

The opening paragraph, concerned with America, is a corrupt summary of the forged account of Vespucci's second voyage, the one made under the Portuguese flag, in the course of which he saw so much of the southeastern coast of South America. It seems to be a patchwork of information and misinformation derived indeed from both forged accounts of that voyage. The new land is called Armenica instead of America, which suggests either a too casual reading of Waldseemüller's cosmography or a secondary source for the name. The date of the voyage is said to be 1496, one year earlier than that of the purported first voyage of the Soderini letter, which had itself been set up a year too early. The description of the Indians is even more sensational than the lurid, exaggerated account in the *Mundus novus*, from which it was apparently drawn. The natives are depicted as lecherous cannibals with hardly a redeeming feature, and their life expectancy, put at 150 years in the source work, has grown to 300 years in this one. It is no wonder that Eden, aware from his reading of Martyr's *Decades* how far from the truth this account had strayed, sought to give Englishmen something better.

Succeeding paragraphs refer briefly to Barbary, Guinea, Arabia, India, and Cochin. The order and phraseology suggest that part of this information was taken from a Portuguese rutter or mariner's log. There follows an equally brief description of the so-called ten, different Christian nations, including such diverse groups as the Latins, Germans, Greeks, Nestorians, and Armenians, taken from some unnamed ecclesiastical source. The last item is a condensation of an account of the land of Prester John, said to have been written in the year 507. As might be expected from the early date, this legendary figure, who was by 1553 already identified with the ruler of Abyssinia, is described as a ruler in Asia. This part of the tract, with its references to griffins, Amazons, the Phoenix, unicorns, men with heads like dogs, the supposed battle between the pygmies and the storks, and other wonders, is straight out of the static, classical earth.

Eden's interest in the "new" regions of the earth, like that of the anonymous author of the little tract printed by Doesborowe, was general and not confined to America. On this account he first selected for translation a general work, the pertinent part of Münster's cosmography, rather than Martyr's *Decades*, which was confined to America. He wanted to promote English trade through English voyages to distant, wealthy regions of the earth, and so *A Treatyse of the newe India* . . . is concerned with India, the Spice Islands, and Cathay as well as the "newe India" or America. This work was a great improvement over its predecessor, for it was much closer to the truth and more detailed. Part of it was already out-of-date, however, particularly the description of Cathay, which was taken from Marco Polo. When the account of Marco Polo was first published (early fourteenth century), and for many years thereafter, it was a source of knowledge of the changing earth, but by the middle of the sixteenth century the passage of time had shunted it into that ever-growing body of literature which simply embalms an earth that no longer exists.

The America that takes form in *A Treatyse of the newe India* . . . is primarily South America and the West Indies, for the descriptive details have been taken from accounts of voyages to those regions—the supposed four voyages of Vespucci, three of Columbus' four voyages, and single voyages by Nuñez, Pinzón, and Magellan. Nevertheless reference is made to "Regio Baccalearum" (Newfoundland, the St. Lawrence region, and north-eastern United States south to Chesapeake Bay) and "Terra Florida" (southeastern United States) with the suggestion that they may be joined to America, the "sayde fyrme land." Thus Eden presented to the average, literate Englishman the two most important aspects of America: a Spanish America based on the reports of returned voyagers, fundamentally valid in spite of the use of the spurious Soderini letter as source material, and the concept of a new mainland, America, to which might be joined other new mainland to the north, the whole a fourth part of the earth, specifically referred to as such in the introductory epistle to the reader.

Eden dedicated *A Treatyse of the newe India* . . . to the Duke of Northumberland, an appropriate gesture in view of the latter's official position, power, and interest in promoting English voyaging. The timing could not have been worse. The book probably appeared in June, 1553, perhaps a month before Northumberland made his unsuccessful attempt to switch the royal succession from Mary Tudor to Lady Jane Grey. In the eyes of the new queen this book just off the press had been dedicated to a traitor. She could hardly be expected to look with favor upon its author. There is no proof, however, that Eden was in actual disfavor. The unfortunate dedication could be explained. Yet his own story of the motives which impelled him to the task of gathering and translating the material published as *The Decades of the newe worlde or west India* . . . (1555), told in the dedicatory epistle accompanying that work, shows that he felt the need for ingratiating himself with Mary. The very soul of tact, he sought to do this by flattering her new husband, Philip of Spain. That the work might also serve to promote Eden's pet project, English voyages to distant lands, was additional incentive.

The marriage of Philip and Mary was a notable match, and the accompanying celebration was suitably elaborate. On August 18, 1554, the happy couple rode into London from adjoining Southwark with all the pomp and pageantry that such an occasion seemed to demand. Eden was in the crowd that watched the procession. He was, he says, so moved with excitement that only the presence of the sovereigns restrained him from breaking into an extemporaneous oration then and there. The desire to commemorate the occasion, however, survived the excitement of the moment. First he contemplated writing an original composition, but abandoned the idea because he doubted his own creative powers. In casting about for a suitable subject his attention was caught by the notable achievements of the immediate ancestors of the sovereigns, the most important of which was the discovery of the West Indies and America (South America). By disseminating knowledge of these discoveries he thought to arouse admiration for the sovereigns responsible and for their lineal descendant, Philip of Spain. So runs Eden's argument. The resolution of his problem was simple but laborious. All he had to do was translate the two most important Spanish accounts of the discovery, those by Peter Martyr and Oviedo. Fortunately for Eden, what he had in mind was only the first four of Martyr's eight decades and the *Sumario de la natural y general istoria de las Indias* (1526) of Oviedo rather than his complete history. Even as planned the task was considerable. These two works not only were full of sound, detailed information about the West Indies and America but also neatly supplemented each other, for the former included some philosophical speculation about the natural curiosities of the new land which the other lacked, and the latter, though a little too matter-of-fact, contained the more recent information. As Eden explains in the dedicatory epistle:

While I was considering these matters, I remembered that in my youth I had read the *Decades of the New World* by Peter Martyr of Anghiera, of which the most illustrious Catholic Ferdinand was king and, most Serene Highness, your grandfather, written in Latin and dedicated to the sacred ruler of your sovereign country. Greatly moved by the faith and learning of the author, I undertook to translate it before others into English, because not only as an historian does he write with great fidelity of things Indian, but also as a philosopher (something desired in other writings) he reveals the hidden origins of natural objects, and admirably investigates the reasons for the works of nature (of which your India is full). And in order that the status of this India may be known at last, what treasure of gold, of gems, of spices, and of other very desirable articles of merchandise is there and how much is brought annually into Spain, I have added the work of that most gentle man Gonzales Ferdinando Oviedo, which he calls in short form the *General History of the Indies,* which he dedicated to your illustrious father Charles V. And I have included a large number of excerpts from recent writers, which seem to me especially suitable in such a collection of memorable items.[27]

Eden's enormous tact and political *savoir faire* are apparent throughout the dedicatory epistle, which he composed in Latin as befitted the solemnity of the occasion. He will indicate the obvious magnitude of the discoveries, he says, in his preface to the general reader, written in English. Since that language is native to Mary and, though originally foreign to Philip, the language in which he wooed Mary, there is no need to repeat these laudatory remarks in Latin. Subtle flattery indeed! Eden then pours out some extravagant personal praise upon the sovereigns and in the same breath, in the manner of Nanki-Poo with Yum-Yum, expressly disavows the intent to utter it. It is possible, but not likely, that Eden intended to fool them into taking literally this elaborate and honeyed talk. It seems much more likely that he was simply saying, in the formal, courtly language of the day, that his previous apparent support of Northumberland was pure coincidence, and that he was committing himself unreservedly to the present regime.

In the preface to the general reader, Eden urges Englishmen to follow the example of the Spaniards, to make voyages to distant lands for the sake of saving the souls of the heathen and increasing English trade, referring particularly to that part of America to which England had some show of title, "to doo for owr partes as the Spaniardes haue doone for theyrs." [28] He recognizes the thirst for gold as the principal driving force behind Spanish exploration of America, yet implies that the desire to Christianize the natives may have been a subsidiary one, saying:

Euen so although summe wyll obiecte that the desyre of golde was the chiefe cause that moued the Spanyardes and Portugales to searche the newe founde landes, trewly albeit we shulde admitte it to bee the chiefe cause, yet dooth it not folowe that it was the only cause, forasmuch as nothyng letteth but that a man may bee a warrier or a marchaunte, and also a Christian.

Then, in great impatience with what he regarded as the sluggardly attitude of the English toward voyaging to America, he adds: "Therefore what so euer owre chiefe intente bee, eyther to obteyne worldely fame or rychesse, (althoughe the zeale to encrease Christian religion ought chiefly to moue vs) I wolde to god we wolde fyrst attempte the matter." [29] He was particularly interested, too, in the voyage to Tartary and Cathay by the north, saying that Willoughby and Chancellor deserved special commendation for their efforts "if euer god sende them home ageyne although they fayle of theyr purpose." [30] This makes it appear that Eden wrote this preface early, before Chancellor returned from Russia in 1554. The book was published after he returned. Indeed, the material about Russia was included because he had returned, and the chances are that Eden simply did not get around to revising the preface.

The plan for Eden's *Decades* expanded markedly during the period of compilation. The return of English mariners from both Russia and Guinea indicated to Eden the desirability of adding material about those regions. In view of the probable renewal of the search for a northeast passage, it seemed advisable to include information about Tartary and Cathay, the ultimate objects of search, and such northern regions as might conceivably be passed on the way. Then the thorough Eden added material from recent works on America in order to supplement those of Peter Martyr and Oviedo. He concluded with instructions for the mining and smelting of gold and silver and the determination of longitude, as being information potentially useful to the explorer and mariner.

The Decades of the newe worlde or west India . . . (1555) opens with the translation of Martyr's first four decades. This is followed by a copy of the third papal bull of 1493, with English translation, the document which granted to Spain all the new lands west of the meridian 100 degrees west of the Cape Verde Islands, included so that Englishmen might have some conception of the original legal basis for the Spanish monopoly in America. The third item is the translation of Oviedo's *Sumario*. These three, taken together, constitute almost half the book. The succeeding portion is a miscellaneous collection of short items from a variety of sources, most of which were authoritative and recent.

The sections on Russia, Tartary, and Cathay were taken from works by Galeatius Butrigarius, Paulus Jovius, Sigmundus Liberus, Johannes Faber, and Sebastian Münster. Some of these men were better known in Eden's day than in our own. Butrigarius had been a papal legate in Spain. Paulus Jovius was a recent Italian historian with a special interest in geography. Sigmundus Liberus claims to have been the representative of Ferdinand of Spain at the Russian court. Johannes Faber lists the Russian representative to the Spanish court as the source of his information. For even more recent information Eden referred his readers to Clement Adams' Latin account of the English voyage made to Russia in 1553-1554, apparently just published. The "booke of the Northe regions" by Ziglerus provided data on Greenland, Iceland, Norway, Finland, Lapland, and other northern regions.

The material on Guinea is a combination of the old and the new not uncommon in the sixteenth century. Eden introduces it with a brief description of Africa which explains the changes in northern Africa since the days of the Roman empire, defines Guinea, and describes Ethiopia as the kingdom of the legendary Prester John. This is followed by the accounts of the two Guinea voyages completed in 1554 and 1555. The first is short and contains only what was told Eden by one of the voyagers. The second, much longer, was based on information furnished by one of the pilots and embellished by Eden with material from such ancient writers as Pliny, Solinus, and Diodorus Siculus, one of the most patent unions of the static, classical earth with the later, changing one that we have.

For additional information about America Eden used the latest book he could find, Gomara's *Istoria de las Indias* . . . , first printed in Saragossa in 1552. He also included one other extended reference to America, that found in the account of Magellan's voyage contained in a letter written by Maximilianus Transylvanus, a member of the Spanish government at the time the ship returned, and in the journal of Antonio Pigafetta, an Italian gentleman who made the voyage. Pigafetta's account he may have had from Ramusio's *Navigationi e Viaggi*, first published in 1550.

Information about the occurrence, mining, and smelting of gold and silver was derived from the ancient *Bibliotheca* of Diodorus Siculus (fl. first century B.C.) and the modern *Pyrotechnia* (1540) of Vannuccio Biringuccia. This was the best Eden could do, since the better *De re metallica* of Agricola, first published in 1556, was not yet in print. The missing link in English theory and practice of navigation at this time was the ability to determine the longitude of a ship at sea. Eden could supply the theory. This he did by including a passage from Gemma Phrysius telling how to determine longitude by means of a clock. The practice had to wait upon the appearance of an accurate chronometer, which was not produced commercially until 1735.

CHAPTER VII

Eden's America

THERE IS literally an enormous amount of information about America in Eden's *Decades*. The reader can work his way along the east coast from the Strait of Magellan on the south to Labrador on the north with hardly a break, and in addition he is made aware of Perú and Panamá City on the west coast, of the Seven Cities of Cibola (pueblo of Zuñi), and the St. Lawrence River basin in the interior of North America. Of course many of the names are different, and the continuity along the east coast is more apparent than real because the boundaries between named regions are so indefinite as to cover up unknown or little known coastal areas. Nevertheless the continuity is reasonably good. From the land of the Patagoni the reader may go northward to the land about the Plata River, to Brazil and Paria (northeastern Venezuela), to Urabá (the Caribbean coast of Venezuela and Colombia from Lake Maracaibo to the mouth of the Atrato River) and Veragua (the Caribbean coast of Panamá, Costa Rica, and Nicaragua from the mouth of the Atrato River to Cape Gracias a Dios), to New Spain or México with special reference to Yucatán, to Florida (southeastern United States), the land of Baccallaos (Newfoundland, the St. Lawrence region, and northeastern United States south to Chesapeake Bay), and the land of Labrador.

The regional organization of this material is as poor as the material is abundant, and of necessity. Eden, if he would seek the goodwill of Philip and Mary, had to open with his most substantial Spanish item, Martyr's *Four Decades*, which had been written chronologically. The reader starts, then, not at the Strait of Magellan but with the West Indies, which he sees through an account of the first two voyages of Columbus. He then moves on to Paria, which he also sees through the eyes of Columbus, and to Urabá, Veragua, and México, regions with which he becomes acquainted through the accounts of Balboa and others. In Oviedo's *Sumario* he backtracks to the West Indies, with an important side trip across the Isthmus of Panamá to Panamá City. He finally reaches the land of the Patagoni, and also the Plata River and Brazil, through Pigafetta's narrative of Magellan's voyage. There is brief reference to Brazil and Perú in subsequent sections on Russia, Tartary, and Cathay, and buried there too are references to French lands along the St. Lawrence, to the Seven Cities of Cibola, and to the lands of Baccallaos and Labrador. The reader does not gain much information about Perú or the Plata River, however, until he comes to Gómara's *Istoria*, where he also learns more of México. Gómara tells him much about Florida and the lands of Baccallaos and Labrador, though he has already gained some idea of the land of Baccallaos from a description Martyr had from Sebastian Cabot, recorded in the *Third Decade*.

The modern United States reader has a great initial advantage over the sixteenth-century reader of Eden's *Decades* in organizing this regional information in that he starts with a true mental picture of America, for he has seen relatively accurate maps of it from the time he was in grammar school. The sixteenth-century English reader lacked such a picture. No map of the period showed accurately the entire west coast of North America, much of which was still "terra incognita." There were maps, such as those made by Gemma Phrysius and Mercator, which gave a fair representation of South and Central America, the southeastern coast of North America, and sometimes a part of its western coast, but it seems likely that their use in England was restricted to a few specialists like John Dee. No map was published with Eden's *Decades*. It is hardly safe to assume, then, that the English layman had access to any map, either good, bad, or indifferent. Yet he could have constructed a passable picture of America from Eden's text alone, even without such help, if he read thoroughly, thoughtfully, and with imagination.

First of all, the general shape of America, pinched and narrow south of the West Indies and bulging to north and south yet narrow again at the Strait of Magellan, was plain. The problem of disposing of the land south of that strait, now called Tierra del Fuego, was not raised by the text. Only the learned, deriving knowledge from other sources, would believe it to be a part of *Terra Australis*, the supposed southern continent. The vagueness of outline north of Panamá City was a part of the general lack of knowledge of the time. Martyr stated clearly that Columbus reached the West Indies by sailing west from the Canaries, which enabled the reader to orient America with respect to Europe and Africa. Numerous other specific references by Martyr, as that Ojeda reached Portus Carthaginis (Cartagena) by sailing due south from the island of Hispaniola and that the first Spaniards to reach Yucatán sailed southwest from the west end of Cuba, bit by bit filled in part of the rough, general outline. Pigafetta was particularly helpful because he talked in terms of degrees, saying, for example, that the cape of St. Augustine, a part of Brazil, was eight degrees south of the equator, giving similar information about points south. Even if the reader could not think in terms of degrees, he could grasp that Brazil was south of the equator and that a great river (the Plata) and the land of the Patagoni lay south of Brazil, in that order. Gómara was equally helpful, and from those three authors alone it was possible to work out the correct sequence of regions along the east coast of America from the Strait of Magellan to and including Labrador. Perú fell into place because Gómara stated that it was in the west part of America and, for those who could understand, gave its latitude and longitude.

Here in the United States, where many of us still believe that the English knew little of America before the early years of the seventeenth century, it may be difficult to convince the reader how much specific information was actually available to the English reader in 1555 without a somewhat detailed statement. In an effort to accomplish this I propose a trip through America from the Strait of Magellan northward through Labrador, the kind of trip an English reader of Eden's *Decades* might have taken in 1555 by paraphrasing the pertinent material and organizing it by regions. I shall try to keep my own editorial comment to a minimum, though that is always difficult for the conductor of a tour, particularly one as spectacular as this.

The land of the Patagoni, as revealed by the name, is the land of the people with the large, clumsy feet. The meaning in translation is literally that. Sixteenth-century Europe knew Patagonia as the land of giants, and no doubt it was also that to Magellan who who gave it this slyly humorous name. Magellan and his men knew parts of the east coast fairly well, for they spent five months, the summer (southern winter) of 1520, at the port of San Julian (Port St. Julian) and another two months at an unnamed port to the south, probably the mouth of the Rio Gallegos. At San Julian they became acquainted with the giants. Their first guest is described as so tall that the head of the Spaniard of average height came only to his waist, and the second as even taller. This is probably a slight exaggeration since the Tehuelche Indians of Patagonia today average only six feet to six feet four inches in height. Nevertheless these Indians were enough taller than the Spaniards to justify reference to them as giants. The description of their brightly painted bodies, their long, stone-tipped, reed arrows, and their llama-skin coats with the large, mule-like ears still attached must have interested the sixteenth-century English reader as much as their reported great height. They worshiped a devil called Setebos, who might be seen among ten or twelve painted devils dancing about the body of the dead, recognizable by his great size and greater merriment. Thus he has more substance than the shadowy god of Caliban's dam as Shakespeare saw him and is much simpler than Browning's Setebos.

The land about the Plata River, "the ryuer of syluer," is made

so attractive that its description seems today to have some of the
blatant dishonesty of a blurb for a modern land promotion scheme.
Yet most of it was true. This land is very fertile, says Gómara.
Here wheat increases fiftyfold in one season, and other grain in
like proportion, including the maize from which the inhabitants
make bread. The sheep are as big as young camels or asses and
produce wool as fine as silk. These were almost certainly not sheep
but representatives of the alpaca, a strain related to the llama.
Nearby are said to be some mountains which produce silver and
others which produce gold. The sixteenth-century English reader
was already aware, from Eden's preface to the reader, that silver
was later produced from this vicinity, for there Eden mentions
13,000 pounds of silver, by weight, brought to Philip from Perú
and the Plata River and "coyned to the kinges vse in the towre
of London." [1] The men living in the mountains are white, continues Gómara, while those who live along the river have, like
the river, the color of fine iron or steel, and many of the rivermen
have legs and feet like an ostrich. This statement is inconsistent
with another in which Gómara says that the inhabitants about the
Plata River are chestnut-colored, but so minor a discrepancy was
not of the kind or degree calculated to disturb a sixteenth-century
English reader, more likely to prefer quantity of detail to con-
sistency. Most of the inhabitants, says Gómara, are diligent tillers
of the soil, but a few—and this seems to be the only fly in the
ointment—are cannibals. Magellan's men also reported the presence
of cannibals on the Plata River. They found them there when, sailing down the coast of Brazil, they entered the mouth of the river
in the mistaken belief that it would lead to the South Sea (Pacific
Ocean).

Perú is a land of fabulous wealth where gold is so common
"that they make pyspots thereof." Gómara emphasizes this wealth
by saying that Perú is extremely rich in silver, pearls, precious
stones, and spices as well as gold, an exaggerated statement since
only gold and silver were plentiful. The inhabitants are described
as warlike yet wise, courteous and honest, in fact admirable in all

ways save that they are not Christians. The soil is so fruitful that
it yields corn twice a year. The sheep, so large that they are used
as horses, produce a wool that is very fine and soft. In this statement Gómara seems to have made the llama and alpaca one, for
the llama today is used as a beast of burden and has coarse wool
while the alpaca, which produces a fine, soft wool, is raised only
for its wool. This land is said to extend from five degrees south
latitude "very farre into the south."

Brazil is a very large land, larger than Spain, Portugal, France,
and Italy put together. It possesses a countless variety of refresh-
ing fruits and very good sugar cane—the two articles of diet a
ship-weary sailor was most likely to crave after a long spell at sea.
Pigafetta also noted that

The people of this countrey praye to noo maner of thinge: but liue
by th[e] instincte of nature, and to th[e] age of C.xx. [one hundred
and twenty] and C.xl. [one hundred and forty] yeares. Bothe the
men and women go naked, and dwell in certeyne longe houses. They
are very docible, and soone allured to the Christian fayth.[2]

Paria (northeastern Venezuela) is pictured as a land of friendly
people where, as in Perú, great riches are to be had. When Columbus set his men ashore on the present peninsula of Paria, the first
landing by Europeans on the mainland of South America that can
be unquestionably authenticated, the natives, who said that the
whole region was called Paria, received them well, giving them a
great feast at which fruits, their principal food, and red and white
wines were served. The attention of the Spaniards was directed at
once to the bracelets and chains of gold and pearls which the
natives wore. When they asked, with a covetous gleam in the eye,
the source of these articles, the natives indicated with some scorn
that whole baskets of pearls could be gathered from the neighboring shore and that gold came from the mountains nearby. The
Spaniards, upon returning to their ships, reported to Columbus
that ornaments of gold and pearls were as common among the
natives as glass ornaments among the women of Spain and, by

way of proof, showed him several strings of pearls which they had secured through trade.

The region from Lake Maracaibo to Honduras (the present northwestern corner of Venezuela, northern Colombia, Panamá, Costa Rica, and Nicaragua) is treated in great detail in Martyr's *Four Decades* because that was the part of the mainland first settled by the Spaniards. Place names, inexactly employed and sometimes overlapping, create a certain amount of confusion for the reader. In the beginning the Spaniards used two principal names, Uraba and Veragua (Beragua in Eden's *Decades*). Although it is not apparent from Martyr's text that Uraba included the land from Lake Maracaibo to the mouth of the Atrato River, which flows into the head of the Gulf of Darien (then called the Gulf of Uraba), and that Veragua is the land from the mouth of the Atrato River to Cape Gracias a Dios, it is clear that both bordered the Gulf of Uraba, Uraba stretching east and Veragua west. In the course of time, as Martyr points out at the beginning of the ninth book of the *Second Decade*, the Spaniards changed Uraba to Andaluzia Nova or New Andalusia and Veragua to Castella Aurea or Golden Castile, considering them both regions of Paria. After the founding of the town of Darien on the Veragua side of the Gulf of Uraba, the adjacent territory came to be known as Dariena, and after the founding of the town of Panamá on the Gulf of Panamá, the surrounding territory similarly took that name. In order to simplify our trip, we shall retain the old terms Uraba and Veragua, which lingered on, limit the term Paria to northeastern Venezuela, as has already been done, and restrict the terms Dariena and Panamá to the towns so designated.

Uraba is mentioned often, but each time only briefly and in passing so that no concrete image of the land or the people is left in the mind of the reader. He is made aware of little beyond that the Spaniards were avid for gold and ruthless in their pursuit of it and that the Indians of Urabá, unlike those of Paria, were hostile.

In Veragua, too, the Spaniards pressed relentlessly their search for the precious yellow metal, and the Indians resisted when they dared. Francisco Pizarro, who was to share in the conquest of Perú, and the bachelor Enciso, who wrote the *Suma de geographia* which came to the hands of Roger Barlow, founded the settlement of Dariena in 1510, and it became the main base for Spanish operations on the isthmus until the founding of the town of Panamá on the south side by Pedrarias in 1519. The aim of these operations, directed largely by Vasco Núñez de Balboa, was always first and foremost the search for gold. Some of the Indians were friendly, some hostile, and the Spaniards soon antagonized even the friendly ones by their program of pillage and plunder. The invaders died from fever and hunger as well as from the arrows of hostile Indians, and, though the coastal areas where they lived were not particularly healthy, much of the suffering could have been prevented had the Spaniards not been so intent on gold, of which they recovered a vast quantity. The mountains in the interior proved a barrier for several years, but in the fall of 1513 Balboa and one hundred and ninety men, guided by the Indians, climbed them in order to gain access to the gold and pearls of the South Sea (Pacific Ocean).

Travel across the isthmus followed hard upon the founding of the town of Panamá. Oviedo crossed twice on foot in the year 1521. Out of this experience he proposed in his *Sumario* that, if any spices should be found in the South Sea, they be sent by ship to Panamá, then carried by cart to the headwaters of the Chagres River, thence sent by small boat down the Chagres to the port of Nomen Dei (Nombre de Dios) which, he says, is only five or six leagues from the mouth of the river. From Nomen Dei the spices could be shipped direct to Spain. No spices were found in quantity, yet Oviedo's judgment was soon vindicated with respect to choice of route. By 1555 Peruvian gold and silver had been coming to Spain over that route for over twenty years, probably a matter of common knowledge in England at the time. In our own day this route is occupied by the Panama Canal.

New Spain or México is the land west and south of the land of

Florida, says Gómara. He does not bound it on the south, but the English reader of 1555 could determine from the context of his account and that of Peter Martyr that there it touched Veragua. So different in point of view are the two accounts that the early reader may have had some difficulty in understanding that they referred to the same region. When Martyr wrote his *Fourth Decade*, the conquest of México, inevitable from the day in 1517 when the first Spaniards landed on the peninsula of Yucatán, was still in progress. Since the conquest had started on the peninsula and moved south and west, México was for Martyr the westward extension of Yucatán, and the name México does not appear in this *Decade*. Gómara, on the other hand, wrote after the conquest was an accomplished fact, and for him this region was New Spain or México, its center of interest not Yucatán but a great city called México, or "Temixtetan" (Tenochtitlán) standing in a lake of salt water. Eden, aware of this difficulty, put a footnote [3] to Gómara's account explaining that the two refer to the same region.

The first Spaniards to visit Yucatán, says Martyr, found a great city with paved streets and magnificent temples, with houses built of stone or brick, shaped like a tower, and reached by a flight of ten or twelve steps. The inhabitants received them graciously and gave them cunningly wrought gold ornaments. The Spaniards in turn gave garments of silk and wool, bits of colored glass, and hawks' bells of laton. Other Indians proved less friendly, but their hostility did not weigh heavily in the balance. News of this city was confirmed by a second expedition, which found others like it. A third expedition under Fernando Cortesius (Hernando Cortés), then governor of Santiago, was sent out with instructions "to returne ageyne after they had searched these regions and obteyned plentie of golde," [4] instructions which eventually produced an undreamed of quantity of gold. Martyr describes in detail some of the treasure he saw in Spain. Without greed or cupidity himself, he was more impressed with the skilled craftsmanship of the necklaces, bracelets, bells, images, helmets, shields, and other objects he saw than with their abundance, saying:

I do not maruaile at golde and precious stones. But am in maner as-
tonyshed to see the woorkemanshyppe excell the substance. For I
haue with woonderynge eyes behelde a thousande formes and simili-
tudes, of the which I am not able to wryte. And in my iudgement, I
neuer sawe any thing whose bewtie myght so allure the eyes of
men.[5]

But no reader can escape the sense of abundant wealth. Many of
those early objects were presents from the Aztec rulers to the
king of Spain, and among them were books made of the bark of
trees, the leaves bound together with bitumen. Martyr says of
them, "In these books are furthermore comprehended their laws,
rytes of ceremonies and sacrifyces, annotations of Astronomie,
accomptes, computations of tymes, with the maner of grassynge,
sowyng, and other thynges perteinyng to husbandry." [6] Obviously
a land of culture and learning as well as wealth.

Gómara says that México is rich in gold, silver, and precious
stones and that it produces cotton, silk, dyes, and an abundance
of sugar and grain. The people are warlike by nature and idolatrous.
Even the women are valiant, and they dress sumptuously. Cacao
beans are used for money instead of gold and silver, and the people
are crafty and subtle in bargaining. Because of the variety and
abundance of beasts and fowls, the land is admirably suited to
hunting and hawking.

The West Indies, in 1555 still the best known part of Spanish
America, is pictured primarily as the land of gold, the same emphasis already found in the descriptions of Perú, Uraba, Veragua,
and México. Yet it is other things too. It is a richly fruitful land.
Its primitive people, living close to nature, in part approximate the
ideal life, in part live in degradation as idolators and cannibals.

Martyr's account of the West Indies, written from day to day
as new information filtered into Spain and published periodically,
has a freshness that the more considered history of Oviedo lacks.
Hispaniola, first seen through the eyes of Columbus, is a verdant
island with moist, fat soil, inhabited by a mild, naked people living
largely on maize and the root of the yucca and "ages" (maguey?).

These people, though timid because occasionally harried by cannibals from other islands, came swimming out to the ships with small amounts of gold, which they traded to the Spaniards for hawks' bells, pins, mirrors, and similar trifles. The only quadruped Columbus and his men found on this island was the rabbit. Ducks, geese, turtledoves, and brightly colored popinjays were abundant. The few serpents in this Eden proved to be harmless. Cotton was in evidence, and also mastic, aloes, and other gums and spices.

This broad, general description of Hispaniola, emphasizing its fruitfulness and the gentle nature of the inhabitants, is fairly typical of the islands as a group. Most of them, certainly the larger ones, were fertile, even lush. Though some of the inhabitants proved to be cannibals, most of them were not, and Peter Martyr has much good to say of their way of life in the second book of the *First Decade:*

The inhabitantes of these Ilandes haue byn euer soo vsed to liue at libertie, in playe and pastyme, that they can hardely away with the yoke of seruitude which they attempte to shake of by all meanes they maye. And surely if they had receaued owre religion, I wolde thinke their life moste happye of all men, if they might therwith enioye their aunciente libertie. A fewe thinges contente them, hauinge no delite in such superfluities, for the which in other places men take infinite paynes and commit manie vnlawfull actes, and yet are neuer satisfied, wheras many haue to much, and none inowgh. But emonge these simple sowles, a fewe clothes serue the naked: weightes and measures are not needeful to such as can not skyll of crafte and deceyte and haue not the vse of pestiferous monye, the seede of innumerable myscheues. So that if we shall not be ashamed to confesse the truthe, they seeme to lyue in that goulden worlde of the whiche owlde wryters speake so much: wherin men lyued simplye and innocentlye without inforcement of lawes, without quarrellinge Iudges and libelles, contents onely to satisfie nature, without further vexation for knowelege of thinges to come. Yet these naked people also are tormented with ambition for the desyre they haue to enlarge their dominions: by reason wherof they kepe warre and destroy one an other: from the which plage I suppose the golden world was not free.[7]

Already the Spaniards had brought trouble to this "golden world," as Peter Martyr hints in the first part of this passage. Later he expands this hint, explaining that the Indians had been forced to work the gold mines in a state of virtual slavery. Oviedo's *Sumario* provides much more detail concerning the gold mines and pearl fisheries, the local flora and fauna, and the customs, character, and religious practices of the natives.

There must have been some doubt in the mind of the early English reader of Eden's *Decades* as to the exact shape and extent of Florida (southeastern United States). Martyr says in the *Fourth Decade* that it is an island.[8] Gómara reports in one place that it is the land north and east of Mexico, and in another that it is "a poynt or cape of lande reachynge into the sea lyke vnto a tounge." [9] It is principally a land of frustrated hopes and death at the hands of cannibals. There, says Gómara, Ponce de León sought in vain for the fountain of youth in 1512 (actually 1513), and later, while attempting to plant a colony, was fatally wounded by an Indian arrow. There De Soto, who had been a captain in Perú, sought in vain for gold for five years. So unpromising was the land, indicates Gómara, that neither Charles V nor Philip his son would countenance further expeditions there but instead sent a handful of Dominican friars to Christianize the natives. Even these men accomplished little. Some were killed and eaten by their intended charges, and others barely escaped with their lives.

The single reference to the Seven Cities of Cibola (pueblo of Zuñi), buried in the section on Russia, Tartary, and Cathay, could have been overlooked even by the careful reader, and, if he read it, he still must have lacked the perspective to understand how vast was the land in whose interior this "kyngdome" lay. It appears as an aside in a passage devoted primarily to the search for Cathay by the northwest. Butrigarius, the Italian *savant*, emissary of the Pope to the Spanish court, and intimate of Peter Martyr, says,

And I remember that when I was in Flaunders in Th[e] emperours courte, I sawe his [Mendoza's] letter wrytten in the yeare. 1541. and dated from Mexico: wherin was declared howe towarde the north-

west, he had fownd the kyngedome of *Sette Citta* (that is) Seuen
Cities, whereas is that cauled Ciuola by the reuerend father Marco da
Niza: and howe beyonde the sayde kyngedome yet further towarde
the Northwest, Capitayne Francesco Vasques of Coronado, hauynge
ouerpassed great desertes, came to the sea syde where he found certeyne shyppes which sayled by that sea with marchaundies, and had
in theyr baner vppon the proos of theyr shyppes, certeyne foules made
of golde and syluer which they of Mexico caule Alcatrazzi: And that
theyr mariners shewed by signes that they were. xxx. [thirty] dayes
saylynge in commynge to that hauen: wherby he vnderstoode that
these shippes could bee of none other countrey then of Cathay, forasmuch as it is situate on the contrary parts of the sayde lande discouered.[10]

There is fusion here of the expeditions of Coronado and Cabeza
de Vaca. It was the latter who reached the Gulf of California, and
he reached it in 1536. Coronado penetrated as far west as the
Grand Canyon of the Colorado River, probably in 1541. This brief
passage gives no hint of the tremendous distances traveled and
terrible hardships sustained by both.

The limits of the land of Baccallaos (Newfoundland, the St.
Lawrence region, and northeastern United States south to Chesapeake Bay) are more definite than might be expected. Peter Martyr
gives them in the sixth book of the *Third Decade*, saying Sebastian
Cabot sailed southward along the coast from the ice-infested north
until he was in the latitude of the Strait of Gibraltar and the
longitude of Cuba (that is, in the vicinity of Chesapeake Bay),
naming the whole region the land of Baccallaos, the native name
for the big fish (codfish) that swarm in those waters.[11] This probably includes "Labrador," which Gómara and Butrigarius treat
separately. They speak of the land of "Laborador" to the north,
and Gómara says that Sebastian Cabot sailed as far north as the
"cape of Laborador at. lviii. [fifty-eight] degrees." [12] Both speak
of that part of the land of Baccallaos visited by Cartier in 1534–
1535, mentioning the dates, and locate it between forty-five and
fifty-one degrees north latitude (the St. Lawrence region). Butrigarius says Cartier named it New France and mentions "the great

and large countreys named Canada, Ochelaga [vicinity of Mont-
real], and Sanguenai" [13] which he found there. Why there should
not also be mention of the first voyage of John Cabot is a little
difficult to understand.

The land of Baccallaos, as seen through the eyes of Sebastian
Cabot, who spoke of it to Peter Martyr, has little to offer. He
says of it only that there are many bears and that the people are
clothed in the skins of beasts. Gómara, quoting from Jacobus
Gastaldus, gives an even more unfavorable impression:

The newe lande of Baccalaos, is a coulde region, whose inhabytauntes
are Idolatours and praye to the soone and moone and dyuers Idoles.
They are whyte people and very rustical. For they eate flesshe and
fysshe and all other thynges rawe. Sumtymes also they eate mans
flesshe priuilye so that theyr Caciqui haue no knowleage therof. The
apparell of both the men and women, is made of beares skynnes, al-
thowgh they haue sables and marternes, not greatly estemed bycause
they are lyttle. Sum of them go naked in soomer, and weare apparell
only in wynter. The Brytons and Frenche men are accustomed to take
fysshe in the coaste of these landes where is founde great plentie of
Tunnyes which th[e] inhabitauntes caul Baccalaos wherof the lande
was so named.[14]

Oviedo, mentioning the report of a Spanish pilot who is said to
have sailed in 1524 as far south as that part of the land now called
New Jersey, paints a similar picture in these words:

Shortly after that yowr Maiestie came to the citie of Toledo, there arryued in the moneth of Nouember, Steuen Gomes the pylot who the
yeare before of 1524. by the commaundement of yowre maiestie sayled
to the Northe partes and founde a greate parte of lande continuate
from that which is cauled *Baccaleos* discoursynge towarde the West
to the. xl. and. xli. degree, from whense he brought certeyne Indians
(for so caule wee all the nations of the new founde landes) of the
whiche he brought sum with hym from thense who are yet in Toledo
at this present, and of greater stature then other of the firme lande as
they are commonlye. Theyr colour is much lyke th[e] other of the
firme lande. They are great archers, and go couered with the skinnes
of dyuers beastes both wylde and tame. In this lande are many excel-

lent furres, as marterns, sables, and such other rych furres of the which
the sayde pilote brought simme with him into Spayne. They haue
syluer and copper, and certeyne other metalles. They are Idolaters and
honoure the soone and moone, and are seduced with suche supersti-
tions and errours as are they of the firme.[15]

Cartier, on the other hand, is said by Butrigarius to have found
New France pleasant and suitable for colonization,

fayre and frutefull, with plentie of all sortes of corne, herbes, frutes,
woodde, fysshes, beastes, metals, and ryuers of such greatnesse that
shyppes may sayle more then. 180. myles vppon one of theym [the
St. Lawrence], beinge on bothe sydes infinitely inhabited.[16]

The description of the land of Labrador is similar to less attractive references to the land of Baccallaos. Gómara, quoting again
from Jacobus Gastaldus, says,

Northwarde from the region of Baccalaos, is the lande of Laborador,
all full of mountaynes and great wooddes in which are manye beares
and wylde bores. Th[e] inhabitauntes are Idolatoures and warlike
people, appareled as are they of Baccallaos. In all this newe lande, is
neyther citie or castell: but they lyue in companies lyke heardes of
beastes.[17]

Gómara gives additional information, equally unfavorable, taken
from an account of a voyage of Gaspar Corte-Real, a Portuguese
mariner, to the "lande of Laborador," saying:

In the yeare a thousande and fiue hundreth, Gasper Cortereales, made
a vyage thyther with two carauelles: but found not the streyght or
passage he sought. At his beinge there, he named the Ilandes that lye
in the mouth of the goulfe Quadrado, after his name Cortereales,
lyinge in the. L. [fifty] degrees and more: and browght from that
lande abowt three score men for slaues. He greatly maruayled to beholde the houge quantitie of snowe and Ise. For the sea is there frosen
excedyngly. Th[e] inhabitauntes are men of good corporature, although tawny lyke the Indies, and laborious. They paynte theyr
bodyes, and weare braselettes and hoopes of syluer and copper. Theyr
apparel is made of the skynnes of marternes and dyuers other beastes,
whiche they weare with the heare inwarde in wynter, and owtwarde

in soommer. This apparell they gyrde to theyr bodyes with gyrdels made of cotton or the synewes of fysshes and beastes. They eate fysshe more then any other thynge, and especially salmons, althoughe they haue foules and frute. They make theyr houses of timber wherof they haue great plentie: and in the steade of tyles, couer them with the skynnes of fysshes and beastes. It is sayde also that there are grifes in this lande: and that the beares and many other beastes and foules are white.[18]

The mention of Indian slaves, brought back in actual fact not by the expedition of 1500, but by one of the ships on the voyage which Gaspar Corte-Real undertook in 1501 and on which he lost his life, makes it appear that Gómara has combined accounts of the two voyages. The first expedition apparently reached Newfoundland; the second probably touched at or coasted along Labrador, Newfoundland, and Nova Scotia. This description, then, may have been based on observations covering most of Sebastian Cabot's original land of Baccallaos. Much of it, however, is applicable to Labrador. It is not nearly so unfortunate, if we think in terms of early incentive for English colonization of North America to be found in Eden's *Decades*, that the land of Labrador should have been confused with the northern part of the land of Baccallaos, both relatively uninviting, as that so little of a favorable nature should have been said about the southern part of the land of Baccallaos, so thickly settled today.

Just why should Englishmen want to read Eden's *Decades* in the year 1555 or shortly thereafter? That many were expected to is indicated by the size of the first edition. There is no record of the number of copies printed, but the considerable number extant today and the fact that the edition was handled by four publishers, G. Powell, W. Seres, E. Sutton, and R. Taye, instead of one, suggests that it was large. Since colonization was not yet the fashion in England, no one would be expected to read it with that end in view, and so little good is reported of that part of America to which England had show of title, the land of Baccallaos, that one would hardly catch such a vision while reading it for some other reason. Chief interest in distant foreign parts was at the time directed toward Russia, and many may have read Eden's *Decades* for information about that country. These same readers probably had an interest, too, in the sections on Tartary and Cathay, which lay beyond Russia. Others no doubt were interested in the Guinea voyages and the description of Africa.

Those Englishmen who read the sections on America probably read them for what was said of the occurrence of gold, the principal American attraction for Europeans for over seventy-five years. There they learned that gold was to be found only in Perú, Uraba, Veragua, the West Indies, and Mexico—the warm regions of America or, more particularly, those within the torrid zone. Here, for those who knew and believed in it, was corroborative evidence of the medieval theory of Albertus Magnus and others that gold occurs only where the sun's rays are the strongest. For other readers the conclusion must have been the same. Gold occurs in America only in the warm regions controlled by the Spaniards and, conversely, does not occur in those cold ones which Englishmen might visit. No use for Englishmen to go to America save to take gold from the Spaniards, and that they were not quite ready to risk. Except for the lone statement of Cartier, then, the land of Baccallaos was still what it was when John Cabot first saw it in 1497, an uninviting land off whose shores was an abundant supply of large fish, and there was little to tempt Englishmen to land there, let alone settle.

CHAPTER VIII

Elizabethan Discovery of America to 1585

IN THE autumn of the year 1584 the younger Richard Hakluyt presented to Queen Elizabeth his *Discourse of Western Planting*, the writing of which had been urged upon him by Walter Ralegh. Like Eden's *Decades* (1555) it was intended to promote voyaging, but the objectives of the two works, even so, were quite different. Eden's *Decades* was written to stimulate the search for new lands and new trade routes to known lands, and any hint of an interest in colonization in Eden's admonition to Englishmen to emulate the Spaniards, who were then establishing colonies in America as well as collecting gold, must be regarded as more apparent than real. Hakluyt's *Discourse*, though it speaks favorably of continuing the search for a northwest passage to Cathay and China, was aimed principally at securing the Queen's aid in establishing a colony in America. With this shift in emphasis from preliminary exploration to permanent settlement, we may, with some show of reason, consider one phase of discovery at an end, though Englishmen still had much to learn of America.

In the years between the publication of Eden's *Decades* and the presentation of Hakluyt's *Discourse*, English foreign trade languished and English relations with Spain greatly deteriorated. Both trends turned English eyes toward the west and eventually made possible the birth of the concept of an American colony.

English foreign trade took a turn for the better with the inauguration of trade with Russia, aided by the illicit trade with the Barbary and Guinea coasts. This improvement, however, was only temporary, and numerous difficulties beset it by the end of 1584, graphically described [1] by Hakluyt in the *Discourse*. Trade with Russia was less lucrative than it had been. Profits, never certain because of natural hazards, had been cut substantially by the dishonesty of English factors, the imposition of Russian taxes, and the advent of competition from Hollanders and Frenchmen, particularly men from Dieppe. Denmark levied on trade with Estland, which passed her door. Flanders was torn by war. France laid heavy taxes on English cloth and devised technical rules for confiscating it as substandard. Trade with Turkey was frowned upon by Venice and other Italian states, levied upon by the knights of Malta, and preyed upon by the pirates of the Barbary coast. Barbary pirates also interfered with the Barbary trade, and Spain confiscated any English ships suspected of trading with northern Africa if they chanced to be found in her harbors or cast upon her shores. Englishmen who traded in Spain were in constant danger of their lives from the Inquisition. Hakluyt fails to mention trade with Portugal or, except for the Barbary coast, with those regions over which she attempted to exercise her monopoly, nor was it necessary, for the interests of Spain and Portugal had merged in 1581 when Philip acquired the Portuguese throne. With the throne Philip also acquired the existing bad feeling between England and Portugal, which served to intensify the already strong ill will between England and Spain and widen the breach between these two powers.

English relations with Spain were fairly good as long as Mary Tudor lived, even though her husband Philip was not especially popular with the English people, who rightly suspected him of designs on the English throne. They deteriorated rapidly after her death on November 17, 1558, for Elizabeth, who succeeded her, was of a different temper. Lacking the marital and religious ties which bound Mary to Spain, she was more intensely nationalistic than her older sister and soon acted in support of English enterprise abroad.

Elizabeth acted against Portugal, however, before she turned her attention to Spain. In 1561 she not only regularized the Guinea trade but herself became a partner in an expedition to the Guinea coast. She furnished the ships, her sixth of the profits to be paid over to the royal navy, while the original Guinea syndicate furnished men, goods, and equipment. When the Portuguese complained of these and other voyages, Elizabeth would only say that English subjects would not trade in any part of Africa under the actual domination of the king of Portugal, which was no answer at all, from the Portuguese point of view, since they had actual dominion over a very few, very small areas on the west coast of Africa. Such a statement meant that the English would trade where they could.

Meanwhile individual attacks on Spanish shipping, similar to those made in 1540 by the *Barbara* of London off the Canaries and in the West Indies, had been renewed. In 1560 two English pirates preyed on Spanish shipping between the Azores and Canaries as it returned home from the West Indies, and local Spanish authorities in the Canaries arrested English factors there in retaliation. Cecil expressed the official attitude when, in 1562, he told the Spanish ambassador that the Pope had no right to partition the world. Between October, 1562, and January, 1569, John Hawkins made three trading voyages to America, which, though covered with the cloak of legality, were in actual violation of the Spanish trade monopoly. These voyages were soon followed by acts of outright piracy on the part of Drake, Oxenham, and others, at least one of which won the approval of Elizabeth. By 1584 relations between England and Spain had become so strained that Hakluyt, in the *Discourse*, could propose to the Queen a plan [2] for an American colony which would serve as a base from which to attack Spanish shipping and sow the seeds of revolt in the Spanish colonies in America as well as to press the search for a northwest passage to Asia.

Spanish America and Florida

Englishmen probably learned little of Spanish America from so casual an early contact as the brief stay of John Rut in the harbor of Santo Domingo in 1527. There was at that early date, however, a potential source of information that may have been much better —at least one Englishman resident in the West Indies. Hakluyt had papers showing that the Thornes had contacts with such a man, for he reports,

And here also I thought good to signifie, that in the sayd letters mention is made of one Thomas Tison an English man, who before the foresayd yere 1526 had found the way to the West Indies, and was there resident, unto whom the sayd M. Nicolas Thorne sent certaine armour and other commodities specified in the letter aforesayd.[3]

There is no record showing what information may have passed through this channel. That there were other Englishmen residing in Spanish America at a somewhat later date is indicated by the account of Robert Tomson, reported by Hakluyt,[4] of a voyage to New Spain or Mexico in 1555, and Tomson himself brought back valuable information.

Tomson sailed for the West Indies in the company of John Field, an English merchant residing in Seville, who purchased the Spanish license permitting them to go. They traveled in the Indies fleet on a ship owned by John Sweeting, also an English merchant of Seville. Their first stop was Santo Domingo, where they spent two months. Tomson was little impressed with the city, which he found small, very hot, and ridden with a certain vicious insect —"a kind of flies or gnats with long bils, which do pricke & molest the people very much in the night when they are asleepe, in pricking their faces and hands, and other parts of their bodies that lie uncovered, & make them to swel wonderfully" [5]—no doubt the mosquito. He gives some useful information concerning the products of the islands, saying, "The countrey yeeldeth great store of sugar, hides of oxen, buls and kine, ginger, Cana fistula & Salsa perillia: mines of silver & gold there are none, but in some rivers there is found some smal quantitie of gold." [6] By this time most of the alluvial gold of the island had evidently been recovered by the Spaniards. From Santo Domingo the Englishmen went on to San Juan de Ulua, the principal port of México, off which their ship was wrecked in a storm, and their goods lost but their lives saved. They landed in México on April 16, 1556.

In the new town of Vera Cruz, five leagues from the port, they met by chance a rich Spaniard, an old friend of Field, who provided handsomely for them and sent them on to México City. Field died of an ague on the way, and Tomson was very sick. In México City Tomson was befriended by a Scot named Thomas Blake, who had lived there more than twenty years, and through his good offices found employment with a Spaniard of great wealth, one of the original Conquistadores. For about a year all went well. At the end of that time, however, Tomson was so indiscreet as to allow himself to be drawn into an argument at dinner over religion, by reason of which he was thrown into jail as a heretic. Eventually he was sent back to Spain, where he also spent a term in prison.

It is difficult for us, living in the twentieth century, to realize that at the time Tomson was in México the Spanish conquest was already ancient history, yet Tomson shows just such perspective when he says, "In my time were dwelling and alive in Mexico, many ancient men that were of the conquerors at the first conquest with Hernando Cortes: for then it was about 36. yeeres agoe, that the said Countrey was conquered." [7] His account of the land is the sort any shrewd, observant eyewitness might have written. The harbor of San Juan de Ulua, on a low island offshore, was largely man-made, he found, kept in repair by twenty Negroes, and it offered little protection against the strong winds which often blew from the north. On the mainland nearby were many "red Deere" which the sailors used to hunt. The business connected with shipping was apparently altogether transacted at nearby Vera Cruz, a smaller town than Santo Domingo. This coastal area was low and unhealthy, but inland the land began to rise and improve in proportion, for Tomson says of it,

but afterward halfe a dayes journey that you do begin to enter into the high land, you shall find as faire, good, and sweet countrey, as any in the world, and the farther you go, the goodlier and sweeter the countrey is, till you come to Pueblo de los Angeles, which may be some 43 leagues from Vera Cruz, which was in my time a towne of 600. households, or thereabout, standing in a goodly soile. Betweene Vera Cruz and that you shall come throughe many townes of the Indians, and villages, and many goodly fieldes of medow grounds, Rivers of fresh waters, forrests, and great woods, very pleasant to behold. From Pueblo de los Angeles, to Mexico, is 20. leagues of very faire way and countrey, as before is declared.[8]

The city of México stood in a lake of fresh water, which was in a wide plain surrounded by high mountains. In the midst of the city was a "square place" (plaza), in the center of which was a great church, not yet finished, and about the square were many fair houses, including those of Montezuma, then sheltering the Spanish viceroys, and the residence of the bishop. Beside many straight and broad streets, there was a canal, through which the Indians brought much produce into the city, coming every morning at daybreak in twenty or thirty canoes. Food was unbelievably cheap. For two shillings sixpence you could buy a whole quarter of an ox, and a fat sheep cost 18 pence. Apples, pears, pomegranates, and quinces were abundant and similarly inexpensive. Tomson took great delight in the surrounding countryside, saying:

The weather is there alwayes very temperate, the day differeth but one houre of length all the yere long. The fields and the woods are alwayes greene. The woods full of popinjayes, and many other kinde of birdes, that make such an harmonie of singing, and crying, that any man will rejoyce to heare it. In the fields are such odoriferous smels of flowers and hearbs, that it giveth great content to the senses.[9]

The treasure of Montezuma had long since been exhausted but not his source of supply, so Tomson could speak of the silver mines at Sacatecas, 80 leagues northwest of México City, and the gold and silver mines of St. Martin, 30 leagues northwest of the city. Other products interested him too, particularly two vegetable dyes, one a cochineal-scarlet and the other a vivid blue. He was also aware of silk, the guava, black cherries, "balme," salsa perilla (sarsaparilla?), cana fistula (actually an Asiatic plant), sugar, and hides.

Other Englishmen made authorized voyages like that of Tomson, several of them recorded by Hakluyt, and returned with similar information. Roger Bodenham, the same under whom Chancellor had sailed in 1551 and long a resident of Seville, made a voyage to México in 1563 in his own ship, sailing with a Spanish fleet.[10] John Chilton, another English merchant long resident of Spain, went to México in 1568 and spent eighteen years there, in Central America, and in the West Indies, traveling, trading, and making notes as he went.[11] Apparently he went where he liked without hindrance. He visited Navidad, the west coast port to which ships came from China and the Philippines bringing cotton, wax, earthenware, and gold. He was unfortunate enough to be in the west coast port of Aguatulco in 1579 when Drake raided it, and he lost a thousand ducats' worth of goods to that buccaneer. Chilton, with high good humor, perceived and described the ingenious device by which the Indians avoided purchasing the pardons which the Spanish priests had begun to sell them in 1570, saying,

The revenue of his [the Pope's] buls after this maner yeeldeth unto his treasury yeerely above three millions of gold, as I have bene credibly informed, although of late both the Spanyards and Indians do refuse to take the buls; for that they perceive he doth make a yeerely custome of it: onely ech Indian taketh one pardon for all his house- holde, (whereas in former time every Indian used to take one for every person in his house) and teareth the same into small pieces, and giveth to every one of his householde a little piece, saying thus, they need now no more, seeing in that which they bought the yeere before they had above ten thousand yeres pardon. These pieces they sticke up in the wall of the houses where they lie.[12]

Henry Hawks lived five years in México, and in 1572, at the request of the elder Hakluyt, he drew up an elaborate account [13] of the land, similar in content to that of Tomson. It contains little additional information worth commenting on here except for the description of a beast that must have been the buffalo, perhaps the earliest English description on record. Hawks says:

There is a great number of beasts or kine in the countrey of Cibola, which were never brought thither by the Spanyards, but breed naturally in the countrey. They are like unto our oxen, saving that they have long haire like a lion, and short hornes, and they have upon their shoulders a bunch like a camell, which is higher then the rest of their body. They are marvellous wild and swift in running. They call them the beasts or kine of Cibola.[14]

Written information of this sort may not have circulated widely in England at an early date. That in existence today became available at irregular intervals and was preserved largely through the efforts of the two Hakluyts, in the beginning for their own private ends. It is not known when the accounts of Tomson and Bodenham were put in writing save that it must have been before the publication of the *Principall Navigations* (1589). That of Hawks was written in 1572, that of Chilton not until 1586. But much of this information probably circulated by word of mouth before it was written down, and other information of a like character, lost today, may have been passed along in similar fashion. It seems likely that more information about Spanish America came into England as a result of authorized voyages than through the unauthorized ones. The Englishmen who lived there in peace had time for leisurely observation of the new land and its inhabitants. Men like Drake, Oxenham, and even Hawkins were usually on the run. Yet such of these freebooters as survived also contributed some information.

The three voyages of John Hawkins [15] to Spanish America, made between October, 1562, and January, 1569, represent a cross between the authorized and the completely unauthorized. Although he failed to obtain the consent of the central government of Spain for his voyages, he did, by devious ways, secure local trading licenses from petty Spanish officials in America so as to preserve the appearance of legality. On each voyage he stopped first at the Guinea coast for a cargo of slaves, a much more acceptable commodity in America than any he could have brought from England. On the first voyage (1562–1563) he traded all his slaves on the island of Hispaniola for gold, silver, pearls, hides, and sugar. On the second (1564–1565) he touched at the islands of Dominica and Margarita, then went on to the mainland where he did his trading. Thence he sailed home by way of the Florida Channel, stopping off on the northern part of the peninsula to visit the colony of French Huguenots, planted there early in 1564 by Laudonnière, then passing on to the Banks of Newfoundland where he paused long enough to replenish his larder with fish.

Laudonnière's colony represented the second attempt of the French Huguenots to settle in Florida. The first colony, planted by Jean Ribault at Charlesfort (Parris Island) in 1562, had failed. Ribault's account of this planting, translated into English by Thomas Hackett and published in London in 1563 as *The whole & true discouerye of Terra Florida* . . . , shows great enthusiasm for the Florida he saw, roughly that stretch of land from the mouth of the St. John's River northward to Parris Island, most of it now Georgia. What he saw on the first day, April 30, moved him to say, ". . . we sayled and vewed the coast all along with vnspeakable pleasure, of the odorous smell and beawtie of the same." [16] The next day the French, unlike the Spaniards who had landed earlier to the south, encountered friendly Indians, a stroke of luck which allowed them to make careful observations of the land and its people. Their first favorable impression was abundantly confirmed, for Ribault says,

. . . we entred and viewed the countrie thereaboutes, which is the fairest, fruitfullest, and pleasantest of al the world, abounding in hony, venison, wilde foule, forests, woods of all sortes, Palme trees, Cypresse and Cedars, Bayes ye highest and greatest, with also the fayrest vines in all the world, with grapes according, which without natural art and without mans helpe or trimming will grow to toppes of Okes and other trees that be of a wonderfull greatnesse and height. And the sight of the faire medowes is a pleasure not able to be expressed with tongue: full of Hernes, Curlues, Bitters, Mallards, Egrepths, woodcocks and all other kinde of small birds: with Harts, Hindes, Buckes, wilde Swine, and all other kindes of wilde beastes, as we percieued well, both by their footing there, and also afterwardes in other places, by their crie and roaring in the night.

Also, there be Conies and Hares: Silke wormes in merueilous number, a great deale fairer and better then be our silke wormes. To bee short, it is a thing vnspeakable to consider the thinges that bee seene there, and shalbe founde more and more in this incomparable lande, which neuer yet broken with plough yrons, bringeth forth al things according to his first nature, wherewith the eternall God indued it.[17]

The Indians told of gold, silver, copper, lead, "turquesses" (turquoises?), and pearls to be had. Nevertheless the French sailed on until they found a suitable harbor, Ribault continuing to regard the land with the same high enthusiasm.

The whole & true discouerye of Terra Florida . . . was unavailable nineteen years later, and Hakluyt, aware of this and of its value, reprinted it in his *Divers Voyages* (1582). The work and its author, who was in England in the fall of 1562, had already aroused English interest in participating with the French in a Florida colony. A plan was evolved by which Ribault and Thomas Stukeley, an enterprising and unscrupulous English voyager, were to lead an expedition there in 1563. It failed to materialize as a voyage because Stukeley traitorously revealed it to Spain. The founding of an exclusively French colony by Laudonnière the next year effectively prevented its revival. The colony was in some distress when John Hawkins visited it in 1565, and Hawkins, seeing this, offered to transport the colonists back to France. Laudonnière, aware that this would either kill the colony completely or open the way for active English participation, refused.

The first two voyages of John Hawkins aroused some irritation among the Spaniards, but this was as nothing compared with the deep and lasting wrath provoked by an unfortunate and unforeseen incident which occurred on his third voyage (1567–1569). At first all went well. Hawkins touched at the islands of Dominica and Margarita, as he had on his second voyage, then went on to the mainland where he again disposed of most of his slaves. All would have continued well had he not run into storms in the Gulf of México, which so battered his ships that he was forced to put into the harbor of San Juan de Ulua for repairs. There the plate fleet from Spain caught him in September, 1568, and the temper of both fleets was such as to make battle almost inevitable from the outset. Heavy losses were sustained on both sides. They grew heavier in retrospect and begot not only additional bad feeling but acts of aggression on either side in the years that followed.

One of. Hawkins' ships, the *Minion*, was so overcrowded with men rescued from other ships that about a hundred had to be put ashore on the Mexican coast to fend for themselves. They decided to divide into two groups. One group of about 75 men worked its way south, while the other smaller group went north. Incredible as it may seem, some members of each group actually returned to England, and stranger still, for it was the less likely to succeed, the three members of the north-bound group known to have survived, David Ingram, Richard Browne, and Richard Twide, were there before the end of 1569. Ingram [18] and two members of the south-bound party, Miles Philips [19] and Job Hortop,[20] eventually gave accounts of their adventures, all printed by Hakluyt in *Principall Navigations*, though the account of Hortop was not included until the second edition (1598–1600), since he did not return to England until 1590. Philips returned in 1582.

The south-bound group, bedeviled by mosquitoes and hunger, surrendered to the Spaniards at the first opportunity. Its members were taken to México City, where they fared well except for a small number, including Hortop, who were soon sent to Spain and imprisoned there. Those who remained in México were employed by the Spaniards as personal servants or as labor bosses in the silver mines. Some acquired a little capital. When the Inquisition was brought to México, they suffered questioning and some restrictions, but those who married and settled down apparently were not seriously molested. Philips apprenticed himself to a silk weaver yet did not marry and, rightly suspected of planning to return to England, was hounded about the country on one pretext or another until he did contrive to escape. The accounts Hortop and Philips wrote of their adventures, though stirring, must have been disappointing in that they revealed little about México that was not already known. Philips in particular, through long residence and ability to speak Spanish, must have known much more than he set down, and may have made it available in England through oral communication.

Ingram claims to have traveled by land with Browne and Twide from the coast of México to within sixty leagues of "Cape Britton" (Cape Breton Island), where they were taken off by a French ship, the *Gargarine*, commanded by Captain Champaigne, truly an epic journey if actually accomplished. The character of the account is such, however, as to raise doubts about its reliability, hence question as to whether Ingram and his two companions traveled as far as Ingram says they did. On this ground Hakluyt, who had printed the account in the first edition of the *Principall Navigations*, omitted it from the second. Whether or not the journey was actually made is still a matter of considerable interest, but, more important for our present purpose, there is nothing new in the account, no information known today to be true of the region described, whether it be regarded as Mexico, Florida, or the land of Baccallaos, that was not already available in England through other sources.

With Hawkins on his third voyage sailed Francis Drake, then a young man in his middle twenties, hotheaded and lacking the reflective judgment of his superior. The difference in temperament became apparent at Rio de la Hacha, a port in that part of Uraba now called Colombia. There Drake had seen an English expedition, of which he was a member, tricked out of ninety slaves by the treasurer of the king of Spain in 1567. Hawkins sent him ahead with the *Judith*, probably intending only that he spy out the town, but Drake, remembering the loss of the year before, put two cannon balls into the treasurer's house and captured a Spanish ship within musket range of the shore, something quite contrary to Hawkins' well-considered policy of staying within the law.

The temper of Drake prevailed over the temper of Hawkins in the years that followed. Outright seizure of Spanish treasure, often under the cloak of reprisal, a legal device then in good standing among nations, became a common occurrence. The chief object of attack was the treasure from Perú en route to Spain. Attack was progressive, beginning with the port of Nombre de Dios, in that part of Veragua now called Panamá, and gradually spreading across the isthmus to the South Sea. In 1572 Drake and John Oxenham took some treasure from Nombre de Dios and coastwise vessels. In 1575 these two made an unsuccessful attack on the mule trains between Panamá City and the head of the Chagres River, and later picked a large treasure from small boats between the mouth of the river and Nombre de Dios. Other Englishmen soon followed their example.

John Oxenham, not content with taking Peruvian treasure from Nombre de Dios and the isthmus, conceived the bold plan of seizing it in the South Sea before it should reach Panamá City.[21] Late in 1576, with the help of the Cimaroons, a well-organized body of escaped Negro slaves, he built a pinnace and launched her on that part of the South Sea now called Gulf of Panamá, as Balboa had done many years before. Early in 1577 he captured rich booty from intercepted treasure ships, easy prey since they had never before been molested in these waters and were completely unprepared for trouble. The chief difficulty attendant upon raiding in the South Sea was that of getting men and loot back across the isthmus to the North (Caribbean) Sea. Before this could be accomplished, the aroused Spaniards captured Oxenham and those of his men who were not killed in the fight and recovered the treasure. Oxenham was tried and hanged in Perú in 1580.

On December 13, 1577, Drake sailed with five ships from Plymouth for the Strait of Magellan and the Moluccas on a voyage which was to take him around the earth.[22] By the time he reached Port St. Julian in Patagonia his men were demoralized and unruly. There he reorganized his expedition, destroying two of his smaller ships, and restored discipline. At the end of two months he was able to resume his voyage. All three ships passed safely through the strait, but in the open ocean beyond a great storm arose which sank the *Marigold* and separated the *Golden Hind* and the *Elizabeth*. The crew of the *Elizabeth* refused to make an extended search for the other ship or to continue to the Moluccas alone and took her back through the strait to England. Drake, in the *Golden Hind*, waited in the vicinity of the strait as long as he dared, then worked his way north along the west coast of South and Central America, raiding Spanish shipping and towns as he went and collecting rich booty, most of it gold and silver. He continued his coastwise sailing northward, touching at what is now California, until he found winds favorable for carrying him westward. He appears to have missed the Moluccas altogether but did touch at Java, where he added a quantity of cloves to his American treasure. Without further delay he passed through the Indian Ocean and around the Cape of Good Hope, reaching Plymouth at the end of September, 1580, two years and nearly ten months after he had sailed away.

English feeling toward Drake was at first mixed. Some regarded him as a pirate; others considered his raiding of Spanish shipping as legitimate reprisal. It took Elizabeth six months to make up her mind how she felt, but she finally adopted the latter view and, on April 4, 1581, knighted him on board his own ship. Drake was a national hero and his reputation grew with the years. The *Golden Hind*, left at Deptford, became a shrine, and for many years, even into the next century, people went there to meditate on his exploits and to eat and drink. It is difficult to say which enhanced Drake's reputation more at the time, his successful raid on the Spanish treasure house in America or his circumnavigation of the earth. There can be little doubt, however, about the relative value of his information to his contemporaries. That about America must have been more important to world-minded Englishmen, who by this time were turning their faces westward in ever-increasing numbers, than what he had to say about the East Indies. He and his crew had a firsthand, though sketchy, knowledge of the west coast of America from the Strait of Magellan perhaps as far north as Canada. Parts of this coast had not been seen before by Englishmen and information from Spanish sources about much of it was extremely scanty. No account of the voyage was printed until after 1585, though no doubt various versions passed by word of mouth before that date.

Considerable information about Spanish America became available to the English layman during the years between the publication of Eden's *Decades* (1555) and the presentation of Hakluyt's *Discourse* (1584) through the publication in England of English translations of important Spanish works. Thomas Nicholas and John Frampton, English merchants formerly resident in Spain, published translations of the works of Enciso, Gómara, and Zárete. In 1577 Richard Willes put out an expanded edition of Eden's *Decades* which contained, among other items, a translation of the last four of Peter Martyr's *Eight Decades*. A translation of Las Casas' account of the Spanish settlements in the West Indies, the translator identified only by the initials M. M. S., was published in 1583. Important as these translations were, their impact on the average, interested, literate Englishman must have been less than that of the original Eden's *Decades*. They simply clarified and added detail to the picture which had taken such substantial form on Eden's pages. In was through the earlier work that the reader who was awake to such opportunities had experienced the unforgettable thrill of discovering Spanish America and Florida.

Northwest Passage and the Changing Attitude toward the New Found Land

In Eden's *Decades* the land of Baccallaos is still primarily a place to catch codfish, even though Cartier is quoted as having found it suitable for colonization, and Labrador is a cold, remote place whose abundant wood and numerous fur-bearing animals are objects of curiosity rather than commercial assets. In Hakluyt's *Discourse of Western Planting* this part of North America appears as an area suitable for colonization. The gap between these two concepts is wide indeed, too wide to be cleared in a single leap. It had to be taken in several steps. One of these steps was the notion of establishing one or more stations in the region, by the side of the supposed northwest passage, where ships going to Asia might stop for food, water, and other supplies. Humphrey Gilbert voiced this in 1566, in that long letter to his brother John, published ten years later through the good offices of George Gascoigne as *A Discourse of a Discoverie for a new Passage to Cataia*,[23] saying, "Moreover, we might from all the aforesaid places, have a yerely retourne, inhabiting for our staple some convenient place of America, about Sierra Nevada, or some other part, wheras it shal seeme best for the shortening of the voyage." [24] Another step was the suggestion to establish there a station to protect or develop some economic interest. George Best expressed this in 1578 when, in his account of Frobisher's three voyages, he described Frobisher's plan for a station in Meta Incognita to protect the gold mines thought to be there. Anthony Parkhurst also expressed it in that same year when, in a letter addressed to an unnamed nobleman, he advocated a settlement in Newfoundland for the drying and salting of the fish caught off its shores.

Though nobody seems to know with certainty just when Humphrey Gilbert first became interested in the search for a northwest passage to Asia, his interest is plain to be seen in 1566. In 1565 he had sought the Queen's permission to search for "a passage by the Northe," [25] and it may be that his ideas had not yet crystallized, but in the next year, in his *Discourse*, he was arguing strongly for the existence of the northwest passage.

The arguments that Gilbert advances in support of the existence of such a passage are woven of strands of evidence drawn from both the static and the changing earths. Though sometimes inconsistent and loosely reasoned, they are vigorously presented. There must be a northwest passage, thinks Gilbert, because America is an island, around which it should be possible to sail by the north, and because the general trend of the main ocean currents reveals its presence. He clinches his conclusion by reference to

modern authority, saying that Gemma Phrysius, Sebastian Münster, Peter Apian, Peter Martyr, and others, whom he also names,
believe in such a passage.

In 1566 Gilbert again sought the Queen's permission to search
for a passage to Cathay and was denied it because the Russia Company rightly considered that such a voyage would infringe upon
its own monopoly, which covered voyages to the northwest and
north as well as to the northeast. For several years thereafter official
duties in Ireland, London, Devonshire, and the Netherlands kept
Gilbert so busy that he had little time to pursue this project further.

Meanwhile Martin Frobisher had become actively interested in
the search for a northwest passage. In 1574 he applied directly to
the Russia Company for permission to make the voyage and was
turned down because that, too, would have infringed the sacro-
sanct monopoly. Time, however, was beginning to run out for
the Russia Company, even though no time limit had been included
in its original grant. Frobisher, undismayed by the refusal, secured
the support of Elizabeth and the Privy Council, and the company
was forced to give its consent, however grudgingly, in February,
1575.

Frobisher's first expedition, which sailed in June, 1576, reached
what he called Meta Incognita, actually the southern end of Baffin
Island, together with certain small, adjacent islands. There he
sailed into a long, narrow indentation in Baffin Island, still called
Frobisher Bay, which he considered to be a strait and the beginning
of the northwest passage. The loss of five members of his small
crew to the Eskimos left him short-handed and prevented such
exploration as would have shown him that it was a dead end. When
he returned to England in October, 1576, with the news that he
had found the passage, he brought as souvenirs some flowers, green
grass, and a piece of black stone collected by members of his
crew, according to George Best, who commanded a ship for him
on each of his two succeeding voyages. This worthless black
stone was said by some to carry gold, and the report at once in-

fected many persons in high places with gold fever. Frobisher sailed again in May, 1577, with instructions to follow the passage into the South Sea, but the Queen sent along a large ship which was to be loaded with gold ore and returned at once to England. Frobisher ignored his instructions to follow the passage and loaded all his ships with ore. The third expedition, which sailed in May, 1578, abandoned all pretense of following the supposed passage to the South Sea and devoted itself to loading ore. Sometime before it returned to England in October of that year, the bubble burst, and Frobisher arrived to find that he had many tons of rock on his ships good only for mending roads.[26]

It has sometimes been said that Frobisher intended to plant a colony in America, but the evidence indicates that he planned nothing more than a fort to guard the gold mines he expected to establish. On his third voyage he took along a prefabricated wooden fort and a hundred men to stay the year around, of whom forty were sailors, thirty miners, and thirty soldiers, gentlemen, gold-refiners, bakers, carpenters, and others necessary to maintain the rest. The equipment was lost on the way over, so that even this plan, so far short of colonization, was abandoned. Best's account of Meta Incognita is neither flattering nor enthusiastic, and he concludes by saying, "I finde in all the Countrie nothing, that may be to delite in, either of pleasure or of accompte, only the shewe of Mine." [27] This is hardly a land deemed suitable for colonization. There was, however, beginning to be a different attitude toward the lands of Baccallaos and Labrador, especially the former, an expression of interest despite the absence of gold.

In 1577 or 1578 Anthony Parkhurst, of his own volition, wrote a letter [28] to a nobleman, whose name is not known today, suggesting that a station be set up in Newfoundland for manufacturing salt and drying and salting fish. The line between a temporary station and a permanent settlement or colony may be very thin indeed, and his detailed suggestions embody some of the characteristics of both, so that he may have had in mind something that would eventually become permanent. The proposed lack of contact with the natives and the shifting of personnel suggest the temporary. Suggestions for expanding the fishing industry, exploiting timber, furs, and iron, and raising livestock all smack of the permanent.

Later that same year Parkhurst wrote a letter [29] to the elder Hakluyt, in response to his inquiry about Newfoundland, mentioning the greatly increased activity of English fishermen in those waters within the four years just past and describing the country itself in glowing terms. Its diversified and abundant products are described in detail, and the climate, contrary to some previous reports, is said to be as temperate as that of England. Thus for the first time we have English corroboration of Cartier's estimate of the new land, mentioned in Eden's *Decades* (1555), which had received scant attention from Englishmen in the intervening years.

Feeling against Spain, running high in England in 1577, is reflected in a document addressed by Humphrey Gilbert to the Queen, entitled *A discourse how hir Majestie may annoy the king of Spayne*,[30] in which he advocates attacking Spanish ships under cover of "lettres patentes to discover and inhabyte some strange place," offering his services for this purpose. On June 11, 1578, he was granted letters patent to discover, hold, and occupy such barbarous lands not yet actually possessed by any Christian prince or people, just such a grant as he had indirectly asked for the year before. It is not surprising, then, to find that the voyage on which he sailed the following November is cloaked in darkness and that little is known of what was achieved. It is surprising to find that the grant was sufficient to support an expedition which, sailing on June 11, 1583, actually aimed at discovery and colonization.

It was in this five-year period between the issuance of Gilbert's grant and the start of his last voyage that Englishmen really began to appreciate the potential value of American colonies. While some, like Frobisher, Parkhurst, and the elder Hakluyt, were thinking principally in terms of temporary settlements which would exploit the natural products of the land, others, like John Florio and the younger Hakluyt, were beginning to visualize permanent colonies as a means of achieving this and other ends too. Florio's ideas found expression in the preface to his English translation of Cartier's account of his own first two voyages (1534, 1535–1536) to New France, published in London in 1580 as *A shorte and briefe narration of the two Nauigations and Discoueries to the Northweast partes called Newe Fravnce*. Impressed with Cartier's description of a land as fruitful and pleasant as France, England, or Germany, he would establish permanent colonies there to receive such commodities as the land might produce, which, in addition, might serve as bases from which to explore adjacent territory and search for a northwest passage. The younger Hakluyt, in the dedication of his *Divers Voyages* (1582) to Philip Sidney, advocated permanent American colonies as places to settle the unemployed of England and as bases from which to search for a northwest passage. In addition, he thought that the existence of such colonies would stimulate English interest in the art of navigation. All these ideas the younger Hakluyt gathered together in his *Discourse of Western Planting*, which he presented to the Queen in 1584. To them he added the concept of western bases of operation against the Spaniards. He also restated there the old aims of Robert Thorne and Richard Eden, the development of a market for English woolen goods and the Christianization of the natives, but tying both to the proposed American colonies.

Both Florio and the younger Hakluyt, through the translation of Cartier's work and the collection called *Divers Voyages*, were supplying information about the new land which they hoped might stimulate interest in planting colonies there. Each work presented the new land in a favorable light, but they were not equally sound, and the *Divers Voyages* was not equally sound throughout. The one, however, may have made just as many converts as the other.

Florio's translation made available the best account of the land of Baccallaos, the only part of the new land to which England had show of title, and revealed that France had some claim there, too. Hakluyt made capital of this in the *Discourse of Western*

Planting, urging the need for haste if England would forestall France.

The *Divers Voyages*, hastily put together as Hakluyt himself admits, contained some material that was good, some bad. Ribault's account of Florida was probably the best available, but England had no claim there. It may have served, however, to direct Ralegh's attention to territory at the vague and indefinite boundary between Florida and the land of Baccallaos, to which he sent Amadas and Barlowe in 1583. The two Thorne documents carried little specific information about the land of Baccallaos. Zeno's account of Estotilande, then considered by some to be America, is not only fictitious (though Hakluyt surely was not aware of this) but also worse than valueless because it might have raised false hopes of finding gold in a region that was non-existent. The two maps accompanying the work left much to be desired. Thorne's map of 1527 was very much out-of-date. Thevet's map of 1575, which was readily available, was infinitely better than the one Michael Lok drafted especially for this volume. Lok's map was based on old data and showed as real the mythical islands of Brazil, St. Brandan, and the Island of the Seven Cities, and a North America that was badly distorted. The soundest part of the book, for the purpose of providing information about the land of Baccallaos, was Verrazano's account of the voyage he made in 1524 to Norumbega (roughly the region between the Hudson and St. Lawrence Rivers) under the French flag. It characterizes the natives as friendly and the climate as equable, and describes briefly the abundant natural products, emphasizing timber, copper, and wild game.

By the time the *Divers Voyages* (1582) appeared, the campaign for American colonies had already extended itself to Humphrey Gilbert, placed in a position to act by the grant of 1578. Early in 1580 he sent the *Squirrel* out on a voyage of reconnaissance. In 1580–1583 he assigned land and rights to a number of persons, including John Dee, Philip Sidney, and George Peckham. Peckham was acting for a group of Catholics anxious to leave Protestant England. In 1582 Gilbert drew up a detailed plan for a proprietary government and, later the same year, assigned trading privileges to a private corporation.

Some years before, in 1574 to be exact, Humphrey Gilbert, Christopher Carlile, George Peckham, and Richard Grenville had jointly petitioned the Queen for permission to sail on a voyage of discovery. She had refused. Their interest in such a project not only survived this blow but increased in intensity and broadened in scope, though only two of the four, Gilbert and Peckham, ever joined forces again. Grenville, acting for his cousin Ralegh, was to plant the unsuccessful Roanoke colony in 1585. About the time that Gilbert's plans were maturing, Carlile was making some of his own, aided by his stepfather Francis Walsingham, probably the most important of Elizabeth's secretaries of state. Walsingham was sympathetic toward western voyaging, in active touch with it through such men as the younger Richard Hakluyt and Philip Sidney, who was to marry his daughter Frances in the fall of 1583, and had already sent Simon Fernando, an Azores pilot, on a scouting expedition to Norumbega.[31] In March, 1583, Walsingham persuaded the citizens of Bristol to contribute 1,000 pounds toward an expedition "intended for the discovery of the coast of America, lying to the Southwest of Cape Briton," which was to be captained by his stepson. Carlile, seeking additional support, approached the Russia Company, presenting a "discourse"[32] on America in an effort to induce its members to participate. There he stressed the deterioration of trade with Russia, the Levant, and the Barbary coast, as Hakluyt was to do the next year, and the advantages of establishing a trading post in America at about 40 degrees north latitude (the vicinity of Philadelphia); this, because of its central location, could make available such northern commodities as salmon, codfish, whales, pitch, tar, hemp, cordage, masts, hides, and furs and such southern ones as wine, olives, honey, and salt. There is no mention of the establishment of bases against Spain, but rather the expression of a desire to avoid trouble with other European powers. This was to be primarily a trading venture aimed at profit, with "planting" and other ends made altogether subordinate to that aim. A committee of the Russia Company reported favorably on the project and recommended that 100 men (the same number Frobisher had intended to use) be sent out for one year to acquire a knowledge of the country and its commodities. The cost was estimated at 4,000 pounds, and the 3,000 pounds not yet subscribed was to be raised in London and elsewhere. For some reason the venture seems never to have been undertaken, but the record that remains of the plans for it serve as further evidence of the changing attitude of Englishmen toward that part of America north of Mexico. More important perhaps is the interest thus shown in territory south of Newfoundland in a latitude not far north of that which was to receive Ralegh's ill-fated first colony. Gilbert, too, had a southern objective in mind but sailed for Newfoundland because that was the "trade way" for English ships going to America.[33] Newfoundland so captivated him that he never got beyond.

On June 11, 1583, after numerous delays, Gilbert sailed for Newfoundland with five ships, and though the talk had been of colonization, the record indicates little more than another preliminary voyage of discovery. Taking possession of Newfoundland at St. John's harbor by right of his grant was the closest Gilbert came to planting a colony. Some attempt was made to explore the coast, but a shortage of supplies and dissatisfaction among the men soon caused him to sail for England with the two ships still left to him, the *Golden Hind* (not Drake's ship) and the *Squirrel*, vowing to return the next spring. On the night of September 9 the *Squirrel* disappeared with all hands, including Gilbert, and his plans to continue the work with him. The *Golden Hind* reached Falmouth on September 22. Her captain and owner, Edward Hay, wrote an account of the voyage, which remained in manuscript until Hakluyt printed it in 1600. Peckham, however, after consultation with Hay, published a brief account [34] before the end of 1583 in an effort to promote another voyage to America under Gilbert's patent, and once more the emphasis was on plantation. But the initiative was about to shift to Walter Ralegh, who indeed was already active since he had furnished one of the ships for Gilbert's expedition.

Gilbert's patent was renewed in favor of Ralegh, his half brother, on March 25, 1584, and he lost no time in acting under it. On April 27 he sent out two ships under the command of Philip Amadas and Arthur Barlowe, with Walsingham's Simon Fernando as pilot. Their route was different from that of Gilbert. Instead of sailing due west to Newfoundland, they followed the route Columbus had pioneered on his first voyage and sailed south to the Canaries, then west to the West Indies, where they stopped to take on food and a fresh supply of water; then they ventured north along the Florida coast. Their objective, judging from this route, was clearly a southern one. Their instructions, revealed by the nature of Barlowe's subsequent report [35] to Ralegh, were to explore rather than to colonize. Such procedure was made necessary by the paucity of English knowledge of that area where Florida and the land of Baccallaos merged. However, we know from his interest in Hakluyt's *Discourse of Western Planting*, presented to the Queen that fall, and the events of the following year that Ralegh must even then have been thinking in terms of colonization.

The English were enchanted with what they found. On July 2 they encountered shoal water and their nostrils were assailed with the sweet smell of flowers so that they knew land was near. Two days later they sighted land and sailed along it for 120 English miles looking for an opening. What they thought was mainland proved to be a long, continuous barrier beach. They passed through the first break they found in it and entered an inland sea (where Pamlico and Albemarle Sounds join waters). Barlowe's description of Roanoke Island, where they landed and took possession in the name of the Queen, reads very much like Ribault's description of the same coast many miles to the south, written over twenty years before. This is what he reported to Ralegh:

. . . we viewed the land about us, being, whereas we first landed, very sandie and low towards the waters side, but so full of grapes, as the very beating and surge of the Sea overflowed them, of which we found such plentie, as well there as in all places else, both on the sand and on the greene soile on the hils, as in the plaines, as well on every little shrubbe, as also climing towardes the tops of high Cedars, that I thinke in all the world the like abundance is not to be found: and my selfe having seene those parts of Europe that most abound, find such differ- ence as were incredible to be written.

We passed from the Sea side towardes the toppes of those hilles next adjoyning, being but of meane higth, and from thence wee behelde the Sea on both sides to the North, and to the South, finding no ende any of both wayes. This lande lay stretching it selfe to the West, which after wee found to bee but an Island of twentie miles long, and not above sixe miles broade. Under the banke or hill whereon we stoode, we behelde the vallyes replenished with goodly Cedar trees, and hav- ing discharged our harquebuz-shot, such a flocke of Cranes (the most part white) arose under us, with such a cry redoubled by many ecchoes, as if an armie of men had showted all together.

This Island had many goodly woodes full of Deere, Conies, Hares, and Fowle, even in the middest of Summer in incredible abundance. The woodes are not such as you finde in Bohemia, Moscovia, or Hercynia, barren and fruitles, but the highest and reddest Cedars of the world, farre bettering the Ceders of Açores, of the Indies, or Ly- banus, Pynes, Cypres, Sassaphras, the Lentisk, or the tree that beareth the Masticke, the tree that beareth the rine of blacke Sinamon, of which Master Winter brought from the streights of Magellan, and many other of excellent smell and qualitie.[36]

The English, like Ribault's French, found not only natural products in overpowering abundance but Indians that were friendly, two of whom returned to England with them. Furthermore, the In- dians possessed pearls and ornaments of copper. Here, then, was the most favorable firsthand report yet made by an Englishman concerning territory in that part of America to which England had show of title. Small wonder, in view of this and the increasingly favorable attitude of Englishmen toward this same part of America, that Ralegh should send out an expedition bent on colonization the very next year.

CHAPTER IX

Medieval Concepts of the Earth in a Renaissance World

THE HISTORY of medieval concepts of the earth in renaissance England is one of inertia and slow change. Some of the concepts were sound, others false; and even the sound ones were usually inadequate in some respect and needed revision. The idea of a round earth was sound, but not the belief that it is motionless, as Copernicus was to demonstrate in 1543. Acceptance of its rotation and revolution did not take place overnight. Similarly the concept of five zones encircling a round earth in an east-west direction was sound, but the corollary that the frigid and torrid zones are not habitable was not true. Yet despite the evidence of its falsity already piling up in the Middle Ages, sixteenth-century writers felt compelled to disprove the corollary as late as the fourth quarter of the century. Some of the concepts that were entirely unsound, like that of the Earthly Paradise, also survived. It was inevitable that this should be so. Belief in them had endured for a long time, often centuries, and they were deeply entrenched in classical and medieval literature. The evidence growing out of the new discoveries must often have seemed thin to the renaissance Englishman or less convincing than the old, or perhaps it was a long time in reaching him. Occasionally one of the concepts lingered on simply because it had not yet been disproved by anybody, and this was the case with the theory that gold occurs in quantity only near the equator.

The clearest and fullest statement by a renaissance Englishman of the medieval belief in the restricted geographical occurrence of gold was made by Richard Eden in the epistle to the reader which precedes his work called *A Treatyse of the newe India . . .* (1553). He says,

This ought to be consydered for a general rule, that nearest vnto the south partes of the world betwene the two Tropikes vnder ye *Equinoctial* or burning lyne, where the sunne is of greatest forse, is the chiefest place where gold is engendred, although it be sometymes founde in colde regions as in Scotland, in Crayford more, likewyse in Hungary, yet nether pure of it self, nor in great quantitie: the reason whereof is largely declared in the Bookes of George Agric, and Albertus Magnus.[1]

There can be little doubt that Eden was serious in saying that gold is begotten on the earth by the rays of the sun, in largest quantity in the torrid zone, where those rays are hottest. It was still the current theory for the origin and regional distribution of the precious metal, current not only in England but throughout western Europe. Indeed, the new evidence tended to support rather than disprove the theory. The major new sources of gold uncovered by the voyagers of the fifteenth and sixteenth centuries, the Guinea coast of Africa, the West Indies, Central America, Perú, and the gold-producing part of México, all lay between the tropics of Cancer and Capricorn. These regions far surpassed Hungary and the Crawford Moor region of Scotland, the two most important sources in the north temperate zone of Europe, both in quantity and purity of gold produced, as Eden well knew. No wonder he took the theory seriously. It was to be a long time before men would realize that gold is brought up from the interior of the earth in molten or fluid state and distributed through the crust without regard for the intensity of the sun's rays. From the vantage point of the twentieth century it is difficult to believe that so mistaken a view could ever have influenced world events, yet it is quite possible that this medieval theory, particularly the corollary that pure gold does not occur in quantity outside the torrid zone, was of first importance in keeping Englishmen away for so long a time from the only part of North America to which they had show of title, that part north of México. All of it was known to be north of the Tropic of Cancer and presumed to be without gold in paying quantity at a time when gold was the chief attraction in the new land.

Eden was not the only renaissance Englishman to refer to this theory nor was he the first. Robert Thorne took it into account in his "booke" to Dr. Lee, written in 1527. But since that letter was written to give England information about Spanish trade with the Moluccas, where the principal product was spice instead of gold, Thorne's statement was slanted toward that product. More than that, he extended the original theory to include other products of adjacent islands and territory in addition to spice. It is a logical extension, though the logic is implied rather than express. The syllogism, which is not altogether sound, runs something like this. Gold occurs in greatest quantity near the equator. Gold is precious. Such precious objects as gold, silver, copper, jewels, and spices often occur in association with one another. Therefore gold, silver, copper, jewels, and spices are all found in greatest quantity near the equator. Thorne's statement follows:

Also to write unto your Lordshippe of the new trade of Spicery of the Emperour, there is no doubt but that the Islands are fertile of Cloves, Nutmegs, Mace, and Cinnamom: and that the said Islands, with other there about, abound with golde, Rubies, Diamondes, Balasses, Granates, Jacincts, and other stones & pearles, as all other lands, that are under and neere the Equinoctiall. For we see, where nature giveth any thing, she is no nigard. For as with us and other, that are aparted from the said Equinoctiall, our mettals be Lead, Tinne, and Iron, so theirs be Gold, Silver, and Copper. And as our fruits and graines bee Apples, Nuts, and Corne, so theirs be Dates, Nutmegs, Pepper, Cloves, and other Spices. And as we have Jeat, Amber, Cristall, Jasper, and other like stones, so have they Rubies, Diamonds, Balasses, Saphyres, Jacincts, and other like.[2]

It is not surprising that Roger Barlow, who was Thorne's friend, should also have referred to this theory and in the same extended form. He makes reference to it in *A briefe summe of Geographie*, which was written in 1540–1541, in these words:

What comoditie is within this lande [the land of Baccallaos] as yet is not knowen for it hath not ben labored, but it is to be presupposed that ther is no riches of gold, spyces nor preciose stones, for it stondeth farre aparted from the equinoctiall whereas the influens of the sonne doth norishe and bryng fourth gold, spices, stones and perles. But whereas our englishe marchantes of brystowe dyd enterpryse to discover and discovered that parte of the land, if at that season thei had folowed toward the equinoctiall, no dowt but thei shuld have founde grete riches of gold and perle as other nations hathe done sence that tyme.[3]

This statement is even more significant than that of Thorne or Eden because it specifically mentions the presupposition that gold was not to be found in paying quantity in the land of Baccallaos and expresses regret that Englishmen had not discovered the rich American lands within the torrid zone, a belief and accompanying feeling that many of his countrymen must have possessed in common with Barlow.

The excitement caused in England by Frobisher's purported discovery of gold in 1576 in Meta Incognita, which was north of Labrador, can hardly be imagined today. There is no reason to believe that the medieval concept of gold engendered in abundance only between the tropics of Cancer and Capricorn had been abandoned by that date. On the contrary, Taylor has turned up a letter from Philip Sidney to Hugh Languet which states specifically that Frobisher at first considered "the piece of glittering earth" which started the gold rush to be of no value because he believed that the precious metals could not exist so far north.[4] Englishmen who had thought it impossible to find gold in that part of America to which they had some right suddenly believed themselves mistaken, happily so, and saw at last a chance to secure the precious yellow metal legitimately, without having to take it away from the Spaniards. Small wonder that such enterprising men as Warwick, Leicester, Walsingham, Philip Sidney, William Winter, Edward

Dyer, John Dee, Humphrey Gilbert, Michael Lok, and Anthony Jenkinson gave Frobisher's mining voyages their strong support. The height of their jubilation could have been equaled only by the depth of their despair at learning the ore to be valueless. The medieval concept of the tropical concentration of gold, reinforced by this negative evidence, continued to linger on in England well into the nineteenth century, long after the chemistry of gold was well-known there.

The theory of an impassable ocean was disproved by Columbus' first voyage to America for all who heard of it except those who thought he had reached one of the Western Islands. If he had reached the Indies or Asia, clearly he had crossed the ocean as most persons visualized it. If he had reached a new continent, still he had crossed an ocean of a sort as indicated by the considerable length of time required to sail there and back, and even to those who thought he had reached one of the Western Islands this fact must have suggested that he had crossed a large portion of the ocean. The voyages of Hojeda, Vespucci, Pinzón, John Cabot, Cabral, and others soon demonstrated that something larger and more impressive than one of the Western Islands lay to the west, and by the beginning of the sixteenth century there was little doubt that the ocean could be and had been crossed.

The medieval church had opposed the concept of antipodean peoples only because it postulated the existence of human beings who could not be saved, since they were cut off from the known, inhabited quarter of the earth by an ocean that could not be crossed. As soon as the Western Ocean was proved passable, this opposition necessarily melted away. The existence of such peoples was soon beyond dispute, for the early voyagers not only reported finding them but often brought such persons back with them when they returned. Only the term *antipodes* now rings familiar on our ears, but *antichthones* was used in conjunction with it in sixteenth-century England, though the two did not necessarily have the same meaning as that given them by Crates of Mallos. *Antoikoi* does not appear in the literature. Robert Record speaks of both in *The*

Castle of Knowledge (1556) and Thevet in *Singularités de l'Amérique* (1558), translated into English by Thomas Hackett in 1568, while Cuningham mentions only *antipodes* in *The Cosmographical Glasse* (1559). As originally used, *antipodes* referred to peoples having a time of day different from that of the peoples of Europe at any given moment but the same season. *Antoikoi* referred to those having the same time of day but a different season. *Antichthones* referred to those having a different season and a different time of day. Record was aware that both season and time of day were involved, but he put the Antichthones where the Antoikoi should have been and the Antipodes where the Antichthones should have been, saying, "Antichthones or Counterdwellers, haue like times of the day, but not of the year. Antipodes or Counterpasers, haue nother the parts of the year, nother of the day agreable togither." [5] He is not altogether consistent in this definition, for earlier he has said that for Englishmen the Antipodes must be under the same meridian as they and half the distance of that circle away,[6] which would place the Antipodes where the Antoikoi belong. Cuningham echoes this earlier statement of Record, saying that the Antipodes are under the same meridian as Englishmen.[7] Thevet is thoroughly confused about the two terms and seems to use them interchangeably, both in the sense of "opposite," suggesting that the Antipodes are those who inhabit the two poles and also those who are directly east and west of each other, while the Antichthones are in between, persons in Perú being Antichthones with respect to persons in India.[8] Today we often use the term "antipodes" loosely to refer to peoples living in an "opposite" part of the earth, in the fashion of Thevet, or to an opposite part of the earth itself. We have even gone so far as to use it as the name for a group of small islands southeast of New Zealand. Presumably Crates of Mallos would not have approved such procedure. Not only have we transferred his term from persons to place but we have attached it to a quarter of the earth inhabited by his *antoikoi*.

The problem of the habitability of the torrid and frigid zones was considered in sixteenth-century England more often than might be imagined, and the habitability of the frigid zone, and indeed of all of North America north of the St. Lawrence River, remained a live issue at least as late as 1583. By the end of the fifteenth century it was probably common knowledge among mariners that Russia and the Scandinavian countries were inhabited close to and even beyond the Arctic Circle and that peoples lived in those parts of Asia and Africa which lay within the torrid zone. Something of this had even appeared in the literature.[9] Yet some persons went right on believing to the contrary either through ignorance of the proof or continuing reliance on out-moded authority, or through an innate feeling that the torrid zone must be too hot and the frigid zone too cold for living. Even those who believed them habitable felt compelled to discuss the problem, so strongly was the contrary view entrenched in classical and medieval literature.

Thomas More declared his belief in the inhospitable character of the torrid zone by having Raphael Hythloday say,

For vnder the lyne equynoctyall and of bothe sydes of the same, as farre as the sonne doth extend hys course, lyeth (quod he) greate and wȳde desertes and wyldernesses, parched, burned and dryed vppe with continuall and intollerable heate. All thynges be hydeous, terryble, lothesome, and vnpleasaunte to be holde; all thynges owte of fasshyon and comylynes, inhabyted wyth wylde beastes and serpentes, or at the leaste wyse wyth people that be no lesse sauage, wylde, and noysome then the verye beastes themselfes be. But a lytle farther beyonde that all thynges begyn by lytle and lytle to waxe pleasaunte; the ayre softe, temperate, and gentle; the ground couered wyth grene grasse; less wildnes in the beastes. At the laste shall ye come again to people, cities, and townes, wherin is contynuall entercourse and occupynge of marchandyse and chaffare, not onelye amonge them selfes and wyth theyre borderers, but also wyth marchauntes of farre contreys by lande and water.[10]

More, then, believed that savages could live in the torrid zone but not civilized men, a distinction not often drawn. Usually the zone was either considered habitable for men or it was not. Expression of the belief that men can live there appeared in 1555 in Eden's *Decades*. Oviedo, who had lived many years in the torrid zone in America, offered himself as a living example to show that it could be done, though he considered that the ancient writers had some grounds for their contrary belief since it is "naturally hotte" there.[11] He was also aware that altitude and temperature are related, knowledge so important for comfortable living in the tropics.[12] Martyr had already called attention to this relationship, saying not only that it can be cool in the mountains of the tropics but that conversely it can also be very warm in northern regions, the latter an extraordinarily acute observation for the day:

For wee knowe, that snowe fauleth on the mountaynes of the Equinoctiall or burnte lyne, and the same to endure there continually: We knowe lykewyse that th[e] inhabitantes of the Regions farre distante frome that lyne towarde the northe, are molested with great heate.[13]

Oviedo went beyond merely stating his belief in the habitability of the equatorial belt and presented a logical explanation for that condition. He considered that the naturally hot ground is cooled to the depth of a man's height by the abundant rain and great number of rivers, brooks, springs, and marshes found there. Eden, assuming the validity of the belief and supporting the explanation, added a long footnote [14] from the Aristotelian tract, *De elementis*, by Jerome Cardan, an Italian mathematician and philosopher whom he had met through John Cheke, the English humanist. Cardan held that the cold and moist element water, whether as ocean or stream, flows from the poles or high points of the earth to the equator, a line of low points, there cooling the equatorial belt. Eden again assumed the habitability of the torrid zone when, in his account of the Guinea voyage of 1554, he noted that the equatorial belt is very hot in Africa and temperate in the West Indies:

This is also to be considered as a secret worke of nature, that through-out all Africke, under the Equinoctial line, and neere about the same on both sides, the regions are extreeme hote, and the people very blacke. Whereas contrarily such regions of the West Indies as are under the same line are very temperate, and the people neither blacke, nor with curlde and short wooll on their heads, as they of Africke have, but of the colour of an Olive, with long and blacke heare on their heads: the cause of which variety is declared in divers places in the Decades.[15]

Record,[16] Cuningham,[17] Thevet,[18] and Best [19] all took the position that the torrid or "burning" zone and the two frigid or "frozen" zones are habitable. Cuningham and Thevet included evidence showing that the torrid and north frigid zones are actually in-habited and Record did the same for the torrid zone alone. Record, who arranged his material in the form of a dialogue between master and scholar, represents his scholar as saying that he has learned from Ovid and Virgil that no man can live in the torrid or frigid zones. The master replies, somewhat severely, that these poets would have done better to speak of painful dwelling in the torrid zone on account of heat and hard dwelling in the frigid zones on account of cold. George Best's discussion of the habitability of the three zones is the most elaborate and detailed that has come down to us from this period, his explanation the most sensible, as the expert Stefansson has already remarked.[20] Best points out that temperature at the surface of the earth is largely controlled by two factors, the angle at which the sun's rays strike the earth, the one principally relied on by the "olde Philosophers," and the length of time the sun continues above the horizon, a factor ignored by most of the ancients. Thus at the equator the great heat produced by the high angle of the sun's rays is to a considerable degree reduced by the fact that they strike the earth only twelve hours out of every twenty-four. Similarly in the frigid zone the effectiveness of the sun's rays is greatly increased in summer by the long days, even though the angle at which they strike the earth there is low.

Early in the sixteenth century John Rastell restated the classical attitude toward the habitability of the north frigid zone when he placed· *Experyence* before. "this fygure" and had him say,

> And northwarde on this syde
> There lyeth Iselonde where men do fyshe
> But beyonde that so cold it is
> No man may there abyde.[21]

Though this view persisted in Best's day notwithstanding his statement and those of such men as Martyr, Eden, Record, Cuningham, and Thevet to the contrary, he suggests that for some it was restricted to the arctic winter with its minimum of sunshine. He can only reply that living creatures do manage to survive under such conditions. Whether the problem was general or thus limited, belief at least in the extreme inclemency of the north frigid zone not only persisted in England but with respect to North America actually extended itself to include Newfoundland. This is indicated by the considerable space devoted to disproving the extended concept in the account of Gilbert's expedition of 1583, written the same year by Edward Hay, one of Gilbert's captains. Hay admits that north of Newfoundland it is colder than in those countries of Europe lying in the same latitude. He thinks, however, that Newfoundland is probably not colder on the whole than those parts of France which lie in the same latitude except along the coast, where the rays of the sun, obscured by moisture picked up by the sun in its daily passage over the ocean, may be temporarily weakened—a curious but not unreasonable theory. Some hold, he says, that the interior of Newfoundland may be cold because the elevation is high there, and he grants that mountains may be snow-covered even at the equator, then calls attention to the temperate lowlands usually to be found in association with the mountains. In the latter part of his argument he draws upon his own voyaging experience and that of others, saying,

. . . Neverthelesse (as I sayd before) the cold cannot be so intollerable under the latitude of 46 47 and 48 (especiall within land) that it should be unhabitable, as some doe suppose, seeing also there are very many people more to the North by a great deale. And in these South parts there be certaine beastes, Ounces or Leopards, and birds in like maner which in the Sommer we have seene, not heard of in countries of extreme and vehement coldnesse. Besides, as in the monethes of June, July, August and September, the heate is somewhat more then in England at those seasons: so men remaining upon the South parts neere unto Cape Rece, untill after Hollandtide, have not found the cold so extreme, nor much differing from the temperature of England. Those which have arrived there after November and December, have found the snow exceeding deepe, whereat no marvaile considering the ground upon the coast, is rough and uneven, and the snow is driven into the places most declyning as the like is to be seene with us. The like depth of snow happily shall not be found within land upon the playner countries, which also are defended by the mountaines, breaking off the violence of winds and weather. But admitting extraordinary cold in those South parts, above that with us here: it can not be so great as in Swedland, much lesse in Moscovia or Russia: yet are the same countries very populous, and the rigor of cold is dispensed with by the commoditie of Stoves, warme clothing, meats and drinkes: all which neede not to be wanting in the Newfound land, if we had intent there to inhabite.[22]

It is hard to know what he meant by "Ounces or Leopards" in Canada in the latitude mentioned, otherwise his illustrations are apt and his reasoning sound.

There grew up in England an interest in the circulation of ocean waters which was stimulated by and inseparable from the interest in the search for a northwest passage to Asia. The problem had received some attention from classical and medieval writers,[23] though interest was relatively slight because contacts with the ocean were proportionately few. Aristotle, for example, had propounded the view that water flows from the high poles to the low equator, a theory which Cardan echoed in the sixteenth century. Macrobius some centuries later had held, on the other hand, that four great currents rise out of the ocean at the equator, two flowing north and two flowing south, each pair forming a single current in the polar regions. The numerous voyages of the fifteenth and sixteenth centuries increased both knowledge of and interest in ocean currents and in the more general problem, the circulation of the ocean. There grew up a strong belief, voiced several times by Peter Martyr, that the ocean flows from east to west. Columbus had spoken of noting this phenomenon in the vicinity of Paria and again near Veragua, and Sebastian Cabot said he had seen it as he coasted along the land of Baccallaos. Many persons believed that these local movements indicated general circulation from east to west. If this were true, then there were probably one or more breaks in America to let the waters through, perhaps in the Gulf of México, perhaps northwest of Labrador. The Spaniards were chiefly concerned with the possibility of a passage between the two Americas, and Martyr expresses such a belief in the sixth book of the *Third Decade*, where he says,

Wherefore, it is not onely more lyke to bee trewe, but ought also of necessitie to bee concluded, that betwene both the landes hetherto vnknowen, there shulde bee certeyne great open places wherby the waters shulde thus continually passe from the East into the weste: which waters I suppose to bee dryuen about the globe of the earth by the vncessaunt mouynge and impulsion of the heauens: and not to bee swalowed vp and cast owt ageyne by the breathyng of *Demogorgon* as sume haue imagined bycause they see the seas by increase and decrease, to flow and reflowe.[24]

Not all of the Spanish explorers believed in the existence of such a passage. When Martyr had occasion to discuss the matter with Andreas Moralis, a pilot, and with Oviedo, as they sat "at my house in the towne of Matrite," [25] Moralis expressed the belief that the ocean bends around the Gulf of Mexico like water in a whirlpool and is expelled with a rush through the constricted passage between Cuba and Florida. Nevertheless belief in a break in America through which the supposedly west-flowing ocean could pass, particularly to the north, persisted and found adherents in England in the second half of the sixteenth century.

Humphrey Gilbert states his belief in the westward trend of the ocean, due to "the Diurnall motion of Primum Mobile," [26] in the elaborate argument for the existence of a northwest passage presented in his *Discourse*. He was impressed by the presence of a west-flowing current (the Cape Agulhas current) at the southern extremity of Africa and the disappearance of a north-trending American current (the Gulf Stream?) along northern Labrador, which he considered might be one and the same. He thought it must pass through some passage in America north of Labrador, emerging in the Pacific Ocean as the strong, west-flowing current encountered there by Bernard de Torre in 1542.[27] There was some doubt in his mind whether a ship could sail back through the supposed passage against the current, but in support of the feasibility of the return trip he mentions Pliny's story of the Indians driven by storm onto the coast of Germany, there captured by the king of the Suevi and presented to the Roman proconsul of France. He repudiates the idea that these were American Indians, who have only small canoes incapable of making an ocean voyage, saying that they must have come from India by a northwest passage. The prevailing winds, he thinks, might have made it possible for them to beat against the current.

George Best voiced his belief in the westward movement of the ocean in his account of Frobisher's voyages, saying like Gilbert that it was caused by the similar movement of the *primum mobile*.[28] It seems likely that these two men were using *primum mobile* in the Aristotelian sense of sphere of fixed stars rather than the medieval sense of sphere beyond the firmament, the sphere of fixed stars. Martyr's use of "heauens" for *primum mobile* supports this interpretation, and it was the supposed movement of the sphere of fixed stars, whatever it was called, which was controlling. In either case the universe involved was the Greek, not the Copernican, universe.

The ancient Greek concept of the universe dominated astronomical thought in western Europe until 1543, when Copernicus published his *De revolutionibus*. In that work he made three revolutionary changes in the old system. First, he substituted the sun for the earth at its center. Second, he had the earth revolve about the sun with the other planets and gave it in addition a rotating motion on an axis through the poles. Third, he eliminated the motion of the sphere of fixed stars, making that sphere much larger than it had been, though not infinite.[29] These changes could have little effect on the validity of any of the concepts already considered in this chapter except the last, but the third did destroy the reason for the supposed westward movement of the ocean. Clearly neither Gilbert nor Best could have believed in the Copernican system, assuming that either had heard of it. Cuningham makes no statement in *The Cosmographical Glasse* which can be interpreted one way or the other. Record, however, makes a positive declaration for the Copernican system in *The Castle of Knowledge,* where the master speaks favorably of Copernicus and his theory that the earth rotates and is not the center of the universe.[30] It is not surprising that these two systems, the old Greek and the new Copernican, should thus have existed simultaneously in the collective mind of sixteenth-century Englishmen. The change from old concept to new is rarely abrupt and sharp, even in this day of almost instantaneous communication, but commonly includes a period of conflict in which the two struggle for supremacy in the minds of men, in the course of which one finally wins out.

One would have supposed that by the second half of the sixteenth century every informed Englishman believed in a four-part earth. Such however was not the case. To be sure the new discoveries made it impossible to return to a belief in a three-part earth, but something had been added to the new concept in some quarters, a northern continent and a southern continent, so that instead of a four-part earth there was a six-part one. Best conceived of an earth divided into six parts, and his concept is tied closely to the Greek universe, though by a strained analogy.[31] He declares that just as the world or universe is divided into two principal parts, the one heavenly and composed of two parts, the *primum mobile* and the orbits of the planets (the over-world), the other elemental (the under-world) and containing the four elements earth, water, air, and fire, so the surface of the earth is divided into six parts, Europe, Africa, Asia, *Terra Septentrionalis* (the northern continent), America, and *Terra Australis* (the southern continent). Only a few persons thought there was a *Terra Septentrionalis;* many believed in *Terra Australis.*

By 1578 the austral or southern continent had had a varied career. Sometime prior to the sixteenth century, probably in the Roman era or perhaps even earlier, the two southern antipodean land masses of Crates of Mallos had, in the minds of some, fused to become an austral continent, or else it had been invented independent of that concept. At any rate such a land mass was mentioned by Isidore of Seville [32] and appeared on the world-map of Ptolemy.[33] Magellan's discovery of land south of the strait which bears his name and Portuguese and Spanish discoveries off the coast of Asia gave it new life, and in the latter half of the sixteenth century it appeared on the maps of such authorities as Mercator and Ortelius, whence it found its way into English thought. It extended all the way across the southern portion of Ortelius' world-map of 1570, larger than any known continent. John Dee appears to have identified it in part with the Locach of Marco Polo. Richard Grenville considered seeking the austral continent before Drake sailed for the Strait of Magellan, and it seems to have been on Drake's agenda for that voyage.

Drake's exact objective when he sailed from Plymouth on December 13, 1577, on the voyage which was to take him around the earth has long been in doubt. Taylor, however, has recently turned up evidence showing that the original plan called for a reconnaissance of the southern continent from the Strait of Magellan to 30 degrees south latitude.[34] The objective was subsequently changed to the Moluccas, the new plan presumably allowing for some reconnaissance of the southern continent and perhaps for search for the western end of the Strait of Anian, as the supposed northwest passage was sometimes called. Drake's experience at the Strait of Magellan was probably sufficient to show him that the southern continent did not exist there,[35] knowledge sufficient to justify his sailing north along the western coast of South America.

The ancient concept of a southern continent materialized twice in actual fact during subsequent centuries, once in the seventeenth century when Australia was explored by the Dutch and again in the nineteenth century when Antarctica began to take form through the efforts of the English and Russians. Other ancient concepts relating to the regions of the earth were also still in existence in England in the sixteenth century. None was ever thus identified with two regions, but at least one other, the land of Prester John, did assume tangible form.

The mysterious medieval land of Prester John materialized in the early part of the sixteenth century, through the explorations of the Portuguese along the east coast of Africa, in the shape of the kingdom now known as Abyssinia. This intelligence, together with considerable information, became available to Englishmen through Eden's account of the Guinea voyages of 1553 and 1554, published in 1555 in his *Decades*. His description of this kingdom, which he refers to as "Aethopia under Aegypt" to distinguish it from "Aethopia interior," is more factual and detailed than might be expected, though it lacks the spontaneity and excitement of the first hand descriptions Ribault and Barlow wrote of America. He says:

In the East side of Afrike beneath the red sea, dwelleth the great and mighty Emperour and Christian king Prester John, well knowen to the Portugales in their voyages to Calicut. His dominions reach very farre on every side: and hath under him many other Kings both christian and heathen that pay him tribute. This mightie prince is called David the Emperour of Aethopia. Some write that the king of Portugall sendeth him yeerely eight ships laden with marchandize. His kingdom confineth with the red Sea, and reacheth far into Afrike toward Aegypt and Barbarie. Southward it confineth with the Sea toward the Cape de Bona Speranza: and on the other side with the sea of sand, called Mare de Sabione, a very dangerous sea lying between ye great citie of Alcair, or Cairo in Aegypt, and the country of Aethopia: In the which way are many unhabitable deserts, continuing for the space of five dayes journey. And they affirme, that if the sayd Christian Emperor were not hindered by those deserts (in the which is great lack of victuals, & especially of water) he would or now have invaded the kingdom of Egypt, and the citie of Alcair. The chiefe city of Ethiopia, where this great emperor is resident, is called Amacaiz, being a faire citie, whose inhabitants are of the colour of an Olive. There are also many other cities, as the city of Sava upon the river of Nilus, where the Emperour is accustomed to remaine in the Sommer season. There is likewise a great city named Barbaregaf, and Ascon, from whence it is said that the Queene of Saba came to Hierusalem to heare the wisedom of Salomon. This citie is but litle, yet very faire, and one of the chiefe cities of Ethiope. In this province are many exceeding high mountains, upon the which is said to be the earthly paradise: and some say that there are the trees of the Sunne and Moone, whereof the antiquitie maketh mention: yet that none can passe thither by reason of great deserts of an hundred daies journey. Also beyond these mountains is the Cape of Bona Speranza. And to have said this much of Afrike it may suffice.[36]

Eden's relation of Africa as a whole is relatively free from references to the fabulous but does mention two of the mythical races which he locates near Ethiopia, the Satyrs, "which have nothing of men but onely shape," and those "people without heads, called Blemines, having their eyes and mouths in their breast" as if they actually existed.[37] This last reference throws some light on a similar one in Ingram's account of North America.

Voyagers returning from America in the fifteenth and sixteenth centuries rarely reported seeing fabulous races or beasts of the sort said by some medieval writers to be found in India and Africa. Indeed voyagers did not find them in India or Africa either, and the old concepts were therefore rapidly dying a natural death. Maximilian Transylvanus, an officer of state under Charles V, expressed the growing feeling among men receiving the new information when, writing of Magellan's voyage around the earth, he said:

For who wyll beleue that men are found with only one legge. Or with such fiete whose shadowe couereth theyr bodyes? Or men of a cubite heyght, and other such lyke, beinge rather monsters then men? Of the which, neyther the Spanyardes who in owre tyme saylyng by the Ocean sea, haue discouered al the coastes of the lande toward the West both vnder and aboue the Equinoctiall, nor the Portugales who compassynge abowt al Affryke haue passed by all the Easte and lykewyse discouered all those coastes vnto the great goulfe cauled *Sinus Magnus*, nor yet the Spanyardes in this theyr laste nauigation, in the which they compased abowt the hole earth, dyd neuer in any of their vyages wryte of such monsters: which doubtelesse they wold not haue omytted if they myght haue had certeyne knowelege therof.[38]

Nevertheless there was some hint of the fabulous in Gómara's references to the men on the banks of the Plata River whose legs and feet were "lyke the legs and fiete of the foule cauled the oystreche" [39] and to the "grifes" [40] (griffins?) said to live in Labrador, and more than a hint in Ingram's relation of the "strange Beast bigger then a Beare, he had neither head nor necke: his eyes and mouth were in his breast. . . ." [41] Gómara's description of the men may have been a true though greatly exaggerated comparison; Ingram's description of the beast he said he saw is too close to the stock description of the fabulous race of Africans to be anything but a repetition of it. Ingram could have had it from Eden [42] or Higden [43] or Solinus,[44] and probably from other sources too.

Emmet DeGolyer has shown recent interest in the epic journey Ingram, Browne, and Twide are said to have made through North America, and in Ingram's account of it, through the publication in 1947 of a slim, handsome volume entitled *The Journey of Three Englishmen Across Texas in 1568*. One might suppose from the title that DeGolyer believes they journeyed only across his native state, but he actively supports the contention that they traveled from a point on the Gulf of Mexico some thirty miles north of Tampico to the mouth of the St. John River in New Brunswick within the space of about a year.[45] It is quite likely that they did. In the fall of 1582 Ingram was examined by a commission seeking information about America in preparation for Gilbert's voyage of

1583. He testified before that body that he and his two companions, having been set ashore by John Hawkins about the beginning of October, 1568, traveled overland in a northerly direction for about twelve months to a point sixty leagues west of Cape Britton (Cape Breton Island), a distance of at least two thousand miles, where they were taken off by a French ship called the *Gargarine*, which took them to Newhaven (?) whence they were transported back to England sometime before the end of 1569. Further, that about a fortnight after their return they visited Hawkins, who gave each of them a reward. Hawkins was alive and available in 1582 and could have contradicted Ingram's testimony as to the time of their return had it been false. The distance was probably nearer 3,000 than 2,000 miles, as a man would walk it. That would mean averaging about eight miles a day if a man took a year to do it, a little more if he took less time. Not a high average over a period of a month or even two months but astronomical for a year, particularly under the conditions faced by these three. Yet if a man kept going he could do it, and Ingram testified that they never continued in one place more than three or four days except at the "Citie of Balma" where they stayed five or six.

Our principal concern here, however, is not the probability of the journey, fascinating as that subject is, but the identity of the beast that had neither head nor neck but eyes and mouth in its breast. Ingram, in a short paragraph of four lines, speaks of seeing this beast and elephants in America. DeGolyer thinks that both beasts belong to the African part of his journey, suggesting that the former might have been a hippopotamus [46] (the illustrator of his book depicts the beast as a sea monster off the coast of South America). It is quite true, as DeGolyer says, that after nearly thirteen years a man can become confused about the details of a journey through primitive country, about what he saw where. It is also true that after such a lapse he might imagine he had seen a beast about which he had only read or heard. Or if the knowledge preceded the journey, he could imagine seeing it behind a bush or in a swamp or up a tree, particularly at dawn or twilight. Man's imagination may be enormously stimulated, as his senses are commonly sharpened, under primitive conditions. It seems to me much more likely that Ingram read or heard about the monstrous African race whose members are said to have neither head nor neck but eyes and mouth in the breast and imagined he saw such a beast in the American wilderness, either on the spot or later.

The land of Ophir, unlike the land of Prester John, failed to materialize, either in the sixteenth century or later, though men continued to believe in it, in England at least as late as 1577. Their fierce passion for gold made them want to believe in the land whose very name conjured up visions of the precious yellow metal, and they cherished every scrap of evidence or interference that might guide them to it. Peter Martyr reports in the *First Decade* that Columbus thought the island of Hispaniola was Solomon's Ophir.[47] The official objective of the expedition which Sebastian Cabot made to the vicinity of the Plata River for Spain in 1526–1529 was "Ophir, Tarshish and Eastern Cathay." [48] Although the search continued, the center of interest shifted from India to the East Indies, probably before the beginning of the sixteenth century. With the discovery of these rich islands, at first so little known, there grew up the notion that the term Ophir had been loosely used in Solomon's day to include one or more of them as well as the province of India. This shift is reflected on the map Robert Thorne prepared for Dr. Lee in 1527, on which certain small, imagined islands of the group are labeled "Insule Tharsis et Offir ditissime." [49] The enlarged meaning probably induced the Spaniards to name the islands they found in 1567–1568, a long way west of Perú, Solomon's Islands (the Solomon Islands), even though they found no gold there. There was not entire agreement on such an interpretation because some thought Perú was Ophir, a view which at least continued to locate Ophir on mainland, but John Dee expressed his approval of the enlarged meaning in an elaborate treatise on Ophir, part of a work compiled in the summer of 1577, perhaps in preparation for Drake's voyage to the Moluccas and the "southern continent" in 1577–1580, and Ophir may have been on Drake's agenda.[50]

Men continued to believe in the Earthly Paradise in the sixteenth century, in England at least as late as 1578. Like the land of Ophir it failed to materialize, then or later. Though voyagers and explorers looked for it in the course of their travels, no expedition was ever sent in search of it. Unlike the land of Ophir it had no gold. It is true that the Bible (Genesis 2:11–12) speaks of "good gold" in the land of Havilah, through which flows the Phison, one of the four rivers flowing out of Paradise, but that land had been so long identified with India that apparently other possibilities were not taken seriously. And Paradise itself had been closed to mortal man since Adam and Eve were driven out.

Columbus thought he had been very close to the Earthly Paradise in 1498 on his third voyage to America. Peter Martyr reports in the *First Decade* that Columbus supposed it to be situated "in the toppes of those three hylles" in Paria (on the island of Trinidad).[51] Columbus' journal indicates, however, that the spot was on the mainland nearby, a location suggested to him by the latitude, climate, natural products, and the report of four rivers at the head of the Gulf of Paria.[52] Eden's statement that some men regarded the Earthly Paradise as being on the top of one of the high mountains in the land of Prester John records a continuing belief in an earthly location for Paradise as late as 1555.[53] That the belief was not then universally held in England is indicated by Cuningham's review of the problem in 1559 in the preface to *The Cosmographical Glasse*. He says that some understand Paradise in a spiritual sense, locating it either in heaven or the hearts of the faithful; some say it is a place on earth so guarded by angels that no man may come near; some say it is in the eastern part of the world, above the middle region of the element air and so free from the violence of all winds; many place it in the middle of the element air; some suppose it to be in the Burning Zone, under the equinoctial; those who place it on earth believe that the Nile, the

Ganges, the Tigris, and the Euphrates flow from it. Nevertheless George Best could write in 1578, "And in conclusion, it is nowe thought that no where else but under the Equinoctiall, or not farre from thence, is the earthly Paradise, and the onely place of perfection in this worlde," [54] as if there were no other opinion.

Closely related to the concept of the Earthly Paradise, but essentially different from it, was that of the Golden Age. Early voyagers to America and those who read of their findings were sometimes impressed by the similarity between the simple, to them almost ideal, life of the natives there and that ascribed to the Golden Age by such writers as Virgil and Ovid. Peter Martyr was impressed with this resemblance,[55] and Barlowe mentions it in his account of the Roanoke Indians.[56] But the Golden Age was never a place in the sense that the Earthly Paradise was. It was a way of living which legend assigned to Italy under the supposed reign of Saturn, god of husbandry, and long since lost. The abundant flora and fauna and the mild climate of America in and near the torrid zone were reminiscent of the conditions said to exist in Paradise, but that parallel was seldom used for anything more than an argument for locating the Earthly Paradise near the equator.

Some of the legendary islands of the Atlantic had their adherents in England in the second half of the sixteenth century. Humphrey Gilbert declared in his *Discourse* that America must be the remainder of Plato's shattered Atlantis,[57] and John Dee used the name Atlantis for North America as if he believed the same thing.[58] There was apparently some faint hope that the islands of Brazil, St. Brandan, and the Seven Cities might still be found, for the map Michael Lok drafted especially for Hakluyt's *Divers Voyages* (1582) shows all three of them.[59]

CHAPTER X

The Reappearance of America in Imaginative English Literature

The Period of Incubation, 1550–1585

OBVIOUSLY the changes which occurred in the medieval concepts of the earth in renaissance England before 1585 did not take place with equal rapidity. The rate of change depended on a number of factors, the most important of which were the nature of the concept, the rate at which pertinent discoveries were made, the rate of communicating word of them, and the character of the individual Englishman receiving the information. A supposedly impassable ocean could be proved passable by a single voyage across it, but the concept of an earthly location for Paradise could be disproved only by the elimination of all likely spots. Most of the medieval concepts of the earth were like that of the Earthly Paradise in that they could be changed only by the cumulative weight of evidence collected bit by bit by many voyagers, and that process took time. Communication of information was slow by modern standards. News of discoveries might travel with some rapidity by word of mouth, though such a rate could hardly be estimated adequately even at the time, or by published account, and before 1553 all accounts that were both satisfactory and easily available were written in Latin, Spanish, Portuguese, Italian, or French—certainly not in English. Whether the change took place at all after the information reached the individual depended on his receptivity, on whether he was an Eden or a

Hakluyt or the average man walking the streets of London or whether he was somewhere in between.

Whatever the factor or combination of factors controlling changes in the medieval concepts of the earth, there was of necessity some lag between discovery and change. Certain aspects of discovery, not necessarily the same as those which induced changes in the medieval concepts of the earth but often related to them, stimulated imaginative literature. Now there was a lag between discovery and its imaginative treatment in literature comparable to that between discovery and the changes which took place in the medieval concepts of the earth, and two of the factors involved were the same, namely, the rate of communicating information and the character of the individual receiving the news. The word "individual," however, has a special meaning relative to the imaginative treatment of discovery in literature, referring to an author and his audience instead of to just any individual receiving new information. The nature of the discovery is also usually a matter of some importance.

The length of lag between discovery of any sort and its imaginative treatment in literature is controlled first of all by the speed with which news of the discovery is communicated. Once that is received, the length is determined by the nature of the discovery and the character of the individual. The discovery must ordinarily be of considerable magnitude to attract any attention, but unless it is in essence dramatic the lag may be quite long. The discovery of atomic energy, for example, did not receive imaginative treatment in literature until after an atomic bomb had been dropped on Hiroshima. And the more startling and moving the discovery the shorter the length of time required to arouse the imagination. The next step is acceptance of the discovery by the individual, and the length of time required there is determined by his relative receptivity. However important and dramatic the event, however rapidly the news of it travels, however receptive the individual, there is an additional lag. Knowledge of the discovery must lie in the mind of a potential author for some length of time before it can generate the ideas, beliefs, and emotions which eventually combine to produce a work of art. There must also be a comparable period of incubation and process of generation in the minds of lesser individuals to prepare an audience capable of receiving it.

Optimum conditions for the treatment of the discovery of the earth in imaginative literature did not arise in England until a number of years after 1550, not until 1587 to be exact. On that account the treatment already noted in Barclay's *Ship of Fools* (1509), More's *Utopia* (1517), Rastell's *Interlude of the Four Elements* (c. 1519), and the anonymous morality *Good Order* (printed in 1533) must be regarded as the result of special circumstances.

The physical discovery of America by Columbus was similar in magnitude to the discovery of atomic energy and his first voyage was as dramatic in its way as the explosion of the bomb dropped on Hiroshima. That the one was reflected in imaginative literature in these United States in a matter of months, the other in England only after a lapse of about fifteen years, and then only incidentally, can be laid primarily to differences in speed of communication, differences in the receptivity of those hearing the news, differences in the nature of the event, and to the fact that the United States was directly involved in the one and Spain, not England, in the other. The special circumstances involved can best be seen in the *Interlude of the Four Elements*, the only early English work of imagination inspired to any appreciable extent by the discovery of America.

Rastell's close association with Thomas More gave him unusual opportunities to acquire information about America, for the man who was both minister to Henry VIII and the leading English humanist of his day knew better than most what was going on in the world, and presumably he passed on much of his knowledge to the brother-in-law who was long his intimate. Rastell's desire for such information is indicated by his attempted voyage to America. He possessed in addition strong literary inclinations.

Witness his production of plays in his own playhouse and his operation of a private printing press, both presumably for a small and select group. What more natural than that he should write a play about America and related matters for this same audience? Through it he could satisfy his creative instinct and at the same time voice his indignation against the rogues who had thwarted his voyage. Perhaps he could even persuade some of his friends to complete this interrupted project. Though there is no positive evidence that Rastell actually staged the *Interlude of the Four Elements*, he undoubtedly wrote it to be staged, and he certainly printed it. Clearly the rate of communicating information to Rastell was rapid for the period. His receptivity was unusually high, and the period of incubation following knowledge and acceptance seems to have been shortened by the acute unhappiness growing out of personal experience. Since he was interested in expressing ideas by means of plays and books he was potentially an author. The receptivity of his audience is in some doubt. Though it is thought to be high because the group is presumed to be select, there is no evidence that any member of it took up the challenge he threw down with the possible exception of his son John. Rarely, however, have so many favorable factors combined to make possible the birth of a work of art.

Marlowe's *Tamburlaine*, the next notable English work of imagination to be inspired to a considerable extent by America, was probably written in 1587–1588 and presented on the stage at about the same time. The long, intervening period produced very little in the way of imaginative treatment of the discovery of America or any other portion of the earth. The principal cause for so long a barren period is not far to seek. In the absence of such a happy combination of circumstances as produced the *Interlude of the Four Elements*, the birth of a *Tamburlaine* had to wait upon an audience sufficiently large and receptive to make it worth a Marlowe's writing. It also waited upon the favorable developments in the English theater which were already well advanced in 1587, the growth of the great dramatic companies and the building of suitable playhouses just outside the city of London.

In 1519 the vast majority of Englishmen still had almost everything to learn about America. Then and for many years thereafter the average man lacked the keys to such knowledge. Until 1553 they remained in the hands of the scholar, the courtier, and the mariner, who in the intervening years made little use of them. Few scholars caught fire from reading the works of Peter Martyr or Oviedo in the original. Court circles were not greatly exercised over the reports of Thorne, Barlow, and Rut. Only eight successful voyages to America in English ships are known to have been made between 1509 and 1562, six to Brazil and two to North America, small show of interest by the mariners.

Until information about America had been widely spread among Englishmen there could hardly be an audience for *Tamburlaine*. This dissemination took place between 1553 and 1585. The publication of *A Treatyse of the newe India* . . . (1553), Eden's initial effort toward that end, was the beginning. His *Decades* (1555) gave to any Englishman who could read his own language a rich source of information about many regions of the earth and particularly about America. By 1585 nearly all the important early Spanish and French accounts of America were available in English translation. Furthermore, there were published accounts of several English voyages, including John Hawkins' third, the three of Frobisher, and Humphrey Gilbert's last. Hackett's translation of Ribault's account of Florida was printed in London in 1563. His version of Thevet's *Singularités de l'Amérique* appeared in 1568. John Hawkins' description of his own third voyage to the Spanish Main and Mexico was published in 1569. The rest appeared after 1576. The increased appearance of such works after this date seems to indicate an already aroused interest in America on the part of the general reading public, "the English layman." It is not always easy to determine whether one of these books was put out to arouse a broader interest in a given part of the earth or whether its publication was stimulated by an already existing interest. Eden tells us frankly that he was principally concerned with disseminating information about Spanish America in order to flatter a Spanish king then monarch in England, secondarily with encouraging Englishmen to make voyages to distant lands. By 1576 the pendulum had probably swung the other way, toward a reading public asking for information about America, even though such a work as the account Peckham wrote in 1583 of Gilbert's voyage of the same year was clearly propaganda. Certainly Golding's English translations of the late Roman works of Mela and Solinus, published in 1585 and 1587, could have been intended only to please an audience already conversant with many regions of the earth.

Information about America might conceivably arouse in Englishmen opposing attitudes toward the earth as a whole. America was, after all, only a part of an earth which, for Elizabethans, was expanding in all directions. It might reawaken the "what's the use" feeling, voiced so fretfully by the poet Barclay many years before, the desire to turn from the new regions of the earth, which seemed endless, to the individual soul, an apparently more limited objective. It might, on the other hand, stir in them the longing to explore and possess the little known regions of the earth, as it had in John Rastell the printer. The latter attitude, hopeful and vigorous, is the one expressed by Richard Eden in an early poem, that appended to *A Treatyse of the newe India* . . . :

TO AL ADUENTURERS, AND SUCHE AS TAKE IN HANDE GREATE ENTERPRYSES

Who hath not of sowrenes felte the bitter tast,
Is not worthy of swetenes to take his repast.
To cracke the nutte, he must take the payne,
The which would eate the carnell fayne.
Who that of bees feareth the stinge,
Shal neuer by hony haue great wonninge.
As the swete Rose bringeth forth the thorne,
So is man truely to ioye and payne borne.

The byrde vpon hope byldeth her neste,
Where oftentymes she hath but euyll reste,
Yet is she not therby drieuen to suche feare,
But yat she performeth the same the nexte yeare.
Much casting of periles doth noble corage swage
Yet do not I commende rashenes or outrage.
What foles do fable, take thou no hede at all,
For what they know not, they cal phantastical.
Nought venter nought haue, is a saying of old.
Better it is to blow the cole, then to fyt a cold.
Fortes fortuna adiuuat, the Latin prouerbe saith,
But fayleth to such as faynt and lacke fayth.
God giueth al thinges, but not ye bul by ye horne
The plowman by trauaile encreaseth his corne.
As fortune fauereth thou mayst be riche or poore,
As *Cresus* or *Irus* that beggeth at the dore.[1]

· Specific information about America, considerable and diverse as it was, could stimulate many different ideas and feelings in those Englishmen who were attracted by the possibilities presented. The French accounts of North America, together with the reports of returned English fishermen and voyagers, might reawaken the triple urges expressed by Rastell: to colonize the land, to proselyte the natives, and to exploit the timber and fishing. Cartier reported seeing a little gold in the St. Lawrence region and hearing of more, but there was hardly enough evidence to arouse interest in that. The Spanish accounts of South America, Central America, and Mexico, on the contrary, fairly overflowed with references to gold, silver, and pearls—especially gold. These references, together with corroborating reports from English voyagers to Spanish America and Englishmen formerly resident there, might be expected to stimulate a desire to share in such abundant wealth, by fair means or foul.

The two events which aroused the greatest popular English interest in America before 1585 were Frobisher's discovery of supposed gold ore in Meta Incognita (Baffin Land) and the return of Drake from his circumnavigation of the earth with Spanish plunder of unquestioned value, a large part of which was gold from America. Quite clearly, then, the imagination of the man in the street was chiefly excited by the report of gold and the prospect of England's sharing in it. Here seemingly was an audience of requisite size, and gold in America was what it wanted to hear about, yet no important work of art appeared to satisfy that demand until the appearance of *Tamburlaine*. Though the period of incubation for this particular subject may have run its course by 1580 or 1581 for the audience, it had not yet for the right author.

A few minor poems growing out of ideas, plans, and emotions resulting from information about America were written before Marlowe's great, blank-verse play. Most of them, like that of Eden, were first published in prose works directly connected with voyaging. Some, but not all, were concerned with gold.

Gascoigne's sonnet to Humphrey Gilbert, written in the form that became such a favorite with Shakespeare, appeared with Gilbert's work, *A Discourse of a Discoverie for a new Passage to Cataia*, in 1576. It proposed to place Gilbert in the company of Columbus, Vespucci, and Magellan if he should discover a northwest passage to Asia:

> Men praise Columbus for the passing skil
> Which he declared, in Cosmographie,
> And nam'd him first (as yet we cal him stil)
> The 2. Neptune, dubd by dignity.
> Americus Vesputius, for his paine,
> Neptune the 3. ful worthely was named,
> And Magellanus, by good right did gaine,
> Neptune the 4. ful fitly to be famed.
> But al those three, and al the world beside,
> Discovered not, a thing of more emprice,
> Then in this booke, is learnedly describe,
> By vertue of my worthie friendes devide.
> Yf such successe, to him (as them) then fall,
> Neptune the 5. we justly may him call.[2]

It is not unlikely that Gascoigne thought thus to make amends for passing the *Discourse* on to a publisher without Gilbert's permission. That happened this way. Sometime during the winter of 1575–1576, Gascoigne made a social call on Gilbert at his house in Limehouse. In the course of the visit he asked Gilbert how he passed his time between wars, and Gilbert, taking him to his study, showed him a number of manuscripts including that of the *Discourse*. Gascoigne displayed particular interest in it, partly because his kinsman Martin Frobisher was then considering pursuing the search for the supposed northwest passage, and he asked to take it home for further perusal, which Gilbert readily permitted him to do. After checking it against the "Tables" of Ortelius and "sundrie other Cosmographicall Mappes and Charts" he deemed it worthy of publication and, without so much as a by-your-leave, had it printed. This Gascoigne tells without apology in his preface to the work.

Frobisher's three voyages to Meta Incognita were celebrated in several poems, welcoming him home from one voyage or bidding him farewell as he sailed on another or praising him for finding the supposed gold. Those that survive were published in conjunction with Settle's account (1577) of the second voyage and Ellis' account (1578) of the third. Abraham Fleming's poem, published with Settle's work, compares Frobisher's voyages with that of Ulysses and also praises Frobisher for returning, like Jason, with the Golden Fleece:

> Through sundrie foming fretes, and storming streightes,
> That ventrous knight of Ithac' soyle did saile:
> Against the force of Syrens baulmed beightes,
> His noble skill and courage did preuaile.
> His hap was hard, his hope yet nothing fraile.
>   Not ragged Rockes, not sinking Syrtes or sands
>   His stoutnesse staide, from viewing forreigne lands.
>
> That Poets penne and paines was well employd,
> His braines bedeawd with dropps of Parnasse spring:

Whereby renowne deserued he enioyd.
Yea, nowe (though dead) the Muses sweetly sing,
Melodiously by note, and tuned string,
  They sound in th'eares of people farre and neere,
  Th'exceeding praise of that approued Peere.

A right Heroicall heart of Britanne blood,
Vlysses match in skill and Martiall might:
For Princes fame, and countries speciall good,
Through brackish seas (where Neptune reignes by right)
Hath safely saild, in perils great despight:
  The Golden fleece (like Jason) hath he got.
  And rich returnd, saunce losse or lucklesse lot.

O that I had old Homers worthy witt,
O that I had, this present houre, his head:
With penne in hand, then musing would I sitt,
And our Vlysses valiant venture spread
In vaunting verse, that when his corps is dead,
  (Which long may liue) his true renowne may rest,
  As one whome God aboundantly hath blest.[3]

The extravagance of expression, abuse of alliteration, and crowding in of classical allusion evident here were common in the poetry and prose of the time. This bombastic style falls harshly on the modern ear, yet it has force and color. It is the crude stuff which the later Elizabethans, particularly Marlowe, Shakespeare, and Donne, were to shape into the richest and most vigorous vehicle of expression in the English language.

. Drake's plundering of the west coast of Spanish America in 1577–1580, on his voyage around the earth, did not stir an immediate, corresponding round of literary applause, perhaps because of the disapproval of those who thought his warlike achievements mere acts of piracy. This feeling was soon submerged in the rising tide of resentment against Spain so that in a few years only admiration for his daring and success remained. In 1585 *A Farewell to Sir Fraunces Drake*, a poem by one Henry Roberts, was addressed to him on the eve of his departure with Frobisher for the West Indies, and during the centuries following a continuing admiration for Drake has found expression from time to time in English song and story.

Two of Humphrey Gilbert's principal assignees, Philip Sidney and George Peckham, joined forces after his death in an effort to organize a new expedition to America. Peckham's account of Gilbert's voyage of 1583, published before the end of the year, was designed to attract subscribers. No small part of the bait was the batch of ten poems prefixed to the report, praising either the report or the intended voyage or the land which was its goal. They were written by William Pelham, Francis Drake, John Hawkins, Richard Bingham, Martin Frobisher, John Chester, Mathew Roydon, Anthony Parkhurst, Arthur Hawkins, and John Ashley. These were men of considerable prominence in their own day. With the exception of Roydon, they were all practical men-of-affairs—soldiers, voyagers, merchants, and four of them, Drake, Hawkins, Bingham, and Frobisher, were sea captains of the first importance. These poems, then, were the sixteenth-century equivalent of the elaborate modern letterhead listing names in the news as members of the board of directors. Roydon was a poet, and the professional may have been asked to contribute a poem to leaven the efforts of the laymen. His close association with Ralegh, Hariot, Chapman, Marlowe, and other members of "The School of Night" makes his contribution of more than usual interest.

The authors—or perpetrators, if you prefer—of these poems expressed various sentiments and desires, each according to his nature. Roydon the poet simply wished Peckham good luck, phrasing his thought in the pleasing and gracious rhyme royal, as effective here as it is ineffective in Barclay's *Ship of Fools:*

> To prayse thy booke because I am thy freende,
>   Though it be common and they due indeede:
> Perhaps it may some daintie eare offende,
>   Reproofe repines that vertue hath her meede.
> Yet neverthelesse how ever thinges succeede,

> Sith to no other ende thy booke was made:
> All that I wish, is that thou mayest perswade.[4]

Drake, as might be expected, said only that westward lies the path to fame and gold. Arthur Hawkins, too, referred specifically to gold, expressing what was probably the common Elizabethan attitude toward it:

> The Metall heere is showne that with a quenchles fire,
> Inflames our thirsting hartes unstaunched in desire.[5]

Wealth and fame were the lures usually dangled before the eye of the contemporary reader, though often referred to only in general terms. Arthur Hawkins, however, lent content to his encomium by listing grapes, figs, oranges, rosin, pitch, and lumber in addition to gold. He, John Hawkins, and Parkhurst stressed the opportunity to Christianize the natives, and John Hawkins and Parkhurst conceived of the new land as a dumping ground for England's excess population. Pelham expressed regret that Englishmen should have been so laggard in exploiting America, saying,

> Our forren neighbours bordring hard at hand,
>   Have found it true, to many a thousands gaine:
> And are inricht by this abounding land,
>   While pent at home, like sluggards we remaine.
>   But though they have, to satisfie their will:
>   Inough is left, our cofers yet to fill.[6]

Bingham echoed this sentiment:

> The white whereat wee levell, well is knowen,
>   The plot and place, with finger poynted out:
> The name thereof through all the world is blone,
>   To put the hard beleevers out of doubt.
>   Our forren neighbours, like it to their gaine:
>   And suck the sweete, while sleeping we remaine.[7]

Eden had expressed the same feeling years before in the preface to his *Decades* (1555),[8] and John Donne was to sound it not many years later with special reference to Guiana:

> ... And with us (me thinkes) Fate deales so
> As with the Jewes guide God did; he did show
> Him the rich land, but bar'd his entry in:
> Oh, slownes is our punishment and sinne.[9]

No one of the ten poems is poetry of the first rank. Whether, taken together, they constituted effective propaganda cannot be determined certainly since the record tells us little more of the project for which they were written. It seems likely that their weakness as poetry, their lack of fire and nobility of expression, may also have been their weakness as propaganda. The voyages of at least three of the authors, Drake, Hawkins, and Frobisher, had excited considerable admiration among Englishmen. Their poetry, however, did not measure up to such tangible accomplishments. It is difficult to imagine anyone sailing for America because Frobisher wrote:

> A pleasaunt ayre, a sweet and firtell soile,
> A certaine gaine, a never dying praise:
> An easie passage, voide of lothsome toile,
> Found out by some, and knowen to mee the waies.
> All this is there, then who will refraine to trie:
> That loves to live abroad, or dreades to die.[10]

Or Hawkins declared:

> If zeale to God, or countries care, with private gaines accesse,
> Might serve for spurs unto th'attempt this pamflet doth expresse.[11]

Drake's plea was only slightly more inspiring:

> Who seekes, by worthie deedes, to gaine renowme for hire:
> Whose hart, whose hand, whose purse is prest: to purchase his desire
> If anie such there bee, that thristeth after Fame:
> Lo, heere a meane, to winne himselfe an everlasting name.[12]

By 1587 it seemed apparent that the only gold in America was in Spanish-held territory, where it occurred in great abundance. The only way to acquire it was to take it from the Spaniards, on sea or on land after it was mined, or to conquer the land which produced it. England had captains who had demonstrated their ability to take gold in raids against the Spaniards. They might conceivably lead Englishmen in due course to the conquest of the land itself. Englishmen were ready, indeed impatient, for conquest of some sort, preferably of territory in Spanish America. What was needed was a tried and ambitious leader who could take region after region of the earth and seize quantities of gold, who could at the same time persuade men to accompany him—not simply go by themselves—persuade them by his matchless eloquence as well as the report of his conquests. Marlowe the potential author sensed this spirit in his potential audience. Elizabethans walked with him and with Tamburlaine across the face of the three-part earth and in their own minds carried on with the sons of Tamburlaine the conquest of the western world, which remained unconquered at the time of his death, a world which for Tamburlaine included not only Spanish America but also *Terra Australis*.

Marlowe's TAMBURLAINE

Marlowe's *Tamburlaine* is essentially a story of military conquest on a grand scale, carried out by a strong and dynamic leader. Englishmen were in a humor to be excited by the broad scope of his ambitions and the qualities of leadership which made possible his conquests. Their knowledge of an expanding earth had by this time given their vision a sweep comparable to that of Marlowe's hero, and their inability to share in the new wealth to any considerable extent had made them as avid for conquest as Tamburlaine. Their covetousness was directed almost entirely against Spain which, since 1581, had possessed India as well as "the Westerne Indie." Marlowe's references to both, and to parts of Spanish America in particular, as objectives for Tamburlaine must have given special fillip to the play. Indeed, Marlowe's Tamburlaine is not a fourteenth-century Tartar but a late sixteenth-century Englishman in all save his complete disregard for human life. He is not Drake or John Hawkins or Ralegh or any other one English captain. He is all of them rolled into one, the ideal leader. He speaks and acts as the average Elizabethan imagined he himself would if he could command an English fighting ship or take the field at the head of English troops. Marlowe sat out in the audience as he wrote this play.

Tamburlaine's vaulting ambition eventually encompassed the whole earth, explored and unexplored, but it did not start with so ultimate a goal. It fed upon and grew with conquest. It was vast even in the beginning. Before he has conquered Persia he pictures himself as the conqueror of all Asia. In the same breath he speaks of conquering the world, but his world then was Asia. He says to Zenocrate, his future bride, at their first meeting:

> But Lady, this faire face and heauenly hew
> Must grace his bed that conquers *Asia:*
> And meanes to be a terrour to the world,
> Measuring the limits of his Emperie
> By East and west, as *Phoebus* doth his course: [13]
>
> (232–236)

Soon after, he induces Theridamas, the Persian leader of a thousand horse, to join him, saying:

> Forsake thy king and do but ioine with me
> And we will triumph ouer all the world.
>
> (367–368)

But the only specific reference in that speech to a recognizable geographic place is to the Caspian Sea, an Asiatic lake:

> Both we wil walke vpon the lofty clifts,
> And Christian Merchants that with Russian stems
> Plow vp huge furrowes in the Caspian sea,
> Shall vaile to vs, as Lords of all the Lake.
>
> (388–391)

Tamburlaine, the newly crowned king of Persia, still speaks only of ruling Asia:

> Though *Mars* himselfe the angrie God of armes,
> And all the earthly Potentates conspire,
> To dispossesse me of this Diadem:
> Yet will I weare it in despight of them,
> As great commander of this Easterne world,
> If you but say that *Tamburlaine* shall raigne.

And all cry:

> Long liue *Tamburlaine*, and raigne in Asia.

> (909–915)

Baiazeth, Emperor of the Turks, in the next speech but one, lets us know that Tamburlaine is about to attack him as he lies outside the beleagured city of Constantinople. There is no direct statement of Tamburlaine's ambitions at this point. There doesn't need to be, for Baiazeth styles himself:

> Dread Lord of *Affrike, Europe* and *Asia*,
> Great King and conquerour of Grecia,
> The Ocean, Terrene, and the cole-blacke sea,
> The high and highest Monarke of the world,

> (941–944)

or ruler of the known, three-part earth and all its waters except the Caspian Sea. If Tamburlaine captured him, he would automatically inherit these prerogatives. Tamburlaine, however, has a surprise in store for the reader. No sooner does he subdue Baiazeth than he proposes extending his operations beyond the territory claimed by that monarch to include México, a slice of the fourth part of the earth and Spanish territory to boot, sending his ships around the earth from east to west:

> Those walled garrisons wil I subdue,
> And write my selfe great Lord of *Affrica*:
> So from the East vnto the furthest West,
> Shall *Tamburlain* extend his puisant arme.
> The Galles and those pilling Briggandines,
> That yeerely saile to the Venetian gulfe,
> And houer in the straightes for Christian wracke,

Shall lie at anchor in the Isle *Asant*,
Vntill the Persean Fleete and men of war,
Sailing along the Orientall sea,
Haue fetcht about the Indian continent:
Euen from *Persepolis* to *Mexico*,
And thence vnto the straightes of *Iubalter:*
Where they shall meete, and ioine their force in one,
Keeping in aw the Bay of *Portingale*,
And all the Ocean by the British shore:
And by this meanes Ile win the world at last.

(1342–1358)

There was considerable mopping up to be done in Asia before this plan could be put into operation. Damascus, Arabia, and Egypt, long considered a part of Asia, had yet to be conquered. Tamburlaine plainly regarded these obstacles simply as delaying actions, keeping his eye on the fourth part of the earth, for in replying to the plea of Zenocrate to spare Damascus and make peace with her father, the Soldan of Egypt, he says:

Zenocrate, were Egypt *Iouves* owne land,
Yet would I with my sword make *Ioue* to stoope.
I will confute those blind Geographers
That make a triple region in the world,
Excluding Regions which I meane to trace,
And with this pen reduce them to a Map,
Calling the Prouinces, Citties and townes
After my name and thine *Zenocrate:*
Here at *Damascus* will I make the Point
That shall begin the Perpendicular.
And wouldst thou haue me buy thy Fathers loue
With such a losse? Tell me Zenocrate?

(1713–1724)

Tamburlaine next extends his ambition to *Terra Australis*, a part of the static earth of current interest to Elizabethan voyagers. His three chief lieutenants he crowns as kings of Algiers, Morocco, and Fes. Then to a suitable acknowledgment of fealty from the new king of Algiers he replies:

Wel said *Theridamas,* when holy Fates
Shall stablish me in strong *Egyptia,*
We meane to traueile to th'Anta(r)tique Pole,
Conquering the people vnderneath our feet,
And be renowm'd, as neuer Emperours were.
Zenocrate, I will not crowne thee yet,
Vntil with greater honors I be grac'd.

(1775–1781)

Part I of the play ends, however, on a disappointing note. Tamburlaine waits to crown Zenocrate only until he has captured Damascus, Arabia, and Egypt, not *Terra Australis* and Spanish America. In his speech at the coronation there is a reference to "the Westerne Indie," as if Tamburlaine were still interested:

To gratify the sweet *Zenocrate,*
Egyptians, Moores and men of Asia,
From *Barbary* vnto the Westerne *Indie,*
Shall pay a yearly tribute to thy Syre.

(2298–2301)

But almost in the same breath he speaks to his soldiers as if he might be through with conquest:

Hang vp your weapons on *Alcides* poste,
For *Tamburlaine* takes truce with al the world.

(2310–2311)

Part I was such a success on the London stage that within a few months Marlowe wrote Part II as a sequel to it. Marlowe seems at first to have narrowed the scope of his hero's ambitions and shifted their emphasis here. Tamburlaine is shown concentrating on Asiatic conquests and training his sons to emulate his deeds. He subdues the Turks under Orcanes, king of Anatolia (Asia Minor), and captures the city of Babylon, but there are no more declarations of moving on to America and *Terra Australis.* There is even an expression of doubt as to whether he has conquered all of the three-part earth. In reply to the captive king of Jerusalem, who reproaches the son Celebinus for his cruelty, Tamburlaine admits he has not yet achieved this objective:

> I Turke, I tel thee, this same Boy is he,
> That must (aduaunst in higher pompe than this)
> Rifle the kingdomes I shall leaue vnsackt.
> If *Ioue* esteeming me too good for earth,
> Raise me to match the faire *Aldeboran*,
> Aboue the threefold Astracisme of heauen,
> Before I conquere all the triple world.
>
> (4036–4042)

Yet in describing to Techelles, king of Fes, his proposed triumphal entry into Samarcand, his native city, he speaks as if he had already gained it:

> Ile ride in golden armour like the Sun,
> And in my helme a triple plume shal spring,
> Spangled with Diamonds dancing in the aire,
> To note me Emperour of the three fold world.
>
> (4094–4097)

But the old, illimitable ambition crops out in time to be passed on to his sons. Tamburlaine, sick unto death, calls for a world-map on which he traces first countries already conquered, then vastly richer and more extensive lands yet to be won. The postponement of reference to America and *Terra Australis* is so effective in building suspense as to make this speech the climax of the play as a whole. He says:

> Giue me a Map, then let me see how much
> Is left for me to conquer all the world,
> That these my boies may finish all my wantes.
>
> *One brings a Map.*
>
> Here I began to martch towards *Persea*,
> Along *Armenia* and the Caspian sea,
> And thence vnto *Bythinia*, where I tooke
> The Turke and his great Empresse prisoners,
> Then martcht I into *Egypt* and *Arabia*,
> And here not far from *Alexandria*,
> Whereas the Terren and the red sea meet,
> Being distant lesse than ful a hundred leagues,

I meant to cut a channell to them both,
That men might quickly saile to *India*.
From thence to *Nubia* neere *Borno* Lake,
And so along the Ethiopian sea,
Cutting the Tropicke line of *Capricorne*,
I conquered all as far as *Zansibar*.
Then by the Northerne part of *Affrica*,
I came at last to *Graecia*, and from thence
To *Asia*, where I stay against my will,
Which is from *Scythia*, where I first began,
Backeward and forwards nere fiue thousand leagues.
Looke here my boies, see what a world of ground
Lies westward from the midst of *Cancers* line,
Vnto the rising of this earthly globe,
Whereas the Sun declining from our sight,
Begins the day with our Antypodes:
And shall I die, and this vnconquered?
Loe here my sonnes, are all the golden Mines,
Inestimable drugs and precious stones,
More worth than *Asia*, and the world beside,
And from th'Antartique Pole, Eastward behold
As much more land, which neuer was descried,
Wherein are rockes of Pearle, that shine as bright
As all the Lamps that beautifie the Sky,
And shall I die, and this vnconquered?
Here louely boies, what death forbids my life,
That let your liues commaund in spight of death.

(4516–4553)

Thus Tamburlaine summarizes his personal conquests, exclusive
of those of his lieutenants: Iran, Iraq, Turkey, Syria, Palestine,
Trans-Jordan, Saudi Arabia, Egypt, Ethiopia, and Greece. The
scheme for digging a canal between the Mediterranean and the
Red Sea, though it existed then only in Tamburlaine's imagination,
was more practical than the ancient project for digging one between the Nile and the Red Sea, which had once materialized.
The Suez Canal testifies to that. The other had long since filled

up, even in Marlowe's day. Tamburlaine next looks westward toward the Antipodes, toward Spanish America, toward the gold, drugs, and precious stones "more worth than Asia" which will never be his. Crates of Mallos would have approved of his use of Antipodes save for the probable inclusion of Peruvians, clearly Antichthones. Finally Tamburlaine takes a last look at *Terra Australis*, bemoaning its loss too. Anticlimax, on the face of it, since an admission of failure to conquer the whole earth, yet this speech is true climax just because these regions remained as objects of conquest for the sons of Tamburlaine—and for Elizabethans.

Part of the attraction of the play for Elizabethans must have been the emphasis on gold, an object of so great moment to them. What was probably the common attitude, already noted in the lines from Arthur Hawkins' poem on America, is expressed in the passage from *The Jew of Malta* in which the Governor of Malta says to the bashaws of Turkey:

> Welcome, great *Bashaws*, how fares *Callymath*,
> What wind drives you thus into *Malta* rhode?

And one of them replies:

> The wind that bloweth all the world besides,
> Desire of gold.
> (1420–1423)

Marlowe's Tamburlaine believed that the great bulk of the gold in circulation was coming from Spanish America, which was an historic fact in the sixteenth century. He says as much in the speech to his sons just quoted:

> Looke here my boies, see what a world of ground
> Lies westward from the midst of *Cancers* line,
> Vnto the rising of this earthly globe,
> Whereas the Sun declining from our sight,
> Begins the day with our Antypodes:
> And shall I die, and this vnconquered?

> Loe here my sonnes, are all the golden Mines,
> Inestimable drugs and precious stones,
> More worth than *Asia*, and the world beside,
>
> (4538–4546)

The gold from America was many times more valuable than its drugs and precious stones combined. If the reader doubt that Tamburlaine's view was also that of Marlowe, he need only refer to the answer of the Governor of Malta to the Bashaw of Turkey:

> Desire of gold, great Sir?
> That's to be gotten in the Westerne *Inde:*
> In *Malta* are no golden Minerals.
>
> (1424–1426)

Elsewhere in Marlowe's plays there is corroborative evidence. One of the inducements Callapine, the captive son of Baiazeth, holds out to Almeda, his keeper, to free him from the power of Tamburlaine is this:

> A thousand Gallies mann'd with Christian slaues
> I freely giue thee, which shall cut the straights,
> And bring Armados from the coasts of Spaine,
> Fraughted with golde of rich *America:*
>
> (2523–2526)

And Valdes, in *Doctor Faustus*, urges his friend to the practice of black magic by picturing some of the fantastic feats evil spirits can be made to perform, saying:

> From *Venice* shall they dregge huge Argoces,
> And from *America* the golden fleece,
> That yearely stuffes old *Philips* treasury,
> If learned *Faustus* will be resolute.
>
> (159–162)

His audience was no doubt at one with Marlowe in this belief, and since, in addition, its members wished to share in the Spanish gold, they readily approved the sentiments of Valdes and of Almeda, who yielded to the blandishments of Callapine.

Gold is scattered freely throughout the play *Tamburlaine*. It figures largely in the policies of the characters and it studs their speech. Tamburlaine dazzles the eyes of Theridamas and his Persians with heaps of gold. The Persians, going into battle, scatter gold before the Tartar soldiers to divert and distract them. The Governor of Babylon attempts to save his life by revealing to Tamburlaine the hiding place of a secret hoard of gold. Tamburlaine himself uses gold as a standard of measurement. His soldiers will not desert for all the gold in India. At the siege of Damascus he drinks to the God of War:

> That meanes to fill your helmets full of golde:
> And make *Damascus* spoiles as rich to you,
> As was to *Iason Colchos* golden fleece.
> (1645–1647)

He will not spare the Egyptians "for all the wealth of Gehons golden waues" (1904). He will drink liquid gold instead of wine when he has conquered the king of Anatolia. The fair Zenocrate is buried not in gross lead but in a sheet of gold.

Tamburlaine's outstanding quality as a leader, as Marlowe depicts him, is his constant and consistent drive toward the conquest of the earth and the subordination of everything else to that end, even if it meant knifing his son Calyphas with his own hand after failure to persuade him to become a bloody conqueror. In furthering his ambition he displays the boldness of a Drake and the craft of a Hawkins, and if his cruelty is made to exceed theirs it serves but to emphasize his singleness of purpose. But Tamburlaine displays one talent on a scale not matched by any Elizabethan military leader, not even Philip Sidney. He has the gift of the tongue. He is a poet in the grand manner. He is Marlowe.

Tamburlaine not only acts like a conqueror but he also talks like one, and from the point of view of the audience the two talents are of equal importance, even though they rarely go together in real life. Theridamas had been attracted to him by the magnificence of his speech as well as the glitter of his gold. Later the ris-

ing Tamburlaine says to Cosroe, the Persian usurper and his new
ally;

> Our quiuering Lances shaking in the aire,
> And bullets like *Ioues* dreadfull Thunderbolts,
> Enrolde in flames and fiery smoldering mistes,
> Shall threat the Gods more than Cyclopian warres,
> And with our Sun-bright armour as we march,
> Weel chase the Stars from heauen, and dim their eies
> That stand and muse at our admyred armes.
>
> (616–622)

Thereupon Theridamas, his fancy once more caught by such
phrasing, turns to Cosroe and says:

> You see my Lord, what woorking woordes he hath.
>
> (623)

The old warrior, stricken by the fatal illness that is to carry him
to his grave, cries out:

> What daring God torments my body thus,
> And seeks to conquer mighty *Tamburlaine*,
> Shall sicknesse prooue me now to be a man,
> That haue bene tearm'd the terrour of the world?
> *Techelles* and the rest, come take your swords,
> And threaten him whose hand afflicts my soul,
> Come let vs march against the powers of heauen,
> And set blacke streamers in the firmament,
> To signifie the slaughter of the Gods.
> Ah friends, what shal I doe? I cannot stand,
> Come carie me to war against the Gods,
> That thus inuie the health of *Tamburlaine*.
>
> (4434–4445)

The gorgeous imagery, bombast on the lips of any save a conqueror,
and the stately measure of the blank verse have still the power to
rouse the leader. How much more must such lines have moved
Elizabethans for whom they were a call to conquest expressed
in stirring music.

The play *Tamburlaine* represents a consummation as well as a beginning. No other English work of art stimulated by knowledge of an expanded earth and a rich Spanish America presents in such concentrated form the thirst for conquest and gold or phrases it so magnificently. Subsequent references to America, and they are fairly numerous, are either more temperate or else strive vainly for the sustained intensity and richness which only Marlowe attained.

Notes

Chapter I

THE STATIC THREE-PART EARTH IN ENGLAND BEFORE THE DISCOVERY OF AMERICA

1. Frank Stevens, *Stonehenge Today and Yesterday* (2d ed.; London: H. M. Stationery Office, 1927), pp. 56–65.

2. Juan Luis Vives, *De tradendis disciplinis*, trans. Foster Watson (Cambridge: University Press, 1913), pp. 166–168.

3. Bede, "De natura rerum," *Opera . . . omnia*, ed. J. A. Giles (London: Whittaker & Co., 1843), Chaps. II–XII (Vol. VI, pp. 100–105 of this edition).

4. *Ibid.*, Chaps. XLII–LI (Vol. VI, pp. 117–122 of this edition); Bede, "De temporum ratione," *ibid.*, Chaps. XXXI, XXXIII (Vol. VI, pp. 207–209, 211–214 of this edition).

5. Lynn Thorndike, *The SPHERE of Sacrobosco and Its Commentators* (Chicago: University of Chicago Press, 1949), p. 43.

6. *The Voiage and Travayle of Syr John Maundeville Knight* ("Everyman's Library," No. 812 [New York: E. P. Dutton & Co., 1928]), p. 219.

7. Sacrobosco, *Sphaera mundi* (early 13th century), English trans., in Thorndike, *op. cit.*, pp. 118–120.

8. Francis R. Johnson, *Astronomical Thought in Renaissance England* (Baltimore: Johns Hopkins Press, 1937), p. 51.

9. Thorndike, *op. cit.*, p. 5.

10. Bartholomeus Anglicus, *De proprietatibus rerum*, trans. John de Trevisa, Feb. 6, 1398 (Westminster: Wynkyn de Worde, 1495), Bk. VIII, Chap. 2.

11. Robert Grosseteste, "De sphaera," ed. Ludwig Baur ("Beiträge zur Geschichte der Philosophie des Mittelalters," Vol. IX [Münster: Aschendorffsche Verlagsbuchhandlung, 1912]), p. 13.

12. Sacrobosco, *op. cit.*, pp. 121–122.

13. Roger Bacon, *Opus majus*, trans. Robert Belle Burke (Philadelphia: University of Penna. Press, 1928), Pt. IV, Fourth Distinction, Chap. X (Vol. I, pp. 177–179 of this edition).

14. *Early Travels in Palestine*, ed. Thomas Wright ("Bohn's Antiquarian Library" [London: Henry G. Bohn, 1848]), p. 3.

15. *Ibid.*, p. 38.

16. John Kirtland Wright, *The Geographical Lore of the Time of the Crusades* ("Research Series," No. 15 [New York: American Geographical Society, 1925]), pp. 18–19, 158–159.

17. *Caxton's Mirrour of the World* ("Early English Text Society, Extra Series," No. 110 [London: Oxford University Press, 1913]), p. 61.

18. Bede, "De natura rerum," *op. cit.*, Chap. IX (Vol. VI, p. 103 of this edition); Bede, "De temporum ratione," *op. cit.*, Chap. XXXIV (Vol. VI, pp. 214–217 of this edition).

19. Sacrobosco, *op. cit.*, p. 129.

20. *Georgics,* i, 233–239.

21. *Metamorphoses*, i, 45–51.

22. *The Commentary of Robertus Anglicus upon the SPHERE of Sacrobosco*, English trans., in Thorndike, *op. cit.*, pp. 239–240.

23. Bacon, *op. cit.*, I, 155.

24. *Recherches Geographiques et Critiques sur le Livre DE MENSURA ORBIS TERRAE Compose en Irlande au Commencement du Neuvieme Siecle, par Dicuil, Suives du Text Restitute*, ed. A. Letronne (Paris: Germain Mathiot, 1814), Chap. VII, Sec. II, Paragraph 6 (pp. 38–39 of this edition).

25. Aristotle, "Meteorologica," trans. E. W. Webster (*The Works of Aristotle Translated into English*, Vol. III [Oxford: Clarendon Press, 1923]), III 6 (378a, lines 16–42 of this edition); Frank Dawson Adams, *The Birth and Development of the Geological Sciences* (Baltimore: The Williams & Wilkins Co., 1928), pp. 277–279.

26. Albertus Magnus, "Mineralium," *Opera omnia*, ed. August Borgnet (Paris, 1890), Bk. III, Chap. 6 (Vol. V, p. 66 of this edition); *The Commentary of Robertus Anglicus upon the SPHERE of Sacrobosco*, *op. cit.*, p. 218.

27. Bartholomeus Anglicus, *op. cit.*, Bk. XV, Chap. 19.

28. Ranulf Higden, *Polychronicon*, trans. John de Trevisa, ed.

Churchill Babington ("Chronicles and Memorials of Great Britain and Ireland during the Middle Ages, Rolls Series," No. XLI, Vol. 1 [London: Longman Green, 1865]), p. 159.

29. Pliny, *Natural History*, trans. H. Rackham ("The Loeb Classical Library" [Cambridge, Mass.: Harvard University Press, 1942]), Bk. VII, Chap. 2 (Vol. II, p. 521 of this edition).

30. Higden, *op. cit.*, pp. 51–53.

31. *Caxton's Mirrour of the World*, p. 93.

32. Bartholomeus Anglicus, *op. cit.*, Bk. XV, Chap. 73.

33. Higden, *op. cit.*, pp. 78–85.

34. *Caxton's Mirrour of the World*, pp. 72–80.

35. *The Voiage and Travayle of Syr John Maundeville Knight*, pp. 195–199.

36. *Ibid.*, p. 195.

37. Bartholomeus Anglicus, *op. cit.*, Bk. XV, Chap. 108.

38. *The Voiage and Travayle of Syr John Maundeville Knight*, p. 219.

39. Bacon, *op. cit.*, Pt. IV, Fourth Distinction, Chap. IV (Vol. I, pp. 157–158 of this edition).

40. *The Voiage and Travayle of Syr John Maundeville Knight*, pp. 219–220.

41. Higden, *op. cit.*, pp. 67–75.

Chapter II

THE CHANGING THREE-PART EARTH BROUGHT TO ENGLAND BEFORE THE DISCOVERY OF AMERICA

1. Richard Hakluyt, *The Principal Navigations Voyages Traffiques and Discoveries of the English Nation* (Glasgow: James MacLehose and Sons, 1903–1905), II, 114–147.

2. Cyril Fox, *The Personality of Britain* (4th ed.; Cardiff: The National Museum of Wales, 1947), pp. 10–14, 84–89.

3. *The Anglo-Saxon Chronicle*, trans. Rev. James Ingram ("Everyman's Library," No. 624 [New York: E. P. Dutton & Co., 1912]), p. 54.

4. *The Ecclesiastical History of the English Nation by the Venerable Bede*, trans. John Stevens, revision Lionel C. Jane ("Everyman's Library," No. 479 [New York: E. P. Dutton & Co., 1910]), 161–164.

214   NOTES: THE CHANGING THREE-PART EARTH

5. *The Life of Alfred the Great*, translated by B. Thorpe from the German of Dr. R. Pauli, to which is appended Alfred's *Anglo-Saxon version of Orosius* with a literal English translation, and an Anglo-Saxon alphabet and glossary ("Bohn's Antiquarian Library" [London: George Bell & Sons, 1900]), pp. 245–259.

6. Bartholomeus Anglicus, *op. cit.*, Bk. XV, Chaps. 25, 31, 57, 58, 105, 122.

7. Higden, *op. cit.*, pp. 267–299.

8. Bartholomeus Anglicus, *op. cit.*, Bk. XV, Chap. 138.

9. Higden, *op. cit.*, p. 327.

10. Bartholomeus Anglicus, *op. cit.*, Bk. XV, Chap. 104.

11. Higden, *op. cit.*, p. 321.

12. *Ibid.*

13. Bartholomeus Anglicus, *op. cit.*, Bk. XV, Chap. 47.

14. *Ibid.*, Bk. XV, Chap. 173.

15. Higden, *op. cit.*, pp. 323–325.

16. *Recherches Geographiques et Critiques sur le Livre DE MENSURA ORBIS TERRAE Compose en Irlande au Commencement du Neuvieme Siecle, par Dicuil, Suives du Text Restitute*, Chap. VII, Sec. II, paragraph 6 (pp. 38–39 of this edition).

17. Halldor Hermannsson, "Ari Thorgilsson, Islendingabok," *Islandica*, XX (1930), 60.

18. Arthur M. Reeves, *The Finding of Wineland the Good* (London: Oxford University Press, 1890), pp. 19–25; *The Norse Discoverers of America*, translated and discussed by G. M. Gathorne-Hardy (Oxford: Clarendon Press, 1921), p. 14.

19. Reeves, *op. cit.*, pp. 25–52.

20. *Ibid.*, 53–78.

21. Snorre Sturluson, *Heimskringla*, ed. Erling Monsen (New York: D. Appleton & Co., 1932), pp. 188–202.

22. M. L. Fernald, "Notes on the Plants of Wineland the Good," *Rhodora*, XII (1910), 17–38.

23. Reeves, *op. cit.*, pp. 80–83.

24. C. E. P. Brooks, *Climate Through the Ages* (London: Ernest Benn Ltd., 1926), pp. 397–399.

25. Higden, *op. cit.*, p. 323.

26. Bartholomeus Anglicus, *op. cit.*, Bk. XV, Chap. 171.

27. Adam of Bremen, "Descriptio insularum aquilonis" ("Patro-

logiae cursus completus . . . series Latina," ed. J. P. Migne, Vol. 146 [Paris, 1853]), p. 652.

28. *The Journey of William of Rubruck to The Eastern Parts of the World, 1253–55* . . . , ed. William Woodville Rockhill ("Publications of the Hakluyt Society," Ser. 2, No. 4 [London, 1900]), pp. 150–153.

29. Bacon, *op. cit.*, Pt. IV, Fourth Distinction (Vol. I, pp. 386–387 of this edition).

30. *The Journall of Frier Odoricus* ("Everyman's Library," No. 812 [New York: E. P. Dutton & Co., 1928]), pp. 231–278.

31. *The Voiage and Travayle of Syr John Maundeville Knight*, p. 152.

32. *Ibid.*, pp. 150–151.

33. *Ibid.*, pp. 161–185.

34. *The Book of Ser Marco Polo*, trans. Sir Henry Yule (2 vols.; London: John Murray, 1903).

35. W. H. Babcock, *Legendary Islands of the Atlantic* ("Research Series," No. 8 [New York: American Geographical Society, 1922]), pp. 34–80, 144–148.

36. *Caxton's Mirrour of the World*, p. 96.

37. *Narrative and Critical History of America*, ed. Justin Winsor (Boston: Houghton Mifflin & Co., 1889), I, 50.

38. Alexander Neckham, *De naturis rerum*, ed. T. Wright ("Chronicles and Memorials of Great Britain and Ireland during the Middle Ages, Rolls Series," No. XXXIV [London: Longman Green, 1863]), pp. 182–183.

39. Charles Homer Haskins, *Studies in the History of Medieval Science* (Cambridge, Mass.: Harvard University Press, 1927), pp. 113–115.

40. George H. T. Kimble, *Geography in the Middle Ages* (London: Methuen & Co. Ltd., 1938), pp. 65–66.

41. Chaucer, "A Treatise on the Astrolabe," *Complete Works*, ed. F. N. Robinson (Boston: Houghton Mifflin Co., 1933), pp. 640–662.

42. Frederick J. Pohl, *Amerigo Vespucci, Pilot Major* (New York: Columbia University Press, 1944), pp. 62–68.

43. E. G. R. Taylor, *Tudor Geography* (London: Methuen & Co. Ltd., 1930), p. 141.

44. *Documents Illustrative of Social and Academic Life at Oxford*,

ed. Henry Anstey ("Chronicles and Memorials of Great Britain and Ireland during the Middle Ages, Rolls Series," No. L [London: Longman Green, 1868]), p. 771.

45. Samuel Eliot Morison, *Admiral of the Ocean Sea* (Boston: Little, Brown & Co., 1942), I, 240–263.

Chapter III
AMERICA, THE FOURTH PART OF THE EARTH

1. *Infra*, pp. 163–184.
2. *Infra*, pp. 185–198.
3. Roger Barlow, *A brief summe of Geographie*, ed. E. G. R. Taylor ("Publications of the Hakluyt Society," Ser. 2, No. 69 [London, 1932]), p. 32.
4. *Ibid.*, p. 148.
5. *Ibid.*, p. 179.
6. Morison, *op. cit.*, I, 314.
7. *Ibid.*, II, 38.
8. Pohl, *op. cit.*, p. 130.
9. *Ibid.*, pp. 147–167.
10. Martin Waldseemüller, *Cosmographiae introductio*, trans. Edward Burke and Mario Cosena (New York: United States Catholic Historical Society, 1907), p. 70.
11. *The First Three English Books on America (1511?–1555)*, ed. Edward Arber (Birmingham: n. p., 1885), p. 8.
12. *Ibid.*, p. 55.
13. *Infra*, p. 81.
14. *Infra*, p. 95.
15. *Infra*, pp. 84–85.
16. James A. Williamson, *The Voyages of the Cabots and the English Discovery of North America under Henry VII and Henry VIII* (London: Argonaut Press, 1929).
17. *Ibid.*, p. 39.
18. *Ibid.*, pp. 29–31.
19. *Ibid.*, p. 29.
20. *Ibid.*, pp. 32, 171.
21. *Ibid.*, p. 35.

22. *Ibid.,* p. 39.
23. *Ibid.,* p. 66.
24. *Ibid.,* pp. 70–84, 225–243.

Chapter IV
ENGLISH VOYAGES TO AMERICA, 1509–1547

1. *The First Three English Books on America* (*1511?–1555*), p. 5.
2. Hakluyt, *op. cit.,* XI, 23.
3. *Ibid.,* XI, 24.
4. *Ibid.,* XI, 25.
5. R. G. Marsden, "Voyage of the 'Barbara,' of London to Brazil in 1540," *English Historical Review,* XXIV (1909), 97.
6. *Ibid.*
7. Hakluyt, *op. cit.,* II, 166.
8. Barlow, *op. cit.,* p. 1.
9. *Ibid.,* p. 154.
10. *Ibid.,* p. 161.
11. *Ibid.,* p. 163.
12. *Spanish Documents Concerning English Voyages to the Caribbean, 1527–1568,* ed. I. A. Wright ("Publications of the Hakluyt Society," Ser. 2, No. 62 [London, 1929]), pp. 29–59.
13. *Infra,* pp. 64–65.
14. Williamson, *op. cit.,* pp. 85–86.
15. A. W. Reed, *Early Tudor Drama* (London: Methuen & Co. Ltd., 1926), pp. 1–28, 187–201.
16. *Infra,* pp. 92–94.
17. *Ibid.*
18. Samuel Purchas, *Purchas His Pilgrimes* (Glasgow: James MacLehose and Sons, 1906), XIV, 303–305.
19. Williamson, *op. cit.,* p. 259.
20. Hakluyt, *op. cit.,* II, 177.
21. Taylor, *op. cit.,* p. 50.
22. Hakluyt, *op. cit.,* II, 176–177.
23. Taylor, *op. cit.,* pp. 11–13.
24. Hakluyt, *op. cit.,* VIII, 3.
25. *Ibid.,* VIII, 3.

26. *Ibid.*, VIII, 4.

27. *Ibid.*, VIII, 49, 81.

28. *Ibid.*, VIII, 108.

29. *Ibid.*, VIII, 4.

30. Walter Raleigh, "The English Voyages of the Sixteenth Century," in Hakluyt, *op. cit.*, XII, 55.

Chapter V

AMERICA IN IMAGINATIVE ENGLISH LITERATURE
BEFORE 1550

1. Sebastian Brant, *The Ship of Fools*, trans. Edwin H. Zeydel ("Columbia University Records of Civilization," No. 36 [New York: Columbia University Press, 1944]), pp. 220–225.

2. Edwin H. Zeydel, "Sebastian Brant and the Discovery of America," *Journal of English and Germanic Philology*, XLII (1943), 410–411.

3. Alexander Barclay, *The Ship of Fools*, ed. T. H. Jamieson (Edinburgh: William Paterson, 1874), II, 23–27.

4. *Letter to Piero Soderini, Gonfaloniere, the Year 1504*, trans. George Tyler Northup (Princeton: Princeton University Press, 1916), p. 44.

5. *The UTOPIA of Sir Thomas More*, ed. J. H. Lupton (Oxford: Clarendon Press, 1895), pp. 26–29.

6. *Ibid.*, p. 28, note 1.

7. *Ibid.*, pp. 6–7.

8. *Ibid.*, p. lxxxix.

9. Arthur E. Morgan, *Nowhere was Somewhere* (Chapel Hill: University of North Carolina Press, 1946), pp. 39–60.

10. *The Complete Works of William Hickling Prescott*, ed. John Foster Kirk (London: Gibbings & Co., 1896), Vol. I.

11. Philip Ainsworth Means, *Ancient Civilizations of the Andes* (New York: Charles Scribner's Sons, 1931).

12. Morgan, *op. cit.*, pp. 36–37.

13. *Supra*, pp. 62–63.

14. *The UTOPIA of Sir Thomas More*, pp. 174–175.

15. *Letter to Piero Soderini, Gonfaloniere, the Year 1504,* p. 9.

16. *De orbe novo, the Eight Decades of Peter Martyr D'Anghera,* trans. Francis Augustus Macnutt (New York: G. P. Putnam's Sons, 1912), I, 221–222.

17. *Ibid.,* I, 307.

18. *The UTOPIA of Sir Thomas More,* p. lxiv.

19. John Rastell, *A new Interlude and a mery of the Nature of the iiij Elementes* (London, c. 1519), as quoted in Williamson, *op. cit.,* p. 89.

20. *Ibid.,* pp. 89–91.

21. *Supra,* pp. 63–64.

22. Rastell, *op. cit.,* pp. 91–92.

23. *Ibid.,* pp. 92–93.

24. *Supra,* p. 85.

25. George L. Frost and Ray Nash, "GOOD ORDER: A Morality Fragment," *Studies in Philology,* XLI (1944), 483–491.

26. *Ibid.,* p. 490.

Chapter VI

EXPANSION OF ENGLISH INTEREST IN VOYAGING, 1547–1558

1. Barlow, *op. cit.,* pp. liv–lv.

2. Hakluyt, *op. cit.,* II, 239.

3. *Ibid.,* II, 21.

4. *Ibid.,* II, 227–228.

5. *Ibid.,* II, 304–316.

6. *Ibid.,* II, 322–344.

7. *Ibid.,* II, 350–354.

8. *Ibid.,* II, 413–425.

9. *Ibid.,* II, 449–479.

10. John William Blake, *Europeans in West Africa, 1450–1560* ("Publications of the Hakluyt Society," Ser. 2, No. 87 [London, 1942]), pp. 301–302.

11. Hakluyt, *op. cit.,* VI, 137.

12. *Ibid.*, VI, 138–142.
13. *Ibid.*, VI, 122–124. See also Blake, *op. cit.*, pp. 264–265, 295–297.
14. Blake, *op. cit.*, pp. 297–298.
15. Hakluyt, *op. cit.*, VI, 145–252.
16. *Ibid.*, VI, 140.
17. *Ibid.*, VI, 141.
18. *Ibid.*, VI, 145–154.
19. *Ibid.*, VI, 154–176.
20. *Ibid.*, VI, 200.
21. Blake, *op. cit.*, pp. 289, 358–360.
22. Hakluyt, *op. cit.*, VI, 177–252.
23. *The First Three English Books on America* (*1511?–1555*), pp. 13–42.
24. *Ibid.*, pp. 43–390.
25. *Ibid.*, p. 5.
26. *Ibid.*, pp. xxvii–xxxvi.
27. *Ibid.*, p. 47 (McCann trans.).
28. *Ibid.*, p. 55.
29. *Ibid.*, p. 57.
30. *Ibid.*, p. 59.

Chapter VII
EDEN'S AMERICA

1. *The First Three English Books on America* (*1511?–1555*), p. 54.
2. *Ibid.*, p. 251.
3. *Ibid.*, p. 342.
4. *Ibid.*, p. 195.
5. *Ibid.*, p. 197.
6. *Ibid.*, p. 196.
7. *Ibid.*, pp. 70–71.
8. *Ibid.*, p. 191.
9. *Ibid.*, p. 346.
10. *Ibid.*, pp. 287–288.
11. *Ibid.*, p. 161.
12. *Ibid.*, p. 345.
13. *Ibid.*, p. 287.

14. *Ibid.*, p. 345.
15. *Ibid.*, p. 242.
16. *Ibid.*, p. 287.
17. *Ibid.*, p. 345.
18. *Ibid.*, pp. 344–345.

Chapter VIII

ELIZABETHAN DISCOVERY OF AMERICA TO 1585

1. *The Original Writings & Correspondence of the Two Richard Hakluyts*, ed. E. G. R. Taylor ("Publications of the Hakluyt Society," Ser. 2, No. 77 [London, 1935]), pp. 218–221.
2. *Ibid.*, pp. 222–233, 239–242, 246–249, 257–265.
3. Hakluyt, *op. cit.*, VI, 125.
4. *Ibid.*, IX, 338–358.
5. *Ibid.*, IX, 342.
6. *Ibid.*, IX, 342–343.
7. *Ibid.*, IX, 357–358.
8. *Ibid.*, IX, 355.
9. *Ibid.*, IX, 357.
10. *Ibid.*, IX, 359–360.
11. *Ibid.*, IX, 360–377.
12. *Ibid.*, IX, 376–377.
13. *Ibid.*, IX, 378–397.
14. *Ibid.*, IX, 383.
15. *Ibid.*, X, 7–74.
16. Richard Hakluyt, *Divers Voyages Touching the Discovery of America and the Islands Adjacent*, ed. John Winter Jones ("Publications of the Hakluyt Society," Ser. 1, No. 7 [London, 1850]), p. 98.
17. *Ibid.*, pp. 101–102.
18. *The Voyages and Colonizing Enterprises of Sir Humphrey Gilbert*, ed. David Beers Quinn ("Publications of the Hakluyt Society," Ser. 2, No. 84 [London, 1940]), pp. 283–307.
19. Richard Hakluyt, *The Principal Navigations* . . . , IX, 398–445.
20. *Ibid.*, IX, 445–465.
21. *Ibid.*, X, 77–81.
22. *Ibid.*, XI, 101–133.

23. *The Voyages and Colonizing Enterprises of Sir Humphrey Gilbert*, Ser. 2, No. 83, pp. 129–164.

24. *Ibid.*, p. 161.

25. *Ibid.*, p. 105.

26. For Best's account of the three voyages see *The Three Voyages of Martin Frobisher*, ed. Vilhjalmur Stefansson (London: Argonaut Press, 1938), I, 1–129.

27. *Ibid.*, I, 129.

28. *The Original Writings & Correspondence of the Two Richard Hakluyts*, Ser. 2, No. 76, pp. 123–127.

29. *Ibid.*, pp. 127–134.

30. *The Voyages and Colonizing Enterprises of Sir Humphrey Gilbert*, Ser. 2, No. 83, pp. 170–175.

31. Taylor, *op. cit.*, p. 125.

32. Richard Hakluyt, *The Principal Navigations* . . . , VIII, 134–147.

33. *Ibid.*, VIII, 42–43.

34. *Ibid.*, VIII, 98–131. See also *The Voyages and Colonizing Enterprises of Sir Humphrey Gilbert*, Ser. 2, No. 84, pp. 435–480.

35. Richard Hakluyt, *The Principal Navigations* . . . , VIII, 297–310.

36. *Ibid.*, VIII, 298–299.

Chapter IX

MEDIEVAL CONCEPTS OF THE EARTH IN A RENAISSANCE WORLD

1. *The First Three English Books on America (1511?–1555)*, p. 7.

2. Richard Hakluyt, *The Principal Navigations* . . . , II, 164–165.

3. Barlow, *op. cit.*, p. 180.

4. Taylor, *op. cit.*, p. 261.

5. Robert Record, *The Castle of Knowledge* (London: Reginald Wolf, 1556), pp. 94–95.

6. *Ibid.*, p. 93.

7. William Cuningham, *The Cosmographical Glasse* (London: J. Day, 1559), p. 21.

8. André Thevet, *The Newfound world or Antartike*, trans. Thomas Hackett (London: H. Bynneman, 1568), f. 91^{a-b}

9. *Supra*, pp. 11–13.

10. *The UTOPIA of Sir Thomas More*, pp. 30–31.

11. *The First Three English Books on America* (*1511?–1555*), p. 217.

12. *Ibid.*, pp. 217–218.

13. *Ibid.*, p. 88.

14. *Ibid.*, p. 217.

15. Richard Hakluyt, *The Principal Navigations* . . . , VI, 176.

16. Record, *op. cit.*, pp. 63–65.

17. Cuningham, *op. cit.*, pp. 65–68.

18. Thevet, *op. cit.*, f. 31^{a-b}.

19. Richard Hakluyt, *The Principal Navigations* . . . , VII, 252–276; *The Three Voyages of Martin Frobisher*, I, 26–45.

20. *The Three Voyages of Martin Frobisher*, I, 39, note 1.

21. Rastell, *op. cit.*, p. 89.

22. Richard Hakluyt, *The Principal Navigations* . . . , VIII, 57–58.

23. Wright, *op. cit.*, pp. 25–26.

24. *The First Three English Books on America* (*1511?–1555*), p. 161.

25. *Ibid.*, p. 184.

26. *The Voyages and Colonizing Enterprises of Sir Humphrey Gilbert*, Ser. 2, No. 83, p. 143.

27. Taylor, *op. cit.*, p. 35.

28. *The Three Voyages of Martin Frobisher*, I, 94.

29. Johnson, *op. cit.*, p. 107.

30. Record, *op. cit.*, pp. 164–165.

31. *The Three Voyages of Martin Frobisher*, I, 18.

32. Isidore of Seville, "Etymologiarum" ("Patrologiae cursus completus . . . series Latina," ed. J. P. Migne, Vol. 82 [Paris, 1878]), Bk. XIV, Chap. V, Paragraph 17 (Column 512 of this edition).

33. *Geography of Claudius Ptolemy*, ed. Edward Luther Stevenson (New York: New York Public Library, 1932), pp. 170–171.

34. Taylor, *op. cit.*, pp. 118–119.

35. J. N. L. Baker, *A History of Geographical Discovery and Exploration* (Boston: Houghton Mifflin Co., 1931), p. 112.

36. Richard Hakluyt, *The Principal Navigations* . . . , VI, 144–145.

37. *Ibid.*, VI, 169.

38. *The First Three English Books on America* (*1511?–1555*), p. 248.

39. *Ibid.*, p. 344.

40. *Ibid.*, p. 345.

41. *The Voyages and Colonizing Enterprises of Sir Humphrey Gilbert*, Ser. 2, No. 84, p. 291.

42. *Supra*, p. 179.

43. *Supra*, pp. 16–17.

44. *The Rare and Singular works of Pomponius Mela* . . . *Where-vnto is added, that learned worke of Iulius Solinus Polyhistor* . . . , trans. Arthur Golding (London: Thomas Hackett, 1590), Chap. XLII.

45. E. DeGolyer, *The Journey of Three Englishmen Across Texas* (El Paso: The Peripatetic Press, 1947), p. 7.

46. *Ibid.*, p. 11.

47. *The First Three English Books on America* (*1511?–1555*), p. 66.

48. Barlow, *op. cit.*, p. xxix.

49. Richard Hakluyt, *The Principal Navigations* . . . , II, 176.

50. Taylor, *op. cit.*, 114–115.

51. *The First Three English Books on America* (*1511?–1555*), p. 90.

52. Morison, *op. cit.*, II, 282–285.

53. *Supra*, p. 179.

54. Richard Hakluyt, *The Principal Navigations* . . . , VII, 254–255.

55. *The First Three English Books on America* (*1511?–1555*), pp. 70–71, 78.

56. Richard Hakluyt, *The Principal Navigations* . . . , VIII, 305.

57. *The Voyages and Colonizing Enterprises of Sir Humphrey Gilbert*, Ser. 2, No. 83, pp. 137–138.

58. Taylor, *op. cit.*, pp. 115, 116.

59. Richard Hakluyt, *The Principal Navigations* . . . , VII, 368.

Chapter X

THE REAPPEARANCE OF AMERICA IN IMAGINATIVE ENGLISH LITERATURE

1. *The First Three English Books on America* (*1511?–1555*), p. 42.

2. George Gascoigne, "A Prophetical Sonet . . . ," *Complete Works*, ed. John W. Cunliffe (Cambridge: University Press, 1907), II, 567.

3. *The Three Voyages of Martin Frobisher*, *op. cit.*, II, 5.

4. *The Voyages and Colonizing Enterprises of Sir Humphrey Gilbert*, Ser. 2, No. 84, p. 440.

5. *Ibid.*, p. 442.

6. *Ibid.*, p. 437.

7. *Ibid.*, p. 439.

8. *Supra*, p. 118.

9. *The Poems of John Donne*, ed. Herbert J. C. Grierson (London: Oxford University Press, 1912), I, 210.

10. *The Voyages and Colonizing Enterprises of Sir Humphrey Gilbert*, Ser. 2, No. 84, p. 440.

11. *Ibid.*, p. 438.

12. *Ibid.*

13. All quotations from the plays of Marlowe have been taken from *The Works of Christopher Marlowe*, ed. C. F. Tucker Brooke (Oxford: Clarendon Press, 1910).

Selected Bibliography

PRIMARY WORKS

Alfred the Great. Version of Orosius. In *The Life of Alfred the Great,*
. . . , ed. B. Thorpe, London: George Bell and Sons, 1900 ("Bohn's
Antiquarian Library").

Anglicus, Bartholomeus. De proprietatibus rerum. Translated into English by John de Trevisa, Feb. 6, 1398. Westminster: Wynkyn de
Worde, 1495.

Bacon, Roger. Opus majus. 2 vols. Translated into English by Robert
Belle Burke. Philadelphia: University of Pennsylvania Press, 1928.

Barclay, Alexander. The Ship of Fools. Ed. T. H. Jamieson. 2 vols. Edinburgh: William Paterson, 1874.

Barlow, Roger. A brief summe of Geographie. Ed. E. G. R. Taylor.
London, 1932. "Publications of the Hakluyt Society," Ser. 2, No. 69.

Bede. De natura rerum. In *Opera* . . . *omnia*, ed. J. A. Giles, Vol. VI,
London: Whittaker & Co., 1843.

—— De temporum ratione. In *Opera* . . . *omnia*, ed. J. A. Giles, Vol.
VI, London: Whittaker & Co., 1843.

Best, George. A Trve Discovrse of the late voyages of discouerie, for
the finding of a passage to Cathaya, by the Northweast . . . In *The
Three Voyages of Martin Frobisher*, ed. Vilhjalmur Stefansson,
London: Argonaut Press, 1938.

Brant, Sebastian. The Ship of Fools. Translated into English by Edwin
H. Zeydel. New York: Columbia University Press, 1944. "Columbia
University Records of Civilization," No. 36.

Cartier, Jacques. A shorte and briefe narration of the two Nauigations
and Discoueries to the Northwest partes called Newe Fravnce.
Translated into English by John Florio from the Italian of Ramusio.
London: H. Bynneman, 1580.

Caxton's Mirrour of the World. London: Oxford University Press,
1913. "Early English Text Society, Extra Series," No. 110.

Cuningham, William. The Cosmographical Glasse. London: J. Day, 1559.

Eden, Richard. A Treatyse of the newe India. . . . In *The First Three English Books on America* [1511?–1555], ed. Edward Arber, Birmingham: n.p., 1885.

—— The Decades of the newe worlde or west India. . . . In *The First Three English Books on America* [1511?–1555], ed. Edward Arber, Birmingham, n.p., 1885.

Frost, George L., and Ray Nash. "*Good Order:* a Morality Fragment," Studies in Philology, LXI (October, 1944), 488–491.

Gilbert, Humphrey. A Discourse of a Discoverie for a new Passage to Cataia. In *The Voyages and Colonizing Enterprises of Sir Humphrey Gilbert*, ed. David Beers Quinn, London, 1940 ("Publications of the Hakluyt Society," Ser. 2, No. 83).

Grosseteste, Robert. De sphaera. Ed. Ludwig Baur. In *Beiträge zur Geschichte der Philosophie des Mittelalters*, Vol. IX, Münster: Aschendorffsche Verlagsbuchhandlung, 1912.

Hakluyt, Richard. Divers Voyages Touching the Discovery of America and the Islands Adjacent. Ed. John Winter Jones. London, 1850. "Publications of the Hakluyt Society," Ser. 1, No. 7.

—— Discourse of Western Planting. In *The Original Writings & Correspondence of the Two Richard Hakluyts*, ed. E. G. R. Taylor, London, 1935 ("Publications of the Hakluyt Society," Ser. 2, No. 77).

—— The Principal Navigations Voyages Traffiques & Discoveries of the English Nation. 12 vols. Glasgow: James MacLehose and Sons, 1903–1905.

Higden, Ranulf. Polychronicon. Ed. Churchill Babington. Translated into English by John de Trevisa. Translated into English by an unnamed 15th century translator. In *Chronicles and Memorials of Great Britain and Ireland during the Middle Ages*, London: Longman Green, 1865 ("Rolls Series," No. 41).

Mandeville, Sir John. The Voiage and Travayle of Syr John Maundeville Knight. New York: E. P. Dutton & Co., Inc., 1928. "Everyman's Library," No. 812.

Marlowe, Christopher. The Works of Christopher Marlowe. Ed. C. F. Tucker Brooke. Oxford: Clarendon Press, 1910.

Martyr, Peter. De orbe novo. 2 vols. Translated into English by F. A. MacNutt. New York: G. P. Putnam & Sons, 1912.

More, Thomas. The UTOPIA of Sir Thomas More. Ed. J. H. Lupton. Oxford: Clarendon Press, 1895.

Odoric, Friar. The Journall of Frier Odoricus. New York: E. P. Dutton & Co., Inc., 1928. "Everyman's Library," No. 812.

Orosius, Paulus. Seven Books of History against the Pagans. Translated into English by Irving Woodworth Raymond. New York: Columbia University Press, 1936. "Columbia University Records of Civilization," No. 26.

Polo, Marco. The Book of Ser Marco Polo. 2 vols. Translated into English by Sir Henry Yule. London: John Murray, 1903.

Rastell, John. A new Interlude and a mery of the Nature of the iiij Elementes. n.p.: John S. Farmer (?), 1908. 'Old English Drama, Students' Facsimile Edition," Vol. 41.

Record, Robert. The Castle of Knowledge. London: Reginald (Reyner) Wolf, 1556.

Ribault, Jean. The whole & true discouerye of Terra Florida. In Divers Voyages Touching the Discovery of America and the Islands Adjacent, ed. Richard Hakluyt, London, 1850 (ed. John Winter Jones, "Publications of the Hakluyt Society," Ser. 1, No. 7).

Rubruck, William of. The Journey of William of Rubruck to The Eastern Parts of the World, 1253-55 . . . , ed. William Woodville Rockhill. London, 1900. "Publications of the Hakluyt Society," Ser. 2, No. 4.

Sacrobosco. Sphaera mundi. In Lynn Thorndike, The Sphere of Sacrobosco and Its Commentators, Chicago: University of Chicago Press, 1949.

Thevet, André. La Cosmographie Universelle. Paris: Chez Pierre l'Huillier, 1575.

—— The Newfound world or Anarctike. Translated into English by Thomas Hackett. London: H. Bynneman, 1568.

Waldseemüller, Martin. Cosmographiae introductio. Translated into English by Edward Burke and Mario E. Cosenza. New York: United States Catholic Historical Society, 1907.

SECONDARY WORKS

Adams, Frank Dawson. The Birth and Development of the Geological Sciences. Baltimore: The Williams & Wilkins Co., 1938.

Arber, Edward (ed.). The First Three English Books on America (1511?–1555). Birmingham: n.p., 1885.

Babcock, W. H. Legendary Islands of the Atlantic. New York: American Geographical Society, 1922. "Research Series," No. 8.

Bakeless, John. The Tragicall History of Christopher Marlowe. 2 vols. Cambridge, Mass.: Harvard University Press, 1942.

Baker, J. N. L. A History of Geographical Discovery and Exploration. Boston: Houghton Mifflin Co., 1931.

Beazley, C. Raymond. Prince Henry the Navigator: the Hero of Portugal and of Modern Discovery, 1394–1460 A.D. New York: G. P. Putnam's Sons, 1895.

—— The Dawn of Modern Geography. 3 vols. London: John Murray, 1897–1906.

Bigger, H. P. The Precursors of Jacques Cartier, 1497–1534. Ottawa: Government Printing Bureau, 1911. "Publications of the Canadian Archives," No. 5.

Blake, John William. Europeans in West Africa, 1450–1560. 2 vols. London, 1942. "Publications of the Hakluyt Society," Ser. 2, Nos. 86, 87.

Bradbrook, M. C. The School of Night. Cambridge: University Press, 1936.

Bunbury, E. H. A History of Ancient Geography among the Greeks and Romans from the Earliest Ages till the Fall of the Roman Empire. 2d ed. 2 vols. London: John Murray, 1883.

Cawley, Robert R. The Voyagers and Elizabethan Drama. London: Oxford University Press, 1938.

—— Unpathed Waters. Princeton: Princeton University Press, 1940.

Clark, Eleanor G. Ralegh and Marlowe. New York: Fordham University Press, 1941.

DeGolyer, Emmet. The Journey of Three Englishmen Across Texas in 1568. El Paso: The Peripatetic Press, 1947.

Fiske, John. The Discovery of America. 3 vols. Boston: Houghton Mifflin Co., 1902.

Fox, Sir Cyril. The Personality of Britain. 4th ed. Cardiff: National Museum of Wales, 1947.

Gathorne-Hardy, G. M. The Norse Discoverers of America. Oxford: Clarendon Press, 1921.

Harrisse, H. The Discovery of North America. London: Henry Stevens & Son, 1892.

Haskins, Charles Homer. Studies in the History of Medieval Science. 2d ed. Cambridge, Mass.: Harvard University Press, 1927.

Johnson, Francis R. Astronomical Thought in Renaissance England. Baltimore: Johns Hopkins Press, 1937.

Kimble, George H. T. Geography in the Middle Ages. London: Methuen & Co. Ltd., 1938.

Miller, Konrad. Mappemundi: Die ältesten Weltkarten. Vol. VI of Rekonstruierte Karten. Stuttgart: Jos. Roth'sche Verlagshandlung, 1898.

Morgan, Arthur E. Nowhere was Somewhere. Chapel Hill: University of North Carolina Press, 1946.

Morison, Samuel Eliot. Portuguese Voyages to America in the Fifteenth Century. Cambridge, Mass.: Harvard University Press, 1940.

—— Admiral of the Ocean Sea. 2 vols. Boston: Little, Brown & Co., 1942.

Parks, George Bruner. Richard Hakluyt and the English Voyages. New York: American Geographical Society, 1928. "Special Publication," No. 10.

Pohl, Frederick J. Amerigo Vespucci, Pilot Major. New York: Columbia University Press, 1944.

Pompen, Fr. Aurelius. The English Version of the Ship of Fools. London: Longmans, Green & Co., 1925.

Prestage, Edgar. The Portuguese Pioneers. London: A. & C. Black, 1933.

Quinn, David Beers (ed.). The Voyages and Colonizing Enterprises of Sir Humphrey Gilbert. 2 vols. London, 1940. "Publications of the Hakluyt Society," Ser. 2, Nos. 83, 84.

Reed, A. W. Early Tudor Drama. London: Methuen & Co. Ltd., 1926.

Reeves, Arthur Middleton. The Finding of Wineland the Good. London: Oxford University Press, 1890.

Stefansson, Vilhjalmur (ed.). The Three Voyages of Martin Frobisher. 2 vols. London: Argonaut Press, 1938.

Taylor, E. G. R. Tudor Geography, 1485–1583. London: Methuen & Co. Ltd., 1930.

—— Late Tudor and Early Stuart Geography, 1583–1650. London: Methuen & Co. Ltd., 1934.

—— (ed.) The Original Writings & Correspondence of the Two Richard Hakluyts. 2 vols. London, 1935. "Publications of the Hakluyt Society," Ser. 2, Nos. 75, 76.

Thorndike, Lynn. The SPHERE of Sacrobosco and Its Commentators. Chicago: University of Chicago Press, 1949.

Williamson, James A. Maritime Enterprise, 1485–1558. Oxford: Clarendon Press, 1913.

—— Sir John Hawkins, the Time and the Man. Oxford: Clarendon Press, 1927.

—— The Voyages of the Cabots and the English Discovery of North America under Henry VII and Henry VIII. London: Argonaut Press, 1929.

—— The Age of Drake. London: Adam and Charles Black, 1938.

Winsor, Justin (ed.). Narrative and Critical History of America. 8 vols. Boston: Houghton Mifflin & Co., 1884–1889.

Wright, John Kirtland. The Geographical Lore of the Time of the Crusades. New York: American Geographical Society, 1925. "Research Series," No. 15.

Index

Abyssinia, 114, 178; *see also* Ethiopia

Adam of Bremen, 36

Adams, Clement, 100, 119

Africa: unit of classical earth, 15; unit of medieval earth, 15-16; medieval description of, 16-17, 36; unit of sixteenth-century earth, 46, 91, 177; unit of modern earth, 45; English voyages to, in the sixteenth century, 106-112; principal commodities in the sixteenth century, 108-112; Eden's description, 178-179; references to, in *Tamburlaine*, 200, 202, 203, 204

Agricola, 120, 164

Albertus Magnus, on the origin of metals, 14, 137, 164

Alfred the Great, see *Orosius* (version of Alfred the Great)

Aloes, 131

Alpaca, 125, 126

Amadas, Philip, 161

Amazon River, 100

America: Norse visits to, 33-36; the fourth part of the earth, 45-47; English awareness of, as the fourth part of the earth, 48-55; slight distinction between North and South, 48-51, 91, 113, 116; in imaginative English literature before 1550, 70-97; a refuge for criminals, 97; in *Of the newe landes* (John of Doesborowe), 113-114; in *A Treatyse of the newe India* (Eden), 115; in *The Decades of the newe worlde or west India* (Eden), 116-119, 121-

137; the sixth part of the earth, 177; fabulous races in, 179-182; slow spread of information about, 189-190; effect of information on Englishmen, 191-192; a dumping ground for excess population, 196; references to, in *Tamburlaine*, 200-206

Ancient Civilization of the Andes (Means), 86

Andaluzia Nova, *see* Urabá

Anian, Strait of, 177

Antarctica, 45, 178

Antichthones of Crates of Mallos, 10-11; in the sixteenth century, 167-168, 205

Antilia, 39-40, 46; *see also* Island of the Seven Cities

Antilles, 46; *see also* Indies, West

Antipodes of Crates of Mallos, 10-11; in the sixteenth century, 95, 167-168, 177; reference to, in *Tamburlaine*, 204, 205

Antoikoi of Crates of Mallos, 10-11; in the sixteenth century, 167-168

Apian, Peter, 6, 154; diagram of the medieval universe, 7

Arcadia, The (Sidney), 83

Arculf, 9

Aristotle, on the origin of metals, 13-14; on circulation of the ocean waters, 173

Ashanti pepper, 109, 110, 111

Ashley, John, 195

Asia: unit of classical earth, 15; unit of medieval earth, 16; medieval